# Change in Psychotherapy

# CHANGE IN PSYCHOTHERAPY

● ● ● ● ● ●

*A Unifying Paradigm*

The Boston Change Process Study Group

W. W. Norton & Company
New York • London

For information about permission to reproduce selections from this book, write to
Permissions, W. W. Norton & Company, Inc., 500 Fifth Avenue, New York, NY 10110

For information about special discounts for bulk purchases,
please contact W. W. Norton
Special Sales at specialsales@wwnorton.com or 800-233-4830

Manufacturing by R. R. Donnelley, Harrisonburg
Book design by Bytheway Publishing Services
Production manager: Leeann Graham

**Library of Congress Cataloging-in-Publication Data**

Change in psychotherapy : a unifying paradigm / Boston Change Process Study Group.
— 1st ed.
　　p. ; cm.
"A Norton professional book."
Includes bibliographical references and index.
ISBN 978-0-393-70599-7 (hardcover)
1. Psychoanalysis. 2. Psychotherapy. 3. Change. I. Boston Change Process Study
Group.
[DNLM: 1. Psychoanalytic Therapy. 2. Psychoanalytic Interpretation. WM 460.6
C456 2010]
RC506.C454 2010
616.89'17—dc22　　　2009049380

ISBN: 978-0-393-70599-7

W. W. Norton & Company, Inc., 500 Fifth Avenue, New York, N.Y. 10110
www.wwnorton.com
W. W. Norton & Company Ltd., Castle House, 75/76 Wells Street, London W1T 3QT

1　2　3　4　5　6　7　8　9　0

# Contents

*The members of the Boston Change Process Study Group,
listed alphabetically, are:*

Nadia Bruschweiler-Stern, MD,
Karlen Lyons-Ruth, PhD, Alexander C. Morgan, MD,
Jeremy P. Nahum, MD, Louis W. Sander, MD,
and Daniel N. Stern, MD*

*\*Alexandra M. Harrison, MD, and Edward Z. Tronick, PhD, were members
of the group until June 2002. They contributed to Chapters, 1, 2, 4, and the
first part of Chapter 5.*

# Acknowledgments

To all our family members, who supported us through the many years of this writing process with patience, good humor, and after-hours fun, we give our love and profound thanks.

We are also indebted to all the members of the Infant Research Workshop at the Boston Psychoanalytic Society who, from 1988 to 2002, created many lively evenings of debate, and were often the sounding board for the initial ideas that culminated in the work in this volume.

We also thank Dan Siegel, Bruce Reis, and Holly Levenkron for their exchanges around these ideas. Our thoughts were also challenged and refined by the many who shared symposia with us on these topics, including Gerald Stechler, Steve Mitchell, Arnold Modell, Anna and Paul Ornstein, Allan Schore, Joe Lichtenberg, Darlene Ehrenberg, Peter Hobson, Bob Stolorow, Donnel Stern, Jim Grotstein, Steve Knoblauch, and Massimo Ammaniti.

And to Michael and Maj-Britt Rosenbaum, we thank you for your generosity in providing your idyllic setting in Virgin Gorda to launch this thinking process.

# Introduction

# Placing the Work in Context: Origins of the Boston Change Process Study Group

In 1994, THE BOSTON CHANGE PROCESS STUDY GROUP (BCPSG) CAME into being. It began as a disparate group of eight, where five were analysts (Alexander Morgan, Jeremy Nahum, Louis Sander, Daniel Stern, and initially Alexandra Harrison). Two of the analysts (Sander and Stern) were also pioneers in the field of psychoanalytically oriented infant research and have continued to individually make major original contributions. Sander brought a deep knowledge of biological systems. Daniel Stern had pioneered microanalytic methods for describing mother–infant interactions. Two were developmental researchers (Karlen Lyons-Ruth and, initially, Edward Tronick) who were contributing major insights to the developmental literature on attachment and affective processes in infancy and who were interested in psychodynamically oriented clinical process. One (Nadia Bruschweiler-Stern) was a developmental pediatrician and a child psychiatrist involved with early processes of the infant–parent encounter and attachment. Although the analysts in the group in full-time practice (Morgan, Nahum, and, initially, Harrison) came later to the recognition of the potential value of studying recent infancy research (than the others) in the theory and practice of psychodynamically oriented therapeutics, one belief bound them all together: that the study of early development was a rich and unique source for contributions to psychoanalysis.

Boston has a long history in developmental thinking. It was here, in 1954, that the first longitudinal project on infant development was created: the BU Longitudinal Project directed by Louis Sander. Not long after this, also in Boston, T. Berry Brazelton began his studies of neonatal capacities and mother–infant exchange and began a dialogue with Daniel Stern and Margaret Mahler. In the Harvard Department of Psychology, Brazelton, Lyons-Ruth, and Tronick were beginning to study infant affective development in the lab of Jerome Bruner. All of this flourished, but without much notice within the psychoanalytic community. Taken together, however, a receptive terrain was being created for the group to emerge.

By the early 1970s, there was also an explosion of developmental research exploring infant affective and mental processes, aided by the new technologies of portable video recording and more powerful computers. This explosion of research findings created a dissonance between the existing psychoanalytic developmental theory and the new findings. This dissonance drew us in to try to create more coherence between emerging developmental knowledge and psychodynamic theory. These exciting findings were poorly received by the psychoanalytic community at large. In spite of this, there were individual exceptions. There was an excellent tutorial at the Boston Psychoanalytic Society given by Gerald Stechler, along with Samuel Kaplan and Virginia Demos. Lichtenberg, another psychoanalyst, published his book in 1983. In 1988, Nahum, joined by Morgan, created the Infant Research Workshop at the Boston Psychoanalytic Society. Shortly thereafter, Lyons-Ruth, as well as Tronick and Harrison, joined this group.

When Daniel Stern and Nadia Bruschweiler-Stern came to Boston in 1994 for a sabbatical year, it was decided that a small group would meet to further consider the usefulness of bringing insights from the study of infancy to bear on thinking about psychoanalytic process. This group (Bruschweiler-Stern, Harrison, Lyons-Ruth, Morgan, Nahum, Sander, Stern, and Tronick) became the BCPSG. Of necessity, the group would have to be small, as it was felt that it would be necessary to consider moment-by-moment clinical process, importantly including the subjective experience of the therapist. Since many in the group had been involved in studying videotapes of mother–infant interactions, we wanted to capture the same moment-to-moment richness of detail in our consideration of clinical process. Psychoanalytic supervision has always consisted of a variant of following this process with the supervisor. However, it has been said that whatever one does not tell the supervisor is what really happened in a treatment, and we wanted to build a level of trust that would encourage frank exploration of the moment-to-moment exchange in the psychoanalytic session. Such authenticity would require a level of comfort, friendship, and security with each other that could only grow in a small and more intimate setting. Throughout, the shared excitement created by the coming together of developmental research, biological systems theory, and affective neuroscience in their relevance to clinical process guided and inspired us.

## HISTORICAL CONTEXT OF THE BCPSG'S WORK WITHIN PSYCHOANALYTIC THINKING

Our work has occurred in the context of a number of threads related to psychotherapeutic change. They are: (a) the pendulum swing from a one- to a two-person psychology; (b) the increasing role of developmental research; (c) the understanding of intersubjectivity in the therapy exchange; (d) the importance of implicit communication, as distinct from explicit, language-based communication; (e) the contribution of dynamic systems thinking; and (f) the role of intention as a primary regulator of interactive exchange. Additionally, we have every reason to assume that this model will be consistent with what is emerging in such fields as current neuroscience and brain imaging studies, among others.

### 1. The Shift From a One- to a Two-Person Psychology

Arnold Cooper's term, *the quiet revolution*, describes well the importance of this shift from a one- to a two-person psychology. Freud had begun his theorizing from a two-person perspective in his original "trauma" theory, in that he viewed the symptomatology of his early patients as being due to the effect of other people upon them and the cure as related to the effect of the analyst upon the person of the patient. He abandoned this idea and replaced it with "originary fantasy" theory in which symptoms occurred as a consequence of intrapsychic fantasies. As a result, the one-person psychology theory became regnant.

Freud's discussions with a number of his circle, particularly Sandor Ferenczi with his emphasis on the transference-countertransference, pulled the two-person conception back toward center focus. However, this opened the door for "wild analysis" and the abuse of the patient by the analyst's power. In response to this, Freud tried to protect the newly created field, as well as both patient and analyst. In 1914–16, in a creative surge with his papers on technique, he tried to pull the pendulum back to the one-person account by establishing the techniques and code for conducting analysis, particularly the importance of the neutrality of the analyst.

In the '40s and '50s, several movements began to push the pendulum back toward the two-person conception: The British object-relations group, which included Winnicott, Fairbairn, and Guntrip, as well as Klein—from a somewhat different perspective—began moving the position of the analyst beyond being merely the object of the patient's drive, a vehicle of his gratification. The relations with the analyst (the object) became in itself an end state for the patient.

In the United States, the Sullivanian Interpersonal School, and also Edgar Levinson, increased the focus on the interactive nature of the therapeutic encounter. Their disciples (Stephen Mitchell, Jay Greenberg, Lewis Aron, Irwin Hoffman, Philip Bromberg, Donnel Stern, Darlene Ehrenberg, Jessica Benjamin, and others) moved things further back toward a two-person conception, an evolution that came to be known as the Relational School.

In a somewhat different vein, Heinz Kohut and his followers emphasized the role of the analyst's reality on the patient, regardless of interpersonal meanings. Others, such as Thomas Ogden, Patrick Casement, James McLaughlin, and Owen Renik, also emphasized the two-person nature of therapy.

An additional aspect of these movements was the increased focus on the "here and now" character of what goes on in the consultation room. Theories outside of strict psychoanalysis, such as Gestalt psychology, had long since drawn attention to the immediacy of the therapeutic experience, that is, the "here and now."

## 2. *The Role of Developmental Research*

Another paradigm shift occurring in psychoanalysis since the '50s was the increasing role of developmental research in thinking about interactions with patients. John Bowlby's observational work emphasized the importance of the actuality of what happens with parents and children and places their actual relations in the forefront. Subsequent analytically informed developmental observers, such as Sander, Gerald Stechler, Daniel Stern, Lyons-Ruth, Beatrice Beebe, T. Berry Brazelton, Robert Emde, Tronick, and others, have been an important influence on psychoanalytic thinking, particularly the BCPSG.

## 3. *The Contribution of Dynamic Systems Thinking*

From the first, dynamic systems theory (DST) (Esther Thelen and Linda Smith) has deeply informed the work of the BCPSG, as we have seen the therapist–patient pair, and the states in which they live, as a dynamic system that undergoes change according to the principles of DST.

## 4. *The Understanding of Intersubjectivity in the Interactive Exchange*

Some of these researchers, along with, importantly, Colwyn Trevarthen, emphasized the intersubjective as well as the interactive in the developmental process. This focus in developmental research was paralleled in clinical thinking by members of the Relational School mentioned above, as well as Robert Stolorow, Beatrice Beebe and Frank Lachmann, Steven Knoblauch, and others, in that ideas about intersubjectivity were incorporated into thinking about the therapeutic exchanges.

## 5. *The Importance of Implicit Communication*

Additionally, observers in both research and clinical settings began to appreciate that communication included explicit language-based aspects as well as implicit aspects. The importance of implicit communication has been an important part of the thinking of the BCPSG.

The focus on the implicit has also been advanced and informed by broader fields of human endeavor, such as music, art, dance, and other body-based activities, as well as their related therapies. These movements have helped to bring the body and all of its reactivity back into our purview as therapists. In the BCPSG work, this is reflected in our attention to the moment to moment, where action as well as feeling and thought are all manifest.

### 6. The Role of Intention as a Primary Regulator of Interactive Exchange

Within the fields of philosophy and ethology, the role of intention has long been recognized as a primary force in the interactive exchange (Brentano, 1874/1973; Bruner, 1986, 1990, 2002; Gergely & Csibra, 1997; Gergely, Nadsasdy, Csibra, & Biro, 1995; Gopnick & Meltzoff, 1998; Husserl, 1962, 1930/1989; Meltzoff, 1995; Meltzoff & Gopnik, 1993; Rochat, 1999; Ruby & Decety, 2001; Sander, 1995a, 1995b; as well as Konrad Lorenz). In most recent BCPSG writings, we have increasingly emphasized the role of intentionality in interactions.

In summary, the work of the BCPSG has been an effort to take these threads, to flesh them out further, and to knit them into a coherent model that highlights the richness of the therapeutic exchange. We have every reason to assume that this model will be consistent with what is emerging in current neuroscience, brain imaging studies, cognitive science, and related fields.

### THE EMERGENCE OF A UNIFYING PARADIGM

This book represents a journey. We began with developmental experience as a source of inspiration and knowledge and as a possible way to illuminate change processes in psychotherapy. In our original paper (BCPSG, 1998a; [Stern et al, 1998 and Chapter One]) as well as in the associated papers in *Infant Mental Health Journal* (BCPSG, 1998b; [Tronick, 1998 and Chapter Two]), we presented a skeleton of a position that was more fully fleshed out as we moved along in our thinking and writing. Looking back, it became clear that all the major ideas were foreshadowed in this first paper. The title ("Non-Interpretive Mechanisms in Psychoanalytic Therapy: The 'Something More' Than Interpretation") carries the central point. It is implicit change that is the something more. Four subpoints emerged within this.

The inspiration for our work comes from current infant observational studies within developmental psychology, which by default places major emphasis on the implicit. It seemed necessary to consider implicit processes. We were impressed that something largely unpredictable, nonlinear, and emergent needed a different model to account for it; this is where DST came in.

What went on between the minds of patient and analyst was the true subject of analysis. Although words were spoken, it was in the implicit meanings that emerged between the words that the true goings-on were located. This in turn required a further inquiry into what we meant by co-creativity and by intersubjectivity. We realized we were talking about moment-by-moment events that we called "local level."

All of this was present in germinal form in the first paper, but needed to be further thought through and these four features elaborated. The three short papers to follow appeared as part of a special issue of the *Infant Mental Health Journal* in which we elaborated on several of the central ideas introduced in our initial paper.

In 2002, BCPSG took up the most difficult problem of where, when, and what is implicit, because it is not the words. Clearly it came closer to residing in the second-by-second world, so we needed to examine this world more carefully. This in turn took us back to mother–infant observational material, which led to our recognition of, and then insisting on the importance of, the local level if we were going to talk about the something more (BCPSG, 2002; see Chapter Four).

In 2005, recognizing and emphasizing two aspects that had not caught our attention initially, namely, that the local level process was sloppy, nonlinear, noncausal, and unpredictable, we then realized that this was the view from being in the thick of it, in the middle of the session, rather than a cleaned-up after-the-fact version. This required different theoretical tools (DST), which in turn made the second aspect apparent, that the process of creating new, surprising, useful events was a co-creative process rather than one of excavating preformed meanings. It was the product of a complex interaction of two minds (BCPSG, 2005a; see Chapter Five).

In responding to several critiques (BCPSG, 2005b), we talked about how, both developmentally and therapeutically, meaning was created through the parsing of intention and affect cues, a universal given of any interaction. This further highlighted the centrality of intention. Here it became apparent that psychoanalytic theory had conceptually reversed what was deep and what was superficial.

In Chapter Six (BCPSG, 2007), we further elaborated this crucial point, forced by our analytic and clinical colleagues to make these findings more relevant to them by bringing in the notions of conflict, defense, and the dynamic unconscious. We had assumed, without being fully aware of it, that implicit process was at the heart of conflict and defense, but here we were to establish this, along with spelling out the process on a descriptive level.

In Chapter Seven (BCPSG, 2008), we continued this process, because the clinical needs of a theory based on dynamics are largely based on meanings, on what a particular defense means. We had to fully confront what was meant by *meaning*. The implicit was now clearly established as foundational, but also served as a guide or reference point for gauging fit with explicit meanings and the coherence and validity of explicit meanings. This chapter concludes with our response to three commentaries on the article itself.

Lastly, we had been challenged to present our thinking about what made a psychodynamic therapy therapeutic. The implicit relational process view is presented in the concluding chapter.

# Change in Psychotherapy

# Chapter 1

# Non-Interpretive Mechanisms in Psychoanalytic Therapy: The "Something More" Than Interpretation[1]

IT IS BY NOW GENERALLY ACCEPTED THAT SOMETHING MORE THAN IN-terpretation is necessary to bring about therapeutic change. Using an approach based on recent studies of mother–infant interaction and nonlinear dynamic systems and their relation to theories of mind, the authors propose that the something more resides in interactional inter-subjective processes that give rise to what they will call "implicit rela-tional knowing." This relational procedural domain is intrapsychically distinct from the symbolic domain. In the analytic relationship it com-prises intersubjective moments occurring between patient and analyst that can create new organizations in, or reorganize, not only the rela-tionship between the interactants but more importantly the patient's implicit procedural knowledge, his ways of being with others. The dis-tinct qualities and consequences of these moments (now moments, "moments of meeting") are modeled and discussed in terms of a se-

[1]Originally published in the *International Journal of Psychoanalysis, 79*, 903–9221. Reprint-ed with permission by Blackwell.

quencing process that they call moving along. Conceptions of the shared implicit relationship, transference, and countertransference are discussed within the parameters of this perspective, which is distinguished from other relational theories and self psychology. In sum, powerful therapeutic action occurs within implicit relational knowledge. They propose that much of what is observed to be lasting therapeutic effect results from such changes in this intersubjective relational domain.

## INTRODUCTION

How do psychoanalytic therapies bring about change? There has long been a consensus that something more than interpretation, in the sense of making the unconscious conscious, is needed. The discussion of what is the something more comes from many perspectives, involving different polarities, where the something more has taken the form of psychological acts versus psychological words; of change in psychological structures versus undoing repression and rendering conscious; of a mutative relationship with the therapist versus mutative information for the patient. Many psychoanalytic writers, beginning early in the psychoanalytic movement and accelerating up to the present, have directly or indirectly addressed these issues (Ferenczi & Rank, 1924; Fenichel, 1941; Greenson, 1967; Loewald, 1971; Sterba, 1940; Strachey, 1934; Winnicott, 1957; Zetzel, 1956). More recently, the same issues are being reconsidered by Ehrenberg (1992), Gill (1994), Greenberg (1996), Lachmann and Beebe (1996), Mitchell (1993), Sandler (1987), Schwaber (1998), and Stolorow, Atwood, and Brandchaft (1994).

This chapter will present a new understanding of the something more, and attempt to show where in the therapeutic relationship it acts, and how. We will do this by applying a developmental perspective to clinical material. Anecdotal evidence suggests that after most patients have completed a successful treatment, they tend to remember two kinds of nodal events that they believe changed them. One concerns the key interpretation(s) that rearranged their intrapsychic landscape. The other concerns special "moments" of authentic person-to-person connection (defined below) with the therapist that altered the relationship with him or her and thereby the patient's sense of himself. These reports suggest that many therapies fail or are terminated, not because of incorrect or unaccepted interpretations, but because of missed opportunities for a meaningful connection between two people. Although we cannot claim that there is a one-to-one correlation between the quality of what one remembers and the nature of the therapeutic outcome, we also cannot dismiss the fact that both the moments of authentic meeting and the failures of such meetings are often recalled with great clarity as pivotal events in the treatment.

The present chapter will differentiate these two mutative phenomena: the interpretation and the "moment of meeting." It will also ask in what domain of the therapeutic relationship these two mutative events occur. While interpretations and "moments of meeting" may act together to make possible the emergence or reinforcement of each other, one is not explicable in terms of the other. Nor does one occupy a privileged place as an explanation of change. They remain separable phenomena. Even those analysts who believe in the mutative primacy of interpretation will readily agree that as a rule, good interpretations require preparation and carry along with them something more. A problem with this inclusive view of interpretation is that it leaves unexplored what part of the enlarged interpretive activity is actually the something more, and what part is purely insight via interpretation. Without a clear distinction it becomes impossible to explore whether the two are conceptually related or quite different. Nonetheless, we do not wish to set up a false competition between these two mutative events. They are complementary. Rather, we wish to explore the something more, as it is less well understood.

We will present a conceptual framework for understanding the something more and will describe where and how it works (see, also, Tronick et al., 1998). First, we make a distinction between therapeutic changes in two domains: the declarative, or conscious verbal, domain; and the implicit procedural or relational domain (see Clyman, 1991; Lyons-Ruth, 1999). Then we will apply a theoretical perspective derived from a dynamic systems model of developmental change to the process of therapeutic change. This model is well suited to an exploration of the implicit, procedural processes occurring between partners in a relationship.

## AN APPROACH TO THE PROBLEM

Our approach is based on recent ideas from developmental studies of mother–infant interaction and from studies of nonlinear dynamic systems, and their relation to mental events. These perspectives will be brought to bear as we elaborate our view on the something more of psychoanalytic therapy, which involves grappling with notions such as "moments of meeting," the "real" relationship, and authenticity. We present here a conceptual overview for the sections on developmental and therapeutic processes. The something more must be differentiated from other processes in psychoanalysis. At least two kinds of knowledge, two kinds of representations, and two kinds of memory are constructed and reorganized in dynamic psychotherapies. One is explicit (declarative) and the other is implicit (procedural). Whether they are in fact two distinct mental phenomena remains to be determined. At this stage, however, we believe that further inquiry demands that they be considered separately. Declarative knowledge is explicit and conscious or readily made conscious. It is represented symbolically in imagistic or verbal form. It is the content matter of interpretations that alter the conscious understanding of the patient's intrapsychic organization. Historically, interpretation has been tied to intrapsychic dynamics rather than to the implicit rules governing one's transactions with others. This emphasis is currently shifting.

Procedural knowledge of relationships, on the other hand, is implicit, operating outside both focal attention and conscious verbal experience. This knowledge is represented nonsymbolically in the form of what we will call implicit relational knowing. Most of the literature on procedural knowledge concerns knowing about interactions between our own body and the inanimate world (e.g., riding a bicycle). There is another kind that concerns knowing about interpersonal and intersubjective relations, that is, how "to be with" someone (D. N. Stern, 1985, 1995). For instance, the infant comes to know early in life what forms of affectionate approaches the parent will welcome or turn away, as described in the attachment literature (Lyons-Ruth, 1991). It is this second kind that we are calling implicit relational knowing. Such knowings integrate affect, cognition, and behavioral/interactive dimensions. They can remain out of awareness as Bollas's "unthought known" (1987), or Sandler's "past unconscious" (Sandler & Fonagy, 1997) but can also form a basis for much of what may later become symbolically represented.

In summary, declarative knowledge is gained or acquired through verbal interpretations that alter the patient's intrapsychic understanding within the context of the "psychoanalytic," and usually transferential, relationship. Implicit relational knowing, on the other hand, occurs through "interactional, intersubjective processes" that alter the relational field within the context of what we will call the "shared implicit relationship."

### The Nature of "Implicit Relational Knowing"

Implicit relational knowing has been an essential concept in the developmental psychology of preverbal infants. Observations and experiments strongly suggest that infants interact with caregivers on the basis of a great deal of relational knowledge. They show anticipations and expectations and manifest surprise or upset at violations of the expected (Sander, 1988; Trevarthen, 1979; Tronick, Als, Adamson, Wise, & Brazelton, 1978). Furthermore, this implicit knowing is registered in representations of interpersonal events in a nonsymbolic form, beginning in the first year of life. This is evident not only in their expectations but also in the generalization of certain interactive patterns (Beebe & Lachmann, 1988; Lyons-Ruth, 1991; D. N. Stern, 1985). Studies of development by several of the authors (Lyons-Ruth & Jacobvitz, 1999; Sander, 1962, 1988; D. N. Stern, 1985, 1995; Tronick & Cohn, 1989) have emphasized an ongoing process of negotiation over the early years of life involving a sequence of adaptive tasks between infant and caregiving environment. The unique configuration of adaptive strategies that emerges from this sequence in each individual constitutes the initial organization of his or her domain of implicit relational knowing. Several different terms and conceptual variations have been proposed, each accounting for somewhat different relational phenomena. These include Bowlby's "internal working models" of attachment (Bowlby, 1973), D. N. Stern's "proto-narrative envelopes" and "schemas of being-with" (D. N. Stern, 1995), Sander's "themes of organization" (Sander, 1997), and Trevarthen's "relational scripts" (Trevarthen, 1993), among others. A formal description of how these strategies are represented remains an active field of inquiry.

Implicit relational knowing is hardly unique to the presymbolic infant. A vast array of implicit knowings concerning the many ways of being with others continue throughout life, including many of the ways of being with the therapist that we call transference. These knowings are often not symbolically represented but are not necessarily dynamically unconscious in the sense of being defensively excluded from awareness. We believe much of transference interpretation may avail itself of data gathered by the analyst about the patient's relational knowings. A prototypical example is that reported by Guntrip (1975) from the end of his first session with Winnicott. Winnicott said, "I don't have anything to say, but I'm afraid if I don't say something, you will think I am not here" (Guntrip, 1975).

### How Changes in "Implicit Relational Knowing" Are Experienced

A feature of dynamic systems theory (DST) relevant to our study is the self-organizing principle. Applying the self-organizing principle to human mental organization, we would claim that, in the absence of an opposing dynamic, the mind will tend to use all the shifts and changes in the intersubjective environment to create progressively more coherent implicit relational knowledge. In treatment, this will include what each member understands to be their own and the other's experience of the relationship, even if the intersubjective relationship itself does not come under therapeutic scrutiny, that is, it remains implicit. Just as an interpretation is the therapeutic event that rearranges the patient's conscious declarative knowledge, we propose that what we will call a "moment of meeting" is the event that rearranges implicit relational knowing for patient and analyst alike. It is in this sense that the "moment" takes on cardinal importance as the basic unit of subjective change in the domain of "implicit relational knowing." When a change occurs in the intersubjective environment, a "moment of meeting" will have precipitated it. The change will be sensed and the newly altered environment then acts as the new effective context in which subsequent mental actions occur and are shaped and past events are reorganized. The relationship as implicitly known has been altered, thus changing mental actions and behaviors that assemble in this different context.

The concept that new contexts lead to new assemblies of a system's constitutive elements is a tenet of general systems theory. An illustration of the same principle from the neurosciences is that of Freeman (1995). He describes the way that in the rabbit brain the neural firings activated by different odors create a different spatial pattern. When a new odor is encountered, not only does it establish its own unique pattern, but the patterns for all of the previously established odors become altered. There is a new olfactory context, and each preexisting element undergoes a change.

The idea of a "moment of meeting" grew out of the study of the adaptive process in development (Nahum, 1994; Sander, 1962, 1983, 1987). Such moments were seen to be key to state shifts and organismic reorganization. We believe the idea of the "well-timed interpretation" is also an attempt to grasp aspects of this idea.

A major subjective feature of a shift in implicit relational knowing is that it will feel like a sudden qualitative change. This is why the "moment" is so important in our thinking. The "moment" as a notion captures the subjective experience of a sudden shift in implicit relational knowing for both analyst and patient. We will discuss this in greater detail below. Clinically, the most interesting aspect of the intersubjective environment between patient and analyst is the mutual knowing of what is in the other's mind, as it concerns the current nature and state of their relationship. It may include states of activation, affect, feeling, arousal, desire, belief, motive, or content of thought, in any combination. These states can be transient or enduring, as mutual context. A prevailing intersubjective environment is shared. The sharing can further be mutually validated and ratified. However, the shared knowing about the relationship may remain implicit.

## DEVELOPMENTAL PERSPECTIVES
## ON THE PROCESS OF CHANGE

Since infants are the most rapidly changing human beings, it is natural to wish to understand change processes in development for their relevance to therapeutic change. Of particular relevance is the widely accepted view that despite neurological maturation, new capacities require an interactive intersubjective environment to be optimally realized. In this environment most of the infant and parent's time together is spent in active mutual regulation of their own and the other's states, in the service of some aim or goal. For further explication of the mutual regulation model and the concepts that underpin it, see Tronick (1989) and Gianino and Tronick (1988). The key notions that elaborate this general view follow.

### *Mutual Regulation of State Is the Central Joint Activity*

"State" is a concept that captures the semistable organization of the organism as a whole at a given moment. As Tronick (1989) argued, dyadic state regulation between two people is based on the microexchange of information through perceptual systems and affective displays as they are appreciated and responded to by mother and infant over time. The states that need to be regulated initially are hunger, sleep, activity cycling, arousal, and social contact; soon thereafter (the level of) joy or other affect states, (the level of) activation or excitation, exploration, attachment, and attribution of meanings; and eventually almost any form of state organization, including mental, physiological, and motivational. Regulation includes amplifying, downregulating, elaborating, repairing, scaffolding, as well as returning to some preset equilibrium. How well the caretaker apprehends the state of the infant, the specificity of his or her recognition, will, among other factors, determine the nature and degree of coherence of the infant's experience. Fittedness gives shared direction and helps determine the nature and qualities of the properties that emerge. Mutual regulation implies no symmetry between the interactants, only that influence is bidirectional. Each of the actors brings his or her history to the interaction, thus shaping what adaptive maneuvers are possible for each. Current concepts from development studies suggest that what the infant internalizes is the process of mutual regulation, not the object itself or part-objects (Beebe & Lachmann, 1988, 1994; D. N. Stern, 1985, 1995; Tronick & Weinberg, 1997). Ongoing regulation involves the repetition of sequenced experiences giving rise to expectancies and, thus, becomes the basis of implicit relational knowing (Lyons-Ruth, 1991; Nahum, 1994; Sander, 1962, 1983; D. N. Stern, 1985, 1995; Tronick, 1989).

### *Regulation Is Goal-Directed*

The processes of mutual regulation moving toward a goal are neither simple nor straightforward most of the time and do not run smoothly (Tronick, 1989). Nor would we expect or want them to, ideally. Rather they demand a constant struggling, negotiating, missing and repairing, midcourse correcting, and scaffolding, to remain within or return to a range of equilibrium. This requires both persistence and tolerance of failures on both partners' part. (Of course the work is asymmetrical, with the caregiver, in most situations, doing the lion's share.) This trial-by-error temporal process of moving in the general direction of goals, and also identifying and agreeing on these goals, we will call "moving along," to capture the ongoing ordinariness of the process as well as its divergence from a narrow and direct path to the goal. Sometimes the goal is clear and the dyad can move along briskly, as when hunger requires feeding. Sometimes an unclear goal must be discovered or uncovered in the moving along process, as in free play or most play with objects.

### *Mutual Regulation Also Involves an Intersubjective Goal*

The moving along process is oriented toward two goals simultaneously. The first is physical and/or physiological, and is achieved through actions that bring about a behavioral fittedness between the two partners, such as positioning and holding of the baby for a feeding by the caregiver, coupled with sucking and drinking by the baby; or, high-level facial and vocal stimulation during face-to-face play by the caregiver, coupled with a high level of pleasurable activation and facial expressivity in the baby. The second, parallel goal is the experience of a mutual recognition of each other's motives, desires, and implicit aims that direct actions, and the feelings that accompany this process (Tronick, Als, & Adamson, 1979). This is the intersubjective goal. In addition to a mutual sensing of each other's motives or desires, the intersubjective goal also implies a signaling or ratifying to each other of this sharing. There must be some act assuring consensuality. Affect attunement provides an example (D. N. Stern, 1985).

It is not possible to determine which goal is primary, the physical or intersubjective. At times one of them seems to take precedence, and a shifting back and forth occurs between what is foreground or background. In any event both are always present. Our central interest here, however, remains the intersubjective goal.

### The Regulatory Process Gives Rise to "Emergent Properties"

In moving along much of the time, one does not know exactly what will happen, or when, even if general estimates can be made. This indeterminacy is due not only to the nature of dynamic systems, but to the shifting of local and even intermediate goals, as well as the fact that so much of moving along is ad-libbed. Even frequently repeated interactions are almost never repeated in exactly the same way. Themes of interaction are always in the process of evolving variations, quite evident in certain activities such as "free play," where part of the nature of the activity is to constantly introduce variations so as to avoid habituation (D. N. Stern, 1977). But, even a more tightly structured activity, such as feeding or changing, is never repeated exactly.

The improvisational nature of these interactions has led us to find guidance in the recent theoretical work on nonlinear, dynamic systems that produce emergent properties (Fivaz-Depeursinge & Corboz-Warnery, 1995; Maturana & Varela, 1980; Prigogine & Stengers, 1984; and, as applied to early development, Thelen & Smith, 1994). These concepts seem to provide the best models to capture the process of moving along and the nature of specific "moments of meeting" (see below), which are emergent properties of moving along. In the course of moving along, the dual goals of complementary fitted actions and intersubjective meeting about that fittedness can be suddenly realized in a "moment of meeting," one that has inevitably been well prepared for, but not determined, over a longer period of time. Such moments are jointly constructed, requiring the provision of something unique from each party. It is in this sense that meeting hinges on a specificity of recognition as conceptualized by Sander (1991).

Examples of "moments of meeting" are such events as: the moment when the parent's behavioral input fits with the baby's movement toward sleep so as to trigger a shift in the infant from awake to asleep; or, the moment when a bout of free play evolves into an explosion of mutual laughter; or, the moment that the baby learns, with much teaching and scaffolding by the parent, that the word that they will use for that barking thing is "dog." In the latter two examples, the meeting is also intersubjective in the sense that each partner recognizes that there has been a mutual fittedness. Each has captured an essential feature of the other's goal-oriented motive structure. To state it colloquially, each grasps a similar version of "what is happening, now, here, between us."

We assume that intersubjective meetings have goal status in humans. They are the mental version of the aim of object-relatedness. In systems terms, such meetings involve linking between organism and context, inside and outside, giving rise to a state that is more inclusive than what either system alone can create. Tronick has termed this more inclusive state the dyadic expansion of consciousness.

## A moment of meeting can create a new intersubjective environment and an altered domain of implicit relational knowing.

An example provides the best illustration. If in the course of playing, a mother and infant unexpectedly achieve a new and higher level of activation and intensity of joy, the infant's capacity to tolerate higher levels of mutually created positive excitement has been expanded for future interactions. Once an expansion of the range has occurred, and there is the mutual recognition that the two partners have successfully interacted together in a higher orbit of joy, their subsequent interactions will be conducted within this altered intersubjective environment. It is not the simple fact of each having done it before, but the sense that the two have been here before. The domain of implicit relational knowing has been altered.

As another example, imagine a young child visiting a new playground with his father. The child rushes over to the slide and climbs the ladder. As he gets near the top, he feels a little anxious about the height and the limits of his newly emerging skill. In a smoothly functioning dyadic system, he will look to his father as a guide to help him regulate his affective state. His father responds with a warm smile and a nod, perhaps moving a little closer to the child. The child goes up and over the top, gaining a new sense of mastery and fun. They have shared, intersubjectively, the affective sequence tied to the act. Such moments will occur again in support of the child's confident engagement with the world.

## Immediate Consequences of "Moments of Meeting" That Alter the Intersubjective Environment

When a "moment of meeting" occurs in a sequence of mutual regulation, an equilibrium occurs that allows for a "disjoin" between the interactants and a détente in the dyadic agenda (Nahum, 1994). Sander (1983) has called this disjoin an "open space" in which the infant can be alone, briefly, in the presence of the other, as they share the new context (Winnicott, 1957). Here an opening exists in which a new initiative is possible, one freed from the imperative of regulation to restore equilibrium. The constraint of the usual implicit relational knowledge is loosened and creativity becomes possible. The infant will recontextualize his new experience.

During the open space, mutual regulation is momentarily suspended. Then the dyad reinitiates the process of moving along. However, the moving along will now be different because it starts from the terrain of the newly established intersubjective environment, from an altered "implicit relational knowing."

## APPLICATION TO THERAPEUTIC CHANGE

We shall now provide a descriptive terminology and conceptual base for the something more, showing how it operates as a vehicle for change in psychoanalytic therapies. The key concept, the "moment of meeting", is the emergent property of the moving along process that alters the intersubjective environment, and thus the implicit relational knowing. In brief, moving along is comprised of a string of "present moments," which are the subjective units marking the slight shifts in direction while proceeding forward. At times, a present moment becomes "hot" affectively, and full of portent for the therapeutic process. These moments are called "now moments." When a now moment is seized, that is, responded to with an authentic, specific, personal response from each partner, it becomes a "moment of meeting." This is the emergent property that alters the subjective context. We will now discuss each element in this process.

### The Preparatory Process: "Moving Along" and "Present Moments"

In many ways, the therapeutic process of moving along is similar to the moving along process in the parent–infant dyad. The form is different. One is mainly verbal while the other nonverbal, but the underlying functions of the moving along process share much in common. Moving along involves the movement in the direction of the goals of the therapy, however they may be explicitly or implicitly defined by the participants. It subsumes all of the usual components of a psychoanalytic therapy, such as interpretation, clarification, and so on. In any therapeutic session, as in any parent–infant interaction, the dyad moves toward an intermediate goal. One intermediate goal in a session is defining the topics they will take up together, such as lateness to a session, was the patient properly "heard" yesterday, the upcoming vacation, is therapy helping the feeling of emptiness, does the therapist like the patient, and so on. The participants do not have to agree. They must only negotiate the interactive flow so as to move it forward to grasp what is happening between them, and what each member perceives, believes, and says in the particular context, and what each member believes the other member perceives, feels, and believes. They are working on defining the intersubjective environment, moving along. The events in the conscious foreground that propel the movement are free associations, clarifications, questions, silences, interpretations, and so on. Unlike the largely nonverbal behaviors that make up the background of the parent–infant environment, the verbal content usually occupies the foreground in the consciousness of both partners. In the background, however, the movement is toward intersubjective sharing and understanding. The verbal content should not blind us to the parallel process of moving along toward an implicit intersubjective goal.

Analogous to the physical fittedness goal in the nonverbal parent–infant interactions, we see the moving along process in an adult therapy session as consisting of two parallel goals. One is a reordering of conscious verbal knowledge. This would include discovering topics to work on, clarify, elaborate, interpret, and understand. The second goal is the mutual definition and understanding of the intersubjective environment that captures the implicit relational knowing and defines the "shared implicit relationship." A set of smaller local goals are needed to microregulate the moving along process. Local goals perform almost constant course corrections that act to redirect, repair, test, probe, or verify the direction of the interactive flow toward the intermediate goal.

As will be seen, the intersubjective environment is part of what we shall call the "shared implicit relationship." The negotiating and defining of the intersubjective environment occurs in parallel with the explicit examination of the patient's life and the examination of the transference. It is a process that is conducted out of awareness most of the time. Yet, it is going on with every therapeutic maneuver. Moving along carries the interactants toward a clearer sense of where they are in their "shared implicit relationship."

We conceive of moving along as a process that subjectively is divided into moments of different quality and function that we call "present moments." Among clinicians the notion of a present moment is intuitively evident and has proved invaluable in our discussions. The duration of a present moment is usually short, because as a subjective unit it is the duration of time needed to grasp the sense of "what is happening now, here, between us." Accordingly, it lasts from microseconds to many seconds. It is constructed around intentions or wishes and their enactment, which trace a dramatic line of tension as it moves toward its goal (see D. N. Stern, 1995). A present moment is a unit of dialogic exchange that is relatively coherent in content, homogeneous in feeling, and oriented in the same direction toward a goal. A shift in any of the above ushers in a new, the next, present moment. For example if the therapist says, "Do you realize that you have been late to the last three sessions? That's unusual for you," the patient responds, "Yes, I do," and the analyst adds, "What are your thoughts about that?," this exchange constitutes a present moment. The patient replies, "I think I've been angry at you." Silence. "Yes I have been." Silence. This is a second present moment. The patient then says, "Last week you said something that really got me ticked off . . ." This is the third present moment.

These present moments are the steps of the moving along process. Between each there is a discontinuity of a kind, but strung together they progress, though not evenly, toward a goal. They proceed in a fashion that is rarely linear.

In brief, we are speaking of a bounded envelope of subjective time in which a motive is enacted to microregulate the content of what is being talked about and to adjust the intersubjective environment.

The fairly tight cyclicity of infant activities (sleep, activity, hunger, play, etc.) assures a high level of repetition, creating a repertoire of present moments. In therapy, too, present moments repeat variations on the theme of habitual moves that constitute the unique way any therapeutic dyad will "move along." Present moments will of course be constrained by the nature of the therapeutic technique, the personalities of the interactants, and the pathology at issue.

Because present moments are so often repeated with only minor variations, they become extremely familiar, canons of what moments of life with that other person are expected to be like. Present moments become represented as "schemas of ways of being with another" (D. N. Stern, 1995) in the domain of "implicit relational knowing." The pair evolves a set of microinteractive patterns in which steps include errors, disruptions, and repairs (Lachmann & Beebe, 1996; Tronick, 1989). These recurrent sequences tell us about the patient's "unthought known" (Bollas, 1987) or the "prereflective unconscious" of Stolorow and Atwood (1992). They are the building blocks of Bowlby's working models and of most internalization. They are not in awareness but are intrapsychically distinct from that which is repressed.

In sum, present moments strung together make up the moving along process. In fact, both the units, i.e., the present moments, as well as the direction of this moving along, occur within a framework that is familiar to and characteristic of each dyad.

## *"Now Moments"*

In our conceptualization, "now moments" are a special kind of "present moment," one that gets lit up subjectively and affectively, pulling one more fully into the present.[2] They take on this subjective quality because the habitual framework—the known, familiar intersubjective environment of the therapist–patient relationship—has all of a sudden been altered or risks alteration. The current state of the "shared implicit relationship" is called into the open. This potential breach in the established proceedings happens at various moments. It does not have to threaten the therapeutic framework, but requires a response that is too specific and personal to be a known technical maneuver.

Now moments are not part of the set of characteristic present moments that make up the usual way of being together and moving along. They demand an intensified attention and some kind of choice of whether or not to remain in the established habitual framework. And if not, what to do? They force the therapist into some kind of "action," be it an interpretation or a response that is novel relative to the habitual framework, or a silence. In this sense, now moments are like the ancient Greek concept of *kairos*, a unique moment of opportunity that must be seized, because your fate will turn on whether you seize it and how.

Clinically and subjectively, the way the therapist and patient know that they have entered a "now moment," and that it is distinct from the usual present moments, is that these moments are unfamiliar, unexpected in their exact form and timing, unsettling or weird. They are often confusing as to what is happening or what to do. These moments are pregnant with an unknown future that can feel like an impasse or an opportunity. The present becomes very dense subjectively as in a "moment of truth." These "now moments" are often accompanied by expectancy or anxiety because the necessity of choice is pressing, yet there is no immediately available prior plan of action or explanation.

[2]We borrow the term "now moment" from Walter Freeman (1994).

The application of habitual technical moves will not suffice. The analyst intuitively recognizes that a window of opportunity for some kind of therapeutic reorganization or derailment is present, and the patient may recognize that he or she has arrived at a watershed in the therapeutic relationship.

Now moments can be described as evolving subjectively in three phases. There is a "pregnancy phase" that is filled with the feeling of imminence. There is the "weird phase" when it is realized that one has entered an unknown and unexpected intersubjective space. And there is the "decision phase" when the now moment is to be seized or not. If it is seized, it will lead to a "moment of meeting," if all goes well, or to a failed now moment if it does not.

A "now moment" is an announcement of a potential emergent property of a complex dynamic system. Although the history of its emergence may be untraceable, it is prepared for with fleeting or pale prior apparitions, something like a motif in music that quietly and progressively prepares for its transformation into the major theme. Still the exact instant and form of its appearance remain unpredictable.

The paths toward the now moment are many. The patient may identify an event during a session and immediately realize that the intersubjective environment has just shifted, but not share and ratify this shift during the session. Or, the patient might have let the event pass without much notice and later rework it to discover its importance in signaling a possible shift in the intersubjective environment. These events are forms of hidden or potential now moments that are part of the preparatory process. They will perhaps, one day, reach a state of readiness to enter into the mutual dialogue and become now moments as we have described.

Now moments may occur when the traditional therapeutic frame risks being, or is, or should be, broken. For example:

- If an analytic patient stops the exchange and asks, "Do you love me?"
- When the patient has succeeded in getting the therapist to do something out of the (therapeutic) ordinary, as when the patient says something very funny and both break into a sustained belly laugh.
- When by chance patient and therapist meet unexpectedly in a dif-

ferent context, such as in a queue at the theater, and a novel interactive and intersubjective move is fashioned, or fails to be.

- When something momentous, whether good or bad, has happened in the real life of the patient that common decency demands be acknowledged and responded to somehow.

Recall that we are dealing with a complex dynamic process where only one of several components may be changing in a slow and progressive fashion during the preparatory phase and may be hardly perceptible, until reaching a certain threshold when it suddenly threatens to change the context for the functioning of other components. Conceptually, now moments are the threshold to an emergent property of the interaction, namely, the "moment of meeting."

The most intriguing now moments arise when the patient does something that is difficult to categorize, something that demands a different and new kind of response with a personal signature that shares the analyst's subjective state (affect, fantasy, real experience, etc.) with the patient. If this happens, they will enter an authentic "moment of meeting." During the "moment of meeting" a novel intersubjective contact between them will become established, new in the sense that an alteration in the "shared implicit relationship" is created.

### The "Moment of Meeting"

A now moment that is therapeutically seized and mutually realized is a "moment of meeting." As in the parent–infant situation, a "moment of meeting" is highly specific; each partner has actively contributed something unique and authentic of his- or herself as an individual (not unique to their theory or technique of therapeutics) in the construction of the "moment of meeting." When the therapist (especially), but also the patient, grapples with the now moment, explores and experiences it, it can become a "moment of meeting." There are essential elements that go into creating a "moment of meeting." The therapist must use a specific aspect of his or her individuality that carries a personal signature. The two are meeting as persons relatively unhidden by their usual therapeutic roles, for that moment. Also, the actions that make up the "moment of meeting" cannot be routine, habitual, or technical; they must be novel and fashioned to meet the singularity of the moment. Of course this implies a measure of empathy, an openness to affective and cognitive reappraisal, a signaled affect attunement, a viewpoint that reflects and ratifies that what is happening is occurring in the domain of the "shared implicit relationship," that is, a newly created dyadic state specific to the participants.

The "moment of meeting" is the nodal event in this process because it is the point at which the intersubjective context gets altered, thus changing the implicit relational knowing about the patient–therapist relationship. That the "moment" plays such a key mutative role has been recognized by others as well. Lachmann and Beebe (1996) have emphasized it, and Ehrenberg (1992) has described her mutative thera-peutic work as taking place precisely during intimate subjective mo-ments.

An example is instructive at this point. Molly, a married woman in her mid-30s, entered analysis because of poor self-esteem that was fo-cused on her body, her inability to lose weight, and her severe anxiety about losing the people most dear to her. She was a second daughter. Because her older sister had been crippled by polio as an infant, Molly's parents cherished her healthy body. When she was a child, they would ask her to dance for them while they watched admiringly.

She began the session talking about "body things" and associated having feelings of sexual excitement and a flash of anger at the analyst on her way to the session. "I have the image of your sitting back . . . and watching me from some superior position." Later in the session she recalled her parents watching her dance and wondered if there were some sexual excitement in it for them, too, "if they wanted it, too." There followed a long discussion of her body experience, includ-ing physical examinations, fears there was something wrong with her body, and body sensations. Then, after a prolonged silence, Molly said, "Now I wonder if you're looking at me." (The now moment began here.)

The analyst felt taken aback, put on the spot. Her first thought was whether to remain silent or say something. If she was silent, would Molly feel abandoned? Repeating Molly's statement—"you wonder if I'm looking at you"—seemed awkward and distancing. The analyst's responding with a remark of her own, however, felt risky. The sexual implications were so intense that to speak them seemed to bring them too close to action. Noting her own discomfort and trying to understand its source, the analyst identified the related issue of dominance and realized that she felt as if she were being invited either to take the "superior position" or to submit to Molly. At this point in her considerations, she suddenly felt free to be spontaneous and communicate to Molly her actual experience.

"It kind of feels as if you're trying to pull my eyes to you," she said.

"Yes," Molly agreed, with avidity. (These two sentences made up the "moment of meeting.")

"It's a mixed thing," said the analyst.

"There's nothing wrong with the longings," Molly replied.

"Right," the analyst agreed.

"The thing is, it takes two to manage," Molly said.

"Certainly at first," the analyst replied.

"That's what I was thinking. . . . It's nice thinking about this now . . . and I actually am able to feel some compassion."

"For yourself?" the analyst asked.

"Yes," Molly answered.

"I'm glad," the analyst responded.

In this vignette, an intersubjective meeting took place because the analyst used her own inner struggle to apprehend the patient and seize the now moment by responding specifically and honestly, "It kind of feels (to me as a specific individual, is implied) as if you are trying to pull my eyes to you." This turned the now moment into a "moment of meeting." This is quite different from the various possible, technically adequate, responses that leave the specificity of the analyst as person, at that moment, out of the picture, such as: "is this the way it was with your parents?" or "tell me what you imagined."

### *Interpretations in Relation to "Moments of Meeting"*

Now moments can also lead directly to an interpretation. And interpretations can lead to "moments of meeting" or the other way around. A successful traditional interpretation allows the patient to see himself, his life, and his past differently. This realization will invariably be accompanied by affect. If the interpretation is made in a way that conveys the affective participation of the analyst, a "moment of meeting" may also have occurred. Sander (1997) sees this occurrence as a matching of specificities between two systems that are in resonance and attuned to one another. This is akin to the affect attunement seen in parent–infant interactions (D. N. Stern, 1985).

Suppose that the analyst makes an excellent interpretation with exquisite timing. It will have an effect on the patient, which may be a silence, or an "aha," or most often something like, "yes, it really is like that." If the analyst fails to convey his or her affective participation (even with a response as simple as, "Yes, it has been, for you," but said with a signature born of his own life experience), the patient could assume or imagine that the analyst was only applying technique, and there will have been a failure to permit an important new experience to alter the known intersubjective environment. In consequence, the interpretation will be much less potent.

Strictly speaking, an interpretation can close out a now moment by "explaining" it further or elaborating or generalizing it. However, unless the therapist does something more than the strict interpretation, something to make clear his or her response and recognition of the patient's experience of a shift in the relationship, then there will be no new intersubjective context created. A sterile interpretation may have been correctly or well formulated but it will most likely not have landed and taken root. Most gifted psychoanalysts know this and do the "something more," even considering it part of the interpretation. But it is not. And that is exactly the theoretical problem we are grappling with. If the scope of what is considered an interpretation becomes too large and ill-defined, the theoretical problems become impossibly confused.

A distinction must be made here. A now moment can, and often does, arise around charged transferential material, and gets resolved with a traditional interpretation. If this interpretation is given in an "authentic" manner, how is that different from a "moment of meeting"? It is different for this reason. During a traditional interpretation involving transferential material, the therapist as a person, as he or she exists in his or her own mind, is not called into the open and put into play. Nor is the shared implicit relationship called into the open for review. Rather, the therapeutic understanding and response occurring within the analytic role is called into play. What "authentic" means in this context is difficult to define. During an "authentic" transference interpretation, there should not be a "moment of meeting" of two people more or less denuded of their therapeutic roles. If there were, the act of the therapist, in response to the transference act of the patient, would have the character of countertransference. In contradistinction, the transference and countertransference aspects are at a minimum in a "moment of meeting" and the personhood of the interactants, relatively denuded of role trappings, is put into play. Assessing the relative lack of transference-countertransference, and the relative presence of two people experiencing each other outside of their professionally prescribed roles, is, of course, not easy, but we are all aware of such moments, provided that the very concept is accepted. We will return to this point below.

### The "Open Space"

As in the developmental sequence, we assume that in the therapeutic situation "moments of meeting" leave in their wake an "open space" in which a shift in the intersubjective environment creates a new equilibrium, a "disjoin" with an alteration in or rearrangement of defensive processes. Individual creativity, agency emerging within the individual's configuration of open space, becomes possible, as the patient's "implicit relational knowing" has been freed of constraints imposed by the habitual (Winnicott, 1957).

### Other Fates of the Now Moment

The other various fates of the now moment, if it is not seized to become a "moment of meeting" or an interpretation are:

### 1. A "Missed Now Moment"

A missed now moment is a lost opportunity. Gill provides a graphic example. "In one of my own analyses . . . I was once bold enough to say, 'I'll bet I will make more of a contribution to analysis than you have.' I almost rolled off the couch when the analyst replied, 'I wouldn't be a bit surprised.' I must also regretfully report that the exchange was not further analyzed, not in that analysis at any rate" (1994, pp. 105–106). We have taken him to mean there was no further discussion of this exchange. Here a moment had been allowed to pass by, never to be returned to.

## 2. A "Failed Now Moment"

In a failed now moment, something potentially destructive happens to the treatment. When a now moment has been recognized but there is a failure to meet intersubjectively, the course of therapy can be put in jeopardy. If the failure is left unrepaired, the two gravest consequences are that either a part of the intersubjective terrain gets closed off to the therapy, as if one had said "we cannot go there," or even worse, a basic sense of the fundamental nature of the therapeutic relationship is put into such serious question that therapy can no longer continue (whether or not they actually stop).

David, a young man, had begun an analysis. In a session after several months had elapsed, he was talking about a severe burn covering much of his chest that he had sustained as a toddler and musing about its influence on his subsequent development. It had left him with a disfiguring scar, easily seen when in a bathing suit or shorts, which had caused him much self-consciousness and acted as the focus for various issues concerning his body. Without thinking, David reached down and started to pull back his shirt, saying, "Here, let me show you. You will understand better." Abruptly, before he had uncovered the scar, his analyst broke in, "No! Stop, you needn't do that!" Both were left surprised by the analyst's response.

Both David and his analyst later agreed that what had transpired had not been helpful. David felt, however, and told his analyst, that the analyst's subsequent response had compounded the failure because, instead of saying that he felt badly for having reacted as he had to David, he said only that he had not performed to his own standards.

## 3. A "Repaired Now Moment"

Failed now moments can be repaired by staying with them or by returning to them. Reparation, in itself, can be positive. Almost by definition the repair of a failed now moment will lead the dyad into one or more new now moments.

### 4. A "Flagged Now Moment"

A now moment can be labeled. These labels are not easy to come by because the dyadic states concerned do not, in fact, have names and are extremely subtle and complex entities. They usually acquire names like "the time when you . . . and I . . ." Flagging them with a label is extremely important, not only because it facilitates their recall and use, but it also adds another layer to the jointness of this interpersonal creation. Flagging may also serve the purpose of dealing with a now moment only partially at the time of its first emergence without running the risk of missing or failing the moment. In this way it can buy the therapy needed time.

### 5. An "Enduring Now Moment"

Sometimes a now moment emerges that cannot be immediately resolved/disclosed/shared, but does not go away. It remains and hangs in the air for many sessions, even weeks. Nothing else can happen until its fate is determined. These enduring now moments are not necessarily failures. They may result from conditions that do not permit the usual solutions because the timing or readiness is not ripe or because the intersubjective meeting required is too complex to be contained in a single transaction. In this sense they also may buy needed time. Usually they are resolved with a different now moment that encompasses the enduring now moment. We will discuss this further below.

### THE "SHARED IMPLICIT RELATIONSHIP" AS THE LOCUS OF MUTATIVE ACTION IN THERAPY

We return now to the question posed at the beginning of this chapter, namely, in what domain of the relationship between therapist and patient does the "moment of meeting" occur and implicit knowledge get altered? We suggest that it takes place in the "shared implicit relationship."

The notion of any relationship in analysis that is not predominantly transferential/countertransferential has always been troublesome. Many analysts claim that all relatedness in this clinical situation is permeated with transference and countertransference feelings and interpretations, including those intermediary phenomena such as the therapeutic alliance and its related concepts. Yet others insist that a more authentic sense of relatedness is the necessary experiential background without which transference is not perceivable, let alone alterable (Thomä & Kachele, 1987).

The "shared implicit relationship" consists of shared implicit knowledge about a relationship that exists apart from, but parallel to, both the transference-countertransference relationship and the assigned psychoanalytic roles. While each partner's implicit knowledge about the relationship is unique to him, the area of overlap between them is what we mean by the shared implicit relationship. (This shared implicit relationship is never symmetrical.)

The emphasis on the importance of the "shared implicit relationship" was for us unexpected, a conclusion that we came to after realizing the nature of a "moment of meeting." Since a "moment of meeting" could only occur when something happened that was personal, shared, outside or in addition to "technique," and subjectively novel to habitual functioning, we were forced to reconsider the entire domain of the shared implicit relationship.

In our view, infant research has simplified consideration of the shared implicit relationship by highlighting the fact of affective communication and intersubjectivity virtually from the outset of postnatal life (Lachmann & Beebe, 1996; Tronick, 1989). Infant and caretaker are both seen to be capable of expressing affect and comprehending the affective expressions of the other. This first communication system continues to operate throughout life and has attracted ever more interest in our field under the rubric of the "nonverbal." We agree with Stechler (1996) that although our professional responsibility enjoins us from sharing the same life space as the patient, it is misguided to assume that the complex emotional being of the analyst can be (or should be) kept from the sensings of the patient, "sensings" based on the operation of a highly complex system that is always functioning. Our position is that the operation of this system constructs the "shared implicit relationship," which consists of a personal engagement between the two, constructed progressively in the domain of intersubjectivity and implicit knowledge. This personal engagement is constructed over time and acquires its own history. It involves basic issues that exist beyond and endure longer than the more therapeutically labile distortions of the transference-countertransference prism, because it includes more or less accurate sensings of the therapist's and patient's person. When we speak of an "authentic" meeting, we mean communications that reveal a personal aspect of the self that has been evoked in an affective response to another. In turn, it reveals to the other a personal signature, so as to create a new dyadic state specific to the two participants.

It is these stable, implicit knowings between analyst and analysand, their mutual sensings and apprehendings of each other, that we are calling their "shared implicit relationship." Such knowings endure over the fluctuations in the transference relationship and could even be detected with a microanalysis, much of the time, by a third party observing them, in which case it could be an "objective" event.

We have been forced by our reflections upon the "moment of meeting" and its role in altering implicit knowledge, to focus on and examine this shared implicit relationship. This is so because of several characteristics of a "moment of meeting."

1. It is marked by a sense of departure from the habitual way of proceeding in the therapy. It is a novel happening that the ongoing framework can neither account for nor encompass. It is the opposite of business as usual.

2. It cannot be sustained or fulfilled if the analyst resorts to a response that feels merely technical to the patient. The analyst must respond with something that is experienced as specific to the relationship with the patient and that is expressive of her own experience and personhood, and carries her signature.

3. A "moment of meeting" cannot be realized with a transference interpretation. Other aspects of the relationship must be accessed.

4. It is a dealing with "what is happening here and now between us?" The strongest emphasis is on the "now," because of the affective immediacy. It requires spontaneous responses and is actualized in the sense that analyst and patient become contemporaneous objects for each other.
5. The "moment of meeting," with its engagement of "what is happening here and now between us," need never be verbally explicated, but can be, after the fact.

All these considerations push the "moment of meeting" into a domain that transcends but does not abrogate the "professional" relationship and becomes partially freed of transferential/countertransferential overtones.

Although it is beyond the scope of this chapter, a further exploration of the "shared implicit relationship" is needed.

## SUMMARY AND DISCUSSION

Whereas interpretation is traditionally viewed as the nodal event acting within and upon the transferential relationship, and changing it by altering the intrapsychic environment, we view "moments of meeting" as the nodal event acting within and upon the "shared implicit relationship" and changing it by altering implicit knowledge that is both intrapsychic and interpersonal. Both of these complementary processes are mutative. However, they use different change mechanisms in different domains of experience.

With the aim of furthering clinical inquiry and research, we have attempted to provide a descriptive terminology for the phenomenology of these moments that create the "shared implicit relationship."

It should be noted that change in implicit relational knowledge and change in conscious verbal knowledge through interpretation are sometimes hard to distinguish from each other in the actual interactive process of the therapeutic situation. The "shared implicit relationship" and the transferential relationship flow in parallel, intertwined, one or the other taking its turn in the foreground. However, it is a necessary condition for relatedness that processing of implicit knowing be ongoing. Interpretation, on the other hand, is a punctate event.

We locate the foundations of the "shared implicit relationship" in the primordial process of affective communication, with its roots in the earliest relationships. We suggest it consists largely of implicit knowledge and that changes in this relationship may result in long-lasting therapeutic effects. In the course of an analysis some of the implicit relational knowledge will get slowly and painstakingly transcribed into conscious explicit knowledge. How much is an open question. This, however, is not the same as making the unconscious conscious, as psychoanalysis has always asserted. The difference is that implicit knowing is not rendered unconscious by repression and is not made available to consciousness by lifting repression. The process of rendering repressed knowledge conscious is quite different from that of rendering implicit knowing conscious. They require different conceptualizations. They may also require different clinical procedures, which has important technical implications.

The proposed model is centered on processes rather than structure and is derived from observing infant–caretaker interaction and from dynamic systems theory. In this model, there is a reciprocal process in which change takes place in the implicit relationship at "moments of meeting" through alterations in "ways of being with." It does not correct past empathic failures through the analytic empathic activity. It does not replace a past deficit. Rather something new is created in the relationship that alters the intersubjective environment. Past experience is recontextualized in the present such that a person operates from within a different mental landscape, resulting in new behaviors and experiences in the present and future.

Our position on mutual regulation in the therapy situation is akin to one described by Lachmann and Beebe (1996). Our idea of a "now moment" potentially becoming a "moment of meeting" differs from their idea of "heightened affective moments" in that we have tried to provide a terminology and a detailed sequential description of the process that leads up to and follows these privileged moments.

We agree with many contemporary thinkers that a dyadic state shift is fundamental, but we locate its emergence in the "moment of meeting" of the interactants. Our position is similar to those taken by

Mitchell (1993) and by Stolorow and Atwood (1992). We add to these authors, however, in considering most of the intersubjective environment as belonging to implicit relational knowing, which gets built into the shared implicit relationship in the course of therapy. The process of change, thus, takes place in the shared implicit relationship. Finally, we anticipate that this view of altering implicit relational knowing during "moments of meeting" will open up new and useful perspectives that consider therapeutic change.

## Chapter 2

# Implicit Relational Knowing: A Central Concept in Psychotherapeutic Change

## Part I. Implicit Relational Knowing: Its Role in Development and Psychoanalytic Treatment[1]

THERE HAS LONG BEEN A CONSENSUS THAT "SOMETHING MORE" THAN interpretation is needed in psychoanalytic therapies to bring about change. Interpretation, in the sense of making repressed impulses and fantasies conscious, may not in itself be sufficient. So how *do* psychoanalytic therapies bring about change? The Boston Change Process Study Group (BCPSG) began meeting early in 1995 to consider how to develop a language and a set of constructs to begin to elaborate on the "something more" that is needed in therapeutic encounters to catalyze change. This set of symposium papers is the first presentation of our attempt to bring together the joint strengths of developmental research, systems theory, and close observation of clinical process. We consider the framework presented here as a work in progress, with both additional elaboration and revisions needed. We present it here in hopes of

[1]Originally published in 1998, *Infant Mental Health Journal*, *19*(3) pp. 282–289. Copyright 1998 Michigan Association for Infant Mental Health. Reprinted with permission.

stimulating the dialogue needed in the field to achieve an interdiscipli-
nary synthesis of scientific research and clinical theory and observation.

Early in our discussions, our attention was drawn to the observation
that most patients remember "special moments" of authentic person-
to-person connection with their therapists, moments that altered their
relationship with him or her and thereby their sense of themselves. We
believe that these moments of intersubjective meeting constitute a pivotal part of the change process. We also find that the role of such moments in therapeutic change can best be understood in relation to
concepts drawn from recent infant research and from current systems
theories.

As we struggled with the problem of change using the traditional
constructs of psychoanalytic theory, it became clear that two kinds of
representational processes needed to be separately conceptualized. The
first kind of representation we will call semantic, in that it relies on
symbolic representation in language. The second kind we will call procedural representation. We are drawing on distinctions made by Kihlstrom and Cantor (1983) and other cognitive psychologists, but are
adapting them to our own needs. Procedural representations are rule-
based representations of how to proceed, of how to do things. Such
procedures may never become symbolically coded, as, for example,
knowledge of how to ride a bicycle. More important to us than bicycle
riding, however, is the domain of knowing how to do things with others. Much of this kind of knowledge is also procedural, such as knowing how to joke around, express affection, or get attention in childhood.
This procedural knowledge of how to do things with others we have
termed *implicit relational knowing*. In using this term, we want to differentiate implicit relational knowing from other forms of procedural
knowledge and to emphasize that such "knowings" are as much affective and interactive as they are cognitive. This implicit relational knowing begins to be represented in some yet-to-be-known form long before
the availability of language and continues to operate implicitly throughout life. Implicit relational knowing typically operates outside focal attention and conscious experience, without benefit of translation into
language. Language is used in the service of this knowing but the im-

plicit knowings governing intimate interactions are not language-based and are not routinely translated into semantic form.

Recognition of such a nonsymbolically based representational system has been one central contribution of infant research (e.g., Ainsworth, Blehar, Waters, & Wall, 1978; Beebe & Lachmann, 1994; Tronick, 1989). In our thinking, implicit relational knowing subsumes what has been termed internalized object relations. The older term—internalized object relations—has connotations of taking in from the outside, rather than of co-construction, and of taking in another person, rather than of representing a mutually constructed regulatory pattern (Tronick, 1989). The older term is also more identified with the literature on pathological rather than adaptive relatedness and is more often used to refer to past relationships and their activation in the transference rather than with more general representational models that are constantly accessed and updated in day-to-day encounters.

Therefore, we view implicit relational knowing as a construct that raises "internal object relations" to a more general representational systems conception. In this conception, implicit relational knowing encompasses normal and pathological knowings and integrates affect, fantasy, behavioral, and cognitive dimensions. Implicit procedural representations will become more articulated, integrated, flexible, and complex under favorable developmental conditions because implicit relational knowing is constantly being updated and "re-cognized" as it is accessed in day-to-day interaction (as articulated at the level of neuronal group selection by Edelman [1987]).

In a therapeutic context, some small areas of the patient's implicit relational knowing may become the subject of verbal articulation and/or transference interpretation. However, the areas that become consciously articulated will be only a small part of the totality of the patient's (and/or therapist's) implicit operating procedures in relationships. Although these "knowings" are often not symbolically represented, they are also not necessarily dynamically unconscious in the sense of being defensively excluded from awareness. Implicit relational knowing, then, operates largely outside the realm of verbal consciousness *and* the dynamic unconscious. However, though we use the term throughout these chapters, we see it as a working term and one that will need further revision (for a fuller and more developmentally grounded discussion see Lyons-Ruth [1999]).

In addition to implicit relational knowing, we needed two more constructs to talk about therapeutic change that is not based on interpretation. The second construct was that of the "real relationship" (another term that too must be seen as a work in progress; see Morgan et al., 1998). The third construct was the notion of "moments of meeting."

We will define the "real relationship" as the intersubjective field constituted by the intersection of the patient's and the therapist's implicit relational knowing. This field extends beyond the transference-countertransference domain to include authentic personal engagement and reasonably accurate sensings of each person's current "ways of being with." Labeling this intersubjective field the "real relationship" also serves to differentiate it from the psychoanalytic components of the relationship in which semantic representations are elaborated via verbal interpretations.

In contrast to more traditional views, we feel that the real relationship is *also subject to* therapeutic change by processes that alter the intersubjective field directly. In traditional theory, interpretation is viewed as the semantic event that rearranges the patient's understanding. We propose that a "moment of meeting" is the *transactional* event that rearranges the patient's implicit relational knowing by rearranging the intersubjective field between patient and therapist, what Tronick et al. (1998) refer to as their dyadic state of consciousness.

What do we mean by a "moment of meeting?" A moment of meeting occurs when the dual goals of complementary fitted actions and intersubjective recognition are suddenly realized. Moments of meeting are jointly constructed, and moments of meeting require the provision of something unique from each partner. Sander (1995b) has pointed out that the essential characteristic of these moments is that there is a specific recognition of the other's subjective reality. Each partner grasps and ratifies a similar version of "what is happening now, between us."

Moments of meeting catalyze change in parent–infant interaction as well as in psychotherapy. In the process of infant development, the baby's implicit relational knowing encompasses the recurrent patterning of mutual regulatory moves between infant and caregiver (Tronick, 1989). These regulatory moves shift to negotiate a series of adaptive challenges emerging over the early years of life, as delineated by theorists such as Sander (1962) and Stern (1985). In the course of this ongoing mutually constructed regulation, the interactive field between infant and caregiver becomes more complex and well-articulated, giving rise to emergent possibilities of new forms of interaction. For example, once recurrent expectations regarding each partner's moves in a peekaboo game are established, the stage is set for both partners to "play with" that form by violating established expectations. This mutual sense of the emerging possibility of new forms of interaction occurring between the two participants creates heightened affect. Beebe and Lachmann (1994) have called attention to the importance of "heightened affective moments" as one of three principles of salience in early development and psychoanalytic treatment. We would further elaborate this concept by tying the heightened affect to a sense of emergent new possibilities in the interactive field. In the positive case, these new interactive possibilities would create more complex and coherent intersubjective regulation because they integrate new developmental capacities of the infant or achieve a fuller and more satisfying adaptation to the infant's current capacities and affective potentials.

The transition to a more inclusive and hence coherent mutual regulatory system hinges on a moment of meeting between parent and child. These moments of changed intersubjective recognition ratify a change in the range of regulation achievable between the two partners. They signal an opening for the elaboration of new initiatives. New forms of shared experience can now be elaborated around previously unrecognized forms of agency. The implicit relational knowing of the two partners will also of necessity be altered. New potential is not only enacted but also represented as a future possibility. Tronick et al. (1998) further elaborate on the more inclusive and coherent regulation inherent in an intersubjective moment of meeting in his discussion of dyadically expanded states of consciousness.

These concepts can be illustrated in the developmental domain with the description of a brief observation of a young mother with her 18-month-old baby. As an extensive attachment literature demonstrates, the infant's strategies for negotiating comforting contact with caregivers are constructed in a series of mutually regulated negotiations with parents and are one of the best-documented forms of implicit relational knowing displayed during the first 2 years of life (for review, see Bretherton, 1988; Lyons-Ruth & Zeanah, 1993). As part of the standard Ainsworth assessment of the infant's strategies for approaching the parent, mother and baby were observed reuniting with each other after the mild stress of two brief 3-minute separations in an unfamiliar laboratory playroom. As recent evidence confirms, infants are physiologically aroused during these brief separations, even in the absence of obvious distress. However, the fluidity of the physical and affective dialogue between mother and infant at such moments of stress can mitigate the onset of longer-term stress responses mediated by the hypothalamic–pituitary–adrenal axis (Hertsgaard, Gunnar, Erickson, & Nachmias, 1995; Spangler & Grossmann, 1993).

The mother and her 18-month-old daughter, whom I will call Tracy, had been receiving therapeutic home visits for 9 months, both to help the mother stabilize her life situation and to help her become more consistently emotionally available to her infant. Over this period of home visiting, Tracy and her mother had both been struggling to find ways of making satisfying physical and emotional contact with each other. This mutual struggle to negotiate more satisfying moments of contact was also obvious in the laboratory observation session. As you will see from the following account, however, this particular session led to a subtle shift between them, to a moment of meeting, that surprised us all.

After arriving at the laboratory playroom, Tracy explored the toys in the room for several minutes while her mother chatted with the female research assistant. When her mother left the playroom for the first time, Tracy did not appear visibly upset. She continued to play with the toys and ignored the research assistant. However, when the assistant got up to leave, Tracy quickly alerted and looked at the door. When she caught sight of her mother entering, she immediately averted her eyes and turned away. Her mother said "Hey!" and stood in front of Tracy. Still looking away, Tracy said, "Mummy!" with a pleased tone and then turned toward her mother and took several tentative steps toward her as though to join her. Her mother said, "What are you doing?" but did not step forward or kneel down toward Tracy. Tracy sidled past her mother's legs with a blank look, went around her mother, and pushed hard to open the door to leave the room. Her mother forcibly removed her hand from the door, saying, "Come here, look what Mama's got." Tracy pulled her hand away, turned away from her mother, and threw the toy she was holding hard onto the floor. She then continued to turn her back to her mother and push on the door while ignoring her mother's invitations to play. Finally her mother pulled her by the arm and she allowed herself to be drawn over to the toy her mother was holding. Still she ignored the toy, instead stepping with her head averted and without apparent purpose closer to her mother's body and then past her, where she squatted briefly beside her mother with her back turned. Then she stood and returned to the door. Finally, after wandering around the room aimlessly for several more seconds, she sat down facing her mother and played with the toy between them while her mother watched and praised her warmly and appropriately.

In contrast to her avoidant and conflicted behavior when her mother was present, Tracy was quite distressed when her mother left again and could not be comforted by the assistant who came in and tried to engage her. When she caught sight of her mother at the door the second time she exclaimed "Mummy!" with a delighted squeal, and began to run toward her. Rather than responding with similar delight, her mother said, "Hi! What have you been doin'?" In response Tracy started to fuss loudly as she ran toward her mother. Perhaps because of this protest on Tracy's part, her mother held out her hands and kneeled as Tracy approached, saying again, "What are you doing?" Tracy lifted her arms up and her mother first grasped her under the arms but then put her arms fully around her as Tracy pushed up against her body. After only a brief squeeze, however, her mother released her, drew back to look at her, and said, "Did you miss me?" Tracy sobered as her mother drew back, then fussed again and tried to move back into her mother's arms. Her mother gave her another awkward squeeze, saying "All right, all right, all right." Then she picked her up, moved to the toys, and kneeled with Tracy on her knee, directing her attention to a toy on the floor. Tracy looked at the toys impassively for a few minutes, sitting stiffly on her mother's knee. Then she stared off into space with a dazed look, began to fuss, slid off her mother's knee, and stood facing her again with her arms outstretched. Her mother responded by opening her own arms. For a long minute they stood frozen with open arms, facing each other silently. Then Tracy gave a little laugh of relief and sank fully into her mother's arms, letting her whole body relax on her mother's shoulder. Her mother was able to give an open, delighted smile in return, and hold her daughter close while rocking and hugging her. Her mother then specifically recognized and ratified this moment of meeting by murmuring "I know, I know" to her daughter as she hugged and rocked her.

In our view, mother and child had negotiated a more fitted and inclusive way of being together and had achieved in the final moment of meeting the dual goals of complementary fitted actions and specific intersubjective recognition—a moment of meeting and a dyadic state of consciousness. Recent studies of cortisol metabolism and attachment behaviors confirm that the fuller emotional sharing achieved by Tracy and her mother by the end of the observation constitutes a regulatory system of more inclusive fittedness in that open and responsive communication between mother and infant is associated with reduced cortisol secretion to mild stressors (Hertsgaard et al., 1995; Spangler & Grossmann, 1993).

We would argue that such moments of meeting shift the implicit relational expectations of each partner and signal an opening for the elaboration of new initiatives between mother and child. Such moments of meeting create the potential for the elaboration of new forms of shared experience and for a new range of more mutual and responsive regulation between them.

In summary, these moments of intersubjective meeting are experienced and represented in the implicit relational knowing of infant with caregiver. They are also experienced in the patient–therapist interaction, with similar resulting changes in the patient's implicit relational knowing. These "moments of meeting" between patient and therapist may or may not become the subject of interpretation. Nevertheless, these moments of meeting open the way to the elaboration of a more complex and coherent way of being together, with associated change in how relational possibilities are represented in each participant's implicit relational knowing.

*Part II. The Process of Therapeutic Change*
*Involving Implicit Knowledge:*
*Some Implications of Developmental*
*Observations for Adult Psychotherapy*[2]

THE MECHANISMS THAT BRING ABOUT CHANGE IN PSYCHOTHERAPY ARE incompletely understood, at best. In exploring processes of change, our working group has considered that the developing infant is probably the fastest changing of all human beings. Of course, genes are kicking in all the time, creating new capacities available to effectuate change. Nonetheless, without an appropriate environment to shape, facilitate, and encourage these changes, they will either not occur or evolve maladaptively. With this in mind, our group, which is made up of developmentalists, as well as those who are primarily clinicians, has attempted to consider the clinical process of therapeutic change with an eye to change processes in early development. The idea was not to look for precursors of later development, as is usually done, but rather to explore, minutely, the change process itself, almost irrespective of what is changing.

Four things impressed us most in listening to and studying in detail the process notes of psychodynamically oriented therapies:

1.  Much of the mutative action involves that broad domain of intelligence called implicit (procedural) knowledge, in particular, implicit knowing about what to do, think, and feel in a specific relationship

---

[2]Originally published in 1998, *Infant Mental Health Journal, 19*(3) pp. 300–308. Copyright 1998 Michigan Association for Infant Mental Health. Reprinted with permission.

context. This knowing is not conscious (nor is it dynamically unconscious, that is, repressed). It simply operates out of awareness. We call this implicit relational knowing (see Chapter 1 and Lyons-Ruth et al., this chapter).

2. The microprocess of proceeding in a therapy session seems to occur in an improvisational mode in which the small steps needed to get to a goal are unpredictable, and the goal itself is not always clear and can shift without notice, as it seems to do in the infant–mother interaction (see Tronick et al., 1998).

3. During a session, points of mutative potential arise at unpremeditated "moments." A "moment" is conceived of as a short subjective unit of time in which something of importance, bearing on the future, is happening. We call these "now moments." Such moments are viewed as emergent properties of a complex, dynamic system. In this sense, they are nonlinear leaps in the process of the therapy session. This loose concept of moments was found to be intuitively appropriate for the clinicians and useful for the entire group, as well as for infant–mother interaction (see Lyons-Ruth et al., this volume; Tronick et al., 1998).

4. When "now moments" are handled by the patient and therapist so as to achieve a "specific moment of meeting," the implicit knowledge of each partner gets altered by creating a new and different intersubjective context between them—the relationship has changed. This process requires no interpretation and need not be made verbally explicit.

The remainder of this part of this chapter will try to describe this change process, give it a terminology, seek links to developmental change processes that have inspired much of our thinking, and briefly explore some explanatory/descriptive concepts, as we began to do in Chapter One.

## CONCEPTS AND TERMS FOR DESCRIBING THE THERAPEUTIC PROCESS

Let us assume an illustrative, (prototypic) session that begins with the patient–therapist dyad in a particular intersubjective state. This is the initial state (state no. 1). By intersubjective state, we mean the shared implicit relational knowledge that each of them has concerning themselves and the other and how they habitually work, and are together. It is largely a nonconscious representation of an important aspect of their relationship.

### 1. "Moving Along"

In this initial stage (no. 1), they start to work together. Most often there is a goal in sight that can last for variable periods of time. For example, a patient and therapist are working toward the goal of understanding how the patient's current states of anxiety are related to the early relationship with her mother. They start to move toward this goal in a progression we call "moving along." This goal-oriented movement is largely linear. While they sense or know roughly where they are going, they do not know exactly how they will get there—that is, what each next step will be—nor can they know exactly when they will reach the goal or even how they will reach it. Furthermore, the goal can shift during the process of seeking it. They are in an improvisational mode. Each step in this moving along process is called a "present moment."

For instance, the therapist says: "Do you realize that you have been late to the last three sessions, which is unusual for you?" And the patient responds, "Yes, I do." Silence. This exchange constitutes a present moment. It has redefined the topic and redirected it.

The patient then says, "Last week you said something that really got me ticked off. . . ." The third present moment gets launched. And so on.

These present moments are the steps of the moving along process. Between each there is a minor discontinuity of some kind, but strung together they progress coherently, though not evenly.

In brief, we are speaking of a bounded envelope of subjective time in which a motive is enacted to microregulate the content and goal of what is being talked about and to adjust the intersubjective environment. The duration of a present moment is usually short because as a subjective unit, it is the duration of time needed to grasp the sense of "what is happening now, here, between us." Accordingly, it lasts from microseconds to many seconds. The present moment is constructed around intentions or wishes and their enactment, which trace a dramatic line of tension as it moves toward its goal (see D. N. Stern, 1995).

This kind of improvisational, self-finding, and self-correcting process is what we have come to be familiar with from Tronick's characterization of the parent–infant interactive process consisting of matches-mismatches, ruptures and repairs (Tronick, 1989, Tronick et al., 1998; Tronick & Weinberg, 1997). This is especially evident in situations such as free play, in which there is not even a specified goal except to amuse each other. This leads to a theme and variation format in which ad-libbed variations succeed one another until the theme is exhausted, and then a new theme (usually related) is found and unfolds its variations, again with many inevitable missteps. This process is almost pure improvisation (Beebe & Stern, 1977; Gianino & Tronick, 1988; D. N. Stern, 1985; D. N. Stern et al., 1977).

The realization that so much occurs in the improvisational mode between parent and infant has made clear the importance of the repair of ruptures and the midcourse corrections that such a process needs (Lyons-Ruth et al., this volume; Tronick, 1989). In fact, coming to implicitly know how to repair and redirect the improvisational process is one of the main hidden agendas of the parent–infant interaction (Tronick & Cohn, 1989). Moreover, in the parent–infant interaction, the repetition of many activities has a quality of moving along that creates a repertoire of present moments. These repetitions become extremely familiar canons of what moments of life with a specific other person are expected to be like while moving along. In this form, present moments become represented as "schemes of ways of being-with-another" (D. N. Stern, 1995). The schemes are in the domain of implicit relational knowing. They are also the building blocks of Bowlby's working models and of most internalization. It is not surprising that these implicit relational schemes have been given great attention by researchers in infancy who have been forced to think about the nonverbal infant's relational knowledge existing prior to explicit verbalization (see Lyons-Ruth, 1998; Tronick, 1998a).

The process of "moving along" in adult psychotherapy is quite similar. If we attend to the recurrent interactive sequences that are analogous to those that have concerned us in infancy, they tell us about the patient's implicit relational knowing concerning his relationship with the therapist and vice versa. This essentially is what is meant by the "unthought known" (Bollas, 1987) or the "unreflected unconscious" (Stolorow, Atwood, & Brandchaft, 1994), or the "past unconscious" of Sandler (Sandler & Fonagy, 1997). These implicit representations are unconscious but not necessarily under any form of repression. (In psychodynamic terms, they are descriptively [topographically] unconscious, but not dynamically unconscious.)

In sum, present moments strung together make up the moving along process, what Tronick refers to as the process of mutual regulation—matching, mismatching, and reparation. Both present moments, and the style of this moving along, occur within a framework that is familiar to and characteristic of each dyad.

### 2. "Now Moments"

In the course of the moving along process, all of a sudden a qualitatively different and unpredicted moment arises. This is a "hot" present moment, a sort of "moment of truth" that is affectively charged. It is also laden with potential importance for the immediate or long-term future. It is a moment called *kairos* in ancient Greek, the moment that must be seized if one is going to change his destiny, and if it is not seized, one's destiny will be changed anyway for not having seized it. It is also a moment that pulls the two participants fully into the present. (We, especially therapists, spend most of the time with only one foot in the present.) For these various reasons, we have called this moment a "now moment."

Two simple examples will suffice. They are obvious in that the habitual framework of the therapy is clearly questioned. Suppose that a patient in a psychoanalytic therapy, lying on the couch, suddenly says, "I want to see what is going on in your face, I'm going to sit up right now and look!" Or, imagine that a patient in a face-to-face therapy, says, "I'm sick of looking at your face. It distracts me. I'm going to turn my chair away from you and toward the wall, right now!" (for more elaborate examples, see Bruschweiler-Stern et al., 1998; Harrison et al., 1998; Nahum et al., this chapter).

The "now moment" is seen as an emergent property of the complex dynamic system made up of two people moving along in the therapeutic process. This emergent moment challenges or threatens the stability of the ongoing initial state. It announces a disturbance in the system (state no. 1) that constitutes a potential transition to a new state of organization (state no. 2). Such reordering of complex dynamic systems is becoming better and better understood (E. Fivaz, R. Fivaz, & Kaufmann, 1979, 1983; R. Fivaz, 1996; Maturana & Varela, 1987; Thelen & Smith, 1994).

This kind of emergent property can only arise if the moving along occurs within a context (system) that is rule governed by an established technique that is (implicitly) well understood by the interactants. The now moment, as an emergent property, disequilibrates the normal, canonical way of doing business together. It offers a new intersubjective context. For this reason, it is difficult and challenging clinically. It requires a deviation from the usual technical moves used by that dyad (though not necessarily from technical "rules" of the therapy).

When a now moment emerges, the therapist and the patient are surprised, in the sense of taken off guard because the exact form and instant of appearance of the moment was not predictable, even if it was generally likely to happen or even expected at some future point. It represents a nonlinear jump. Because the moment jumps out of the habitual, and is at the instant of its encounter unprepared for, the therapist (and patient) experience anxiety because they cannot know exactly what to do unless, of course, they quickly resort to habitual ways of interacting, thus operating under the guise of established technique. They are on unfamiliar ground, with all the possibilities of promise and disaster that inhabit not knowing what to do. If the therapist "knows" what to do, he has probably missed the now moment or has quickly hidden behind the technique. In the adult patient–therapist dyad, the emergent properties arise from the inherent workings of that complex dynamic system. In infancy preprogrammed developmental shifts, as well as the intrinsic mutual regulatory working of the system, create emergent properties within the dyadic system (Tronick, 1989, 1998a).

### 3. A "Moment of Meeting"

A now moment that is therapeutically seized and mutually recognized can become a "moment of meeting." This requires that each partner contributes something unique and authentic as an individual in response to a now moment. The response cannot be an application of technique or a habitual therapeutic move. It must be created on the spot to fit the singularity of the unexpected situation, and it must carry the therapist's signature as coming from his own sensibility and experience, beyond technique and theory. This is necessary because the "now moment" has disequilibrated the initial intersubjective context; thus, it must be enacted mutually. Only when this enactment has been performed, mutually recognized, and ratified, will a new intersubjective state come into being.

Similar shifts in the behavioral and intersubjective state are readily seen in the parent–infant interaction. For instance, when the social smile emerges along with sustained mutual gaze and vocalization, the parent and baby amuse each other with facial and vocal exchanges. They are moving along. Then, something unpredictable happens (e.g., a funny expression or an unexpected vocal and facial synchronization, and all of a sudden they are laughing together). The interaction has been kicked up to a new and higher level of activation and joy that the baby may never before have achieved and which has never before been shared between them as an intersubjective context.

This change in intersubjective environment can be described as follows: The participants are "moving along" in an initial intersubjective state (no. 1). A now moment emerges. It pushes the intersubjective state into a zone of transition that is unstable. If the "now moment" is accepted as a request for a reevaluation of their implicit knowledge about their relationship, and a new intersubjective context is enacted in a "moment of meeting," it will act to catapult the implicit intersubjective context into a new state (no. 2.)—a dyadic state of consciousness (see Tronick et al., 1998a), and restabilize the system. The patient and therapist can then take up again the process of moving along, but in a different intersubjective state. The end result is a change in both members' implicit relational knowing.

The notion of a moment of meeting also comes from work with infants. Sander (1988, 1997) introduced the term to describe the situation when the parent provides a behavior that is specifically fitted to permit and catalyze a shift in the infant's state. For instance, when the mother sings the exact song, or performs the needed ritual of touching, that sends the baby from the state of drowsiness into a state of sleep.

### 4. An "Open Space"

Immediately after a moment of meeting, Sander (1988) observed that an "open space" occurs in the infant–parent interactive process in which the partners disengage from their specific meeting and can be alone, in the presence of the other. A similar pause is observed in adult psychotherapy. It is assumed that during this open space each participant can assimilate the effect of the moment of meeting in finding a new equilibrium in the altered intersubjective state that they now inhabit.

After the open space has finished, the two partners take up again the moving along process, but now they do so within a new intersubjective context (state no. 2). Their implicit relational knowing has been expanded—there has been a dyadic expansion of consciousness—and the relationship between them has changed.

### 5. Other Fates of the "Now Moment"

If the now moment is not seized to become a moment of meeting, it can lead to various other outcomes:

(a) The now moment simply can be missed. This is a lost opportunity but usually reappears.
(b) There can be a failed now moment. The moment does not go by unnoticed; rather there is a failure to establish a moment of meeting. If this failure is left unrepaired, the two gravest consequences are that either part of the intersubjective terrain gets closed off to the therapy, as if one had said, "we cannot go there," or even worse, a basic sense of the fundamental nature of the therapeutic relationship is put into such serious question that a full therapy can no longer continue (whether or not they actually stop).

In the parent–infant relationship, "now moments" are frequently missed or failed. It is less grave in this situation because the developmental push will assure that such moments will reappear. The only question is how this new property will be integrated into the relationship. In the patient–therapist situation, there will be fewer opportunities to seize these moments because the failure to do so is generally experienced as so painful to the patient as to prevent risking offering it again. Still, several opportunities for repair usually present themselves.

(c) When failed now moments are taken up again they can be repaired. This requires a new "moment of meeting," a dyadic expansion that emerges from mutual regulation.

(d) Some now moments endure and stay charged for many sessions. Their urgency can wax and wane. Similarly, some now moments can be flagged as important events that must be returned to, but not at that moment. The therapeutic process thus buys time.

(e) Finally, an interpretation, acting in the domain of explicit knowledge, can resolve some, but certainly not all, now moments. It is instructive in this regard to note that most good, well-timed interpretations also include, as a sort of coda, a specific moment of meeting that concerns the emotional effect of the interpretation. It acts in the domain of implicit relational knowing, but is necessary to render the interpretation not just a sterile application of technique, but a mutative event in altering the explicit and implicit relationship.

In brief, an interpretation is the act that alters the intrapsychic landscape of the patient's explicit knowledge. A moment of meeting is the act that alters the intersubjective landscape of the patient's implicit relational knowing. These two mechanisms can act alone or together (see Lyons-Ruth, 1998).


## SUMMARY

We have tried to explore the process of change in psychotherapy using the perspectives of developmental processes and concepts of change in

dynamic systems. The basic data are the detailed reports of psycho-
therapists about their therapy sessions. The major findings are the realization that even in a "talking therapy," a vast amount of therapeutic
change occurs in the realm of procedural knowledge that is not conscious, especially implicit knowledge of how to act, feel, and think
when in a particular relational context (implicit relational knowing).
We suggest that the mutative act in this domain is a specific moment of
meeting, which is an emergent property of the dyadic system that
pushes it into a new state of intersubjectivity—Tronick et al.'s dyadic
state of consciousness—thus changing the relationship.

# Part III. Case Illustration: Moving Along . . . and, Is Change Gradual or Sudden?[3]

## INTRODUCTION

TODAY I WILL PRESENT A BRIEF FRAGMENT FROM AN ONGOING ANALYTIC treatment of a woman I shall call Jean. It will be based on my verbatim written notes. The material I will describe is fairly typical of the kind of sequencing that has characterized our work together, which has been marked by gradual but cumulatively dramatic improvements in Jean's general adaptation. As examples, when our work together began, she worked as the equivalent of a research assistant, well below the level of her credentials, and was too terrified to drive a car. Today, she is a well-known and highly regarded scholar in her field, whose writings and teachings are influential, who travels worldwide in her work, and drives and owns a car.

## THE CLINICAL ILLUSTRATION

Jean, now in her mid-40s, came to see me because she became suicidal when her then-husband, Paul, accepted a professorship in another city. She felt unable to move with him, and they were divorced a year later.

---

[3]Originally published in 1998, *Infant Mental Health Journal, 19*(3) pp. 315–319. Copyright 1998 Michigan Association for Infant Mental Health. Reprinted with permission.

From the first days of her marriage, Jean had consistently thought to herself, "I'm not sure this is good for me."

The best way to characterize this bright, attractive, artistic woman, now a successful fellow at a think tank, is to say she has only been able to experience spontaneity and freedom in a context of nonengagement with others. A massive impingement of her sense of agency would be our term to describe her experience of being with another. Her relationship with me has been an important partial exception to this.

I will try to show how we moved along in considering an issue that we have rarely discussed directly in her long therapy, which has become an analysis, namely the issue of sex. I chose this point because Jean goes from feeling not understood to feeling understood, and this alters the context, enabling her to articulate what her experience had been with me at the previous moment. Moreover, a shift occurs where she becomes able to talk about something she has never been able to discuss before. Implicit here is the idea that transformation does not necessarily encompass awareness at the moment it occurs. Our model is in fact more gradualist than you may have assumed.

Now, mind you, sex and analysis are two words that are inextricably linked in the minds of many. Yet Jean repeatedly made it clear that were I to interpret her thoughts as representing sexual ideas and wishes, I would lose any claim as a valid understander of her subtle, complex inner world. Other than a brief affair as her marriage was dissolving, some 10 years ago now, she has been sexually abstinent. We might even call her celibate. During her marriage, she found the infrequent sex with Paul agonizing. She felt deeply ashamed to find it so unpleasant.

Along with this, however, she remains convinced that sex is not something that women enjoy. For her, this is an open secret men try not to see. Nor in treatment has she talked about sexual fantasies, desires, or fears. She does not seem to think about others sexually, although she lives in dread that she will be so considered. She has often railed against a culture that she feels uses the sexuality of women to sell everything.

The sequence I will describe begins on a Friday after Jean has told me a dream, a rare occurrence. It has appeared to me that it is only in her dreams that sex appears, invariably with bizarre or violent features, always dissociated. As in real life, she is never the one having sex. In the days preceding, I found ways to impart to her that what she calls her nerdy, dowdy clothing does not so much protect her from being humiliated, put down, or seen as somebody who thinks she's sexy but isn't, but rather ensures that she will not elicit desire.

On the Friday in question I said, "Have you noticed how frequently sex comes up in your dreams?" "No," she giggled, "it doesn't seem frequent," clearly pleased to disagree. After demanding that I say more of what I mean and my obliging, she sobered slightly and continued, "When it comes up, it's a black box, something I'm suspicious of, uncertain of, afraid of."

On Monday, after discussing a Cézanne exhibition, and my noting her identification with the artist whose early work showing violent and erupting sexual imagery fascinated her, she went on. "Ever since you said my sexuality is compartmentalized, is not in my life, I've thought yes, it's true, and a very sad loss. But things could be a whole lot worse and I'm not sure you understand that. There are certain things where your understanding is so different from mine. Had my sexuality been better integrated, I'd have married better. But then, I would have been unable to resist the pressure to have babies." "Feeling pushed into something is the theme," I said. She vigorously agreed, then said she doubted she'd find a suitable sexual partner should she come to want sex, to "buy the hammering social message." I said, "You might not know if it were really you." "Absolutely," she replied, "I don't have such a strong belief in myself that I'd know, if I did come to like sex, if it would be me or the message hammered in. Maybe there is no way to filter out the external message about sex and babies, and it becomes part of you." A silence lasting several minutes ended with her asking me, as she is wont to do, what I'm thinking. Here I chose to answer and said, "I can't help but think how vexing your fear of being influenced must be in dealing with me." Jean said, "When we talk about influence, and I say you could hurt me by not understanding, that's different from my absorbing things from you. With all the help you've given me, I've always felt I had to have responsibility for filtering, presenting you with things, seeing where you're coming from, that's still an issue." "It's unavoidable, isn't it?" I say. "Yes," Jean answers. I'm afraid I could get to a place where I couldn't control or steer where we're going anymore. As an aside, we could say, being with another, when she is understood, does not constitute an impingement. Moreover, the meta-communication when I said, "It's unavoidable, isn't it?" is that I accepted her fear-driven need to control the flow.

Tuesday Jean began by telling me about a situation at work where she had given Don, a male colleague, some work he could easily appropriate. "This is really wild," she stated, "it's a feeling of a rape, a sexual violation, as with Paul. I was the one who willingly offered him the work, feeling it was not an option to give in to my hesitance because I shouldn't do something that makes me look weird. Here I've not only freely consented, I've given Don the idea. I got myself in a tizzy feeling violated, then I picked up where we left off yesterday." She continued, "If you had that point of view, you could make me feel I won't be happy unless I have babies. I know you don't think that, you're much more open-minded than I am, you're not a '50s Freudian." Having disabused herself of one reason to fear me, she immediately constructed another. "But you came of age in the '60s and might have the '60s delusion that integrated sexuality is the right thing for everyone. That's why I felt suspicious Friday when you said I didn't talk about sex, I do." I responded, "To pursue that, when you talk about what happened with Don, you're talking about your sexuality." "Yes," she said, "you're being too narrow-minded, I think. I talk about sex with you all the time." I said, "You Freudians, you think everything is sex." She laughed and retorted, "You're a '60s hippie, you think of sexuality as genital sexuality but you don't deny I'm talking about sex when I describe what happened with Don, so what are you complaining about?" I replied, "If that is so, you and I are engaged in sex, but rather than '60s joyful mutual realization sex, it's sex where one person imposes himself on the other, where I force myself on you and you must accede."

Wednesday, Jean began, "I didn't feel bad after yesterday, but energized that we'd moved the discussion from Friday where I felt, eew, ich!, my sexuality is dissociated. I was feeling you shouldn't blame me because I can't do what you want—and then yesterday, you were so open to my saying I do talk about sex, it's just not genital sex. I went from being apologetic to propounding my own point of view. The other thing, yesterday I realized when you said Friday that I didn't talk about sex, it felt like a sexual maneuver to me and more specifically, I felt you wanted me to strip, to look at me, it gave me the creeps. Your justification would be that "you should have sex, it will be good for you, break through those childish feelings, I know more than you." I replied, "Your realizing yesterday how you felt Friday is very important, I agree, it's good we were able to get beyond Friday, we see more clearly the degree to which being exploited, humiliated, controlled, pervades your sense of yourself and your sexuality." Jean responded, "I don't think my sexuality is off to one side, when you say the fear of being done to permeates all aspects of my life, that's what I mean by integration, it's just a problematic one."

### DISCUSSION

As you may surmise, I have had to condense and omit much rich associative material, but I wanted to illustrate a shift over time where Jean became able to talk about something—sex—that she had not been able to discuss before. The recurrence of the sequence of moving from not feeling understood to feeling understood alters the context, enabling her to articulate what her experience with me, unrecognized at the time, had been at a given moment. Her saying, "Yesterday, you were so open to my saying I do talk about sex . . . " signaled that my actions had challenged her expectancy. We might consider this delta learning, what one learns about the world because something does not happen, in this case something bad. Her vigilance lessened. She moved from the position of being a helpless responder to others, with the even worse possibility of being subjugated, or in her words, "extinguished," to being an agent in the exchange. Each time the patient was able to mobilize her initiative in the interaction, "I went from being apologetic to propounding my own point of view," her sense of agency was altered and strengthened in previously unrecognized ways, and she was on the road to being able to claim her desires as her own.

One might ask, has a moment of meeting occurred in this illustration? My answer would be, yes but. For, although we have come together, the question would be, at which moment? The nodal moments are: (a) Friday, my asking, "Have you noticed?" (b) on Monday, my saying, "It's unavoidable, isn't it?" (c) Tuesday, "To pursue that, when you talk about what happened with Don . . . " "Yes," our exchange of jokes ("You Freudians . . . " "You're a '60s hippie") (d) Wednesday, "I was feeling you shouldn't blame me . . . and then . . . you were so open to my saying . . . I went from feeling apologetic to propounding my own point of view." It is here that the shift has occurred in Jean, but it is the next day (Wednesday), that she tells me and we join on it and she says, "I realized it felt like a sexual maneuver."

In this group's continuing work, we hope to be better able to sort out the differences, if any, in gradual versus sudden shifts, in quantitative versus qualitative shifts, and to better understand their interrelationship.

# Introduction to Chapter 3

IN THIS CHAPTER THE CONCEPT OF RECOGNITION PROCESS IS DEALT WITH in more depth, including its history and its development in the work of Lou Sander. We have written this chapter to underscore the central importance of recognition process in the apprehension of one party's intention and direction by another. It is the process critical to the fitting together of two subjectivities in a shared direction, the importance of which is elaborated further in the subsequent chapters.

As explained in Chapter 1, we had realized that a crucial aspect of the change process involved special moments in which there was a mutual recognition of intentionality and a specificity of the fittedness of each person's initiatives towards the other. All of these were implied but not fully explicated in our notion of the *moment of meeting*. The effects of the moment of meeting from the point of view of the change process were not only to enlarge the intersubjective field and increase its complexity and coherence, but also to enhance a feeling of vitalization in the process between the two partners.

One of our members, Lou Sander, has been deeply influenced by the study of biological systems, systems which exemplify principles of complexity, specificity, organization, and coherence. One of his seminal contributions has been to apply these principles to the understanding of human intersubjective interactions. In this chapter, Lyons-Ruth elaborates on how the concept of recognition process is central to understanding human interaction, as well as the associated processes of developmental and therapeutic change, with both developmental and therapeutic case examples.

# Chapter 3

# "I Sense That You Sense That I Sense . . . ": Sander's Recognition Process and Relational Moves in the Psychotherapeutic Setting[1]

FOR MORE THAN 30 YEARS, SANDER HAS BEEN ONE OF OUR FOREMOST theorists of dyadic systems. In fact, Sander is also one of the few theorists who have appreciated the problem of accounting for the emergence of a coordinated, two-person system. In this pioneering role, he has struggled to create a language and to forge a set of principles and constructs when few other thinkers were grappling with similar issues. The intercoordination of human life at many levels of social organization, such as the family or the culture, is most commonly taken as a given and the particulars of coordinated functioning described. However, from his perspective both as a psychoanalyst and as an infant observer, Sander recognized the problem in accounting for how two unacquainted individuals come to know each other's minds in the service of conducting complex coordinated activity.

The emphasis on the concept of adaptation by psychoanalytic writ-

[1]Originally published in 2000, *Infant Mental Health Journal*, 21(1–2) pp. 85–98. Copyright 2000 Michigan Association for Infant Mental Health. Reprinted with permission.

ers such as Hartmann (1939/1958) and Erikson (1950), an emphasis also shared by Piaget (1952, 1971), first led Sander to consider the biological basis of fittedness between the individual and his caregiving surround. As detailed in Nahum's overview of his contributions (Nahum, 2000), he turned to the systems theories elaborated by the biologists Paul Weiss (1947) and Ludwig von Bertalanffy (1952) as the most promising and complex models that might capture some essential features of the processes of adaptation in two-person systems. Weiss (1947) uses the concept of recognition process to account for the highly specific ways that components of a developing biological system self-organize. Sander's initial emphasis on recognition processes, however, grew out of his participation as a research psychiatrist in Eleanor Pavenstedt's longitudinal parent–infant study, in which he observed a wide variety of mother–infant dyads. These observations left him keenly sensitive to the infant's spontaneity and initiative in constructing his or her own direction of activity, as well as to the infant's vulnerability to yield that spontaneity when pressured to engage in a performance desired by the other. This focused his attention on the nature of the negotiations within the dynamic tension of the mother–infant system and on the role that a moment of positive recognition plays in that process. As Sander stated in his paper on recognition process, recognition process refers to "the specificity of another's being aware of what we experience being aware of within ourselves" (1991, p. 9).

This view of the pivotal role of recognition process in the experience of the developing child has been central to his thinking over a lifetime. For Sander, the task of coming to "know" oneself, through experiencing being known, lies at the heart of self-organization. Because of the critical role this process of becoming known plays in the individual's sense of integration and well-being, exposing to another the delicate source of self-organizing initiative "remains a life or death precipice at the heart of self-organization" (Sander, personal communication, March 2, 1996). Thus, consideration of the role of recognition process in development has been a lifelong orienting direction in his work.

In his published work, Sander does not specify how one knows that he is indeed being recognized, however. In addition, the description of recognizing that another person is aware of what we are aware of within ourselves at first brings to mind a reflective process whereby the knower is capable of representing embedded perspectives of the type "I know that she knows that I know . . . " Such sophisticated reflective perspective-taking is clearly not available in early infancy, yet this is precisely where Sander locates the beginnings of the central organizing function of the recognition process. It is this problem of accounting for how the recognition process might function at an implicit, non-reflective level that is the subject of this chapter.

The biological origins of this term for Sander make clear that such self-reflective capacity is not necessary for such a fitting-together process to function and guide development. Despite this, his published writings do not elaborate exactly how such a recognition process might work at a psychological rather than a biological level, nor the ways that this construct might be applied to psychotherapeutic process. In this chapter I will present an overview of Sander's thinking regarding the role of recognition process in early development and then elaborate how such a recognition process might be conceived to work in the psychotherapeutic setting, in a spirit consistent with Sander's larger theoretical framework.

Clinical material will illustrate how the concept of recognition process can begin to specify the microprocess of dyadic relational moves occurring in the psychotherapeutic setting. The final sections of the chapter will describe in more detail how Sander drew on the general systems models of Weiss and Von Bertalanffy to ground his thinking about developmental process and how his systems view converges with recent thinking regarding change processes in nonlinear dynamic systems.

## SPECIFICITY, RECOGNITION PROCESS, AND "FITTING TOGETHER"

In his paper "Recognition Process: Specificity and Organization in Early Human Development," Sander elaborated his thinking about the pivotal role of recognition in early development, adding that "only the beginnings of the experience of recognition . . . can be dealt with here. . . . The full complexity of experiences of recognition central to developmental processes of later life, or of the healing process of the psychotherapeutic experience, must be taken up elsewhere" (1991, p. 2). He begins his discussion by reiterating a systems view: "Human beings as living systems combine the organizational coherence of an ecological organization, i.e., the environmental context, with a biological organization and with a psychological organization" (p. 3). The concept of coherence of organization is central to Sander's thinking and he sees increasing coherence of psychological organization as a central overarching goal of development. For Sander, increased coherence implies an increased inclusiveness of organization, so that more parts are integrated in more complex and adaptive ways into an overall wholeness. In his view, recognition process is central to this movement toward coherence. In his words, "As part of this design, psychological organization searches for its own coherence, its own wholeness, and that search is conveyed by something that can be called a recognition process" (p. 4). Emphasizing multiple interrelated levels of organization leads Sander to the potential tension inherent in needing to organize at the dyadic level (being together), as well as at the level of individual psychological organization (being separate). In Sander's writings, recognition process is the device that bridges these levels.

Sander locates this recognition process at the heart of the continual, self-initiated exchanges that occur between any organism and its context of environmental support. In these constant exchanges, "the organism modifies itself or modifies the context to achieve that enduring coordination with its context that the biologist knows as the adapted state" (1991, p. 5). To account for how the organism achieves this "enduring coordination with its context," or this coherence of systems organization over time, Sander calls on the concepts of the biologist Paul Weiss. Weiss views the "enduring coordinations" that constitute the organization of the organism-environment system as resting on the biological device of specificity or specificity of recognition. In Weiss's (1970) words, quoted in Sander (1991), "In the living world such (special determining) qualities are used universally as means of communication, recognition, affinity relations, selectivity—the basic principle being matched specificities—a sort of resonance between two systems attuned to each other by corresponding properties" (p. 8).

Sander then raises this construct to the level of psychological organization by proposing that such specificity of recognition also applies to the organization of awareness and self-awareness, "i.e., the specificity of another's being aware of what we experience being aware of within ourselves. This specificity I have called recognition process and think of it as being experienced in 'moments of meeting' that convey a fittedness that connects inner experiencing with its outer context. Such experiencing of fittedness validates or confirms coherence of psychological organization on the level of the individual as a whole" (1991, p. 9). In Sander's words, "If, indeed, there is a validity to the choice of a 'recognition process' central to the development of that complexity of psychological organization we call 'person,' it is because it represents the fulfillment of the same basic principles that characterize the process of organizing living systems from their simplest level. This suggests it could be worthwhile to examine the psychoanalytic-therapeutic process within this same framework of principles as a way of defining in a more focused way the moments in the therapeutic process that in fact do lead to basic reorganization of the psychological system" (p. 23).

## RECOGNITION PROCESS IN PARENT–
## INFANT TRANSACTIONS

In an unpublished paper presented in 1965, Sander first develops his views on the role that recognition process plays in the developmental changes of the second 18 months of life. As established by a wide range of developmental studies, at 18 months of age the infant reaches a new level of self-awareness in that he or she first becomes capable of representing the self symbolically. At this age, the infant is able for the first time to use the verbal "I" to refer to the self and to recognize a mirror image as a representation of the self.

Sander theoretically ties the emergence of the self-representation to "interactions of recognition" between child and parent. He points out that the interaction between parent and toddler is often based on the parent's inferences regarding the toddler's intentions, leaving ample room for errors in the parent's attributions about the goals of the child's behavior. He reasons that accurate recognition by the caregiver of what the child is aware of as his own intentions would, in his words, "facilitate reciprocal coordinations which can achieve the quality of recognition and facilitate a more acute and accurate inner perception—again fostering 'self-recognition'" (1965, p. 11), or, as Sander states later, fostering the child's sense of his inner experience as his own. These "reciprocal coordinations that can achieve the quality of recognition" are later described in terms of "the specific matching of communicative exchanges on the part of the mother to the cues which are given expression by the child" (p. 12). He cites Spitz's (1957) converging view that all self-awareness combines awareness of one's own person tinged with the consciousness of the other's reactions to it.

Sander (1965) also proposes that the second 18 months of life may constitute "a phase of optimal inner awareness" for "owning" one's own experience. He points out that during the period from 18 to 48 months the toddler passes from expressing his inner world of wants, intentions, and plans more or less directly, through a period in which direct expression becomes conflicted, to a time toward 48 months in which there can be general concealment of the inner world. This leads him to identify the second 18 months as a phase-specific time span for the incorporation of experiences of the other's recognition of one's own inner perceptions into aspects of an accurate and externally validated self-representation.

In the remainder of the paper, he describes aspects of the play sessions of three preschool girls with an emphasis on how the spontaneous expression of inner experiences was or was not integrated into their fantasy play and into their reciprocal exchanges with the adult play partner by 36 months of age. He emphasizes that in the context of a high level of reciprocal communication over time with the parent, the child by 36 months could express detailed themes of her inner world to the interviewer and, in return, experience recognition and acceptance of her inner world by the interviewer, further consolidating her sense of ownership of her own experience.

In later work, however, Sander (1997) makes clear that recognition processes expressed through specificity in the coordination of joint activity do not require the level of self-awareness emerging in the 18-month-old toddler. Here, he describes an example from a film of a father and his 8-day-old baby, taken in the course of the Boston University Longitudinal Study of Personality Development (Sander, 1984).

On first viewing, what apparently happened was that the baby became fussy in the mother's arms, was handed to the father, and fell asleep.

When the film was viewed frame by frame, however, the specificity of coordination between baby and father became apparent. Sander describes it as follows: It can be seen that the father glances down momentarily at the baby's face. Strangely enough, in the same frames, the infant looked up at the father's face. Then the infant's left arm, which had been hanging down over the father's left arm, began to move upward. Miraculously, in the same frame, the father's right arm, which had been hanging down at his side, began moving upward. Frame by frame the baby's hand and the father's hand moved upward simultaneously. Finally they met over the baby's tummy. The baby's left hand grasped the little finger of the father's right hand. At that moment the infant's eyes closed and she fell asleep, while the father continued talking, apparently totally unaware of the little miracle of specificity in time, place, and movement that had taken place in his arms (1997, p. 155).

He points out that the progressive elaboration of increasingly complex forms of specifically fitted activity between parent and child is the essential process through which development takes place or, in Sander's terminology, the way that new levels of organization emerge in dyadic systems.[2]

## RECOGNITION PROCESS AND IMPLICIT RELATIONAL KNOWING IN THE PSYCHOTHERAPEUTIC ENCOUNTER

In Chapter 1, we advanced a model of how change occurs in the psychoanalytic setting through processes different from interpretation. We described a set of processes that contribute to therapeutic change but operate at an enactive rather than interpretive level, that is, at the level

---

[2]In his 1975 paper titled "Infant and Caretaking Environment: Investigation and Conceptualization of Adaptive Behavior in a System of Increasing Complexity," Sander had outlined this series of new and increasingly inclusive levels of dyadic organization that emerge over the first 3 years and conceptualized them as a series of adaptive issues that must be negotiated between mother and child.

of relational acts between patient and therapist. Such "acts" are often highly nuanced "speech acts" (Searle, 1969) rather than the kinds of actions commonly referred to as "acting out." In such verbally conveyed acts, nuances of timing, word choice, prosody, and shifts in content from the previous utterance, as well as aspects of the content itself, constitute choices of action on the part of both participants. That continued flow of action-choices, in turn, conveys in multiple subtle ways how each person's central intentions and affect states are implicitly understood by the other. These action choices are informative to the partner regarding what modes and levels of being together, or doing together, might be available in this particular relationship. This metacommunicative flow of spoken action conveys or embodies the implicit relational knowing of the two parties.

In a related paper, Lyons-Ruth (1999) elaborated on the concept of implicit relational knowing as a construct that has not yet been fully defined or fully recognized in either the academic research literature or in the psychoanalytic literature, although much cognitive, developmental, and clinical literature converges on such a concept. Implicit relational knowing is unconscious in that it operates continuously, takes place largely out of awareness, and is active developmentally before symbol use is available. Implicit relational knowing differs from the traditional psychoanalytic concept of transference derived from unconscious conflict because, although unconscious, it is not necessarily dynamically repressed. Implicit relational knowing includes interpersonally unacceptable elements that cause dyadic and intrapsychic conflict and these may be further acted on by repression or other defense mechanisms to become dynamically unconscious as well (however, see Lyons-Ruth, 1999, for a relational developmental account of defense).

In addition to the construct of implicit relational knowing, "knowledge" that is instantiated in the flow of dialogue between patient and therapist, in Chapter 1 we identified another needed construct as a "moment of meeting," a moment that included Sander's recognition process. As described in Lyons-Ruth et al. (1998a), "the implicit relational knowings of patient and therapist intersect to create an intersubjective field that includes reasonably accurate sensings of each person's ways of being with others. . . . This intersubjective field becomes more complex and articulated with repeated patient–therapist encounters, giving rise to emergent new possibilities for more coherent and adaptive forms of interaction. During a transactional event that we term a moment of meeting, a new dyadic possibility crystallizes when the two partners achieve the dual goals of complementary fitted actions and joint intersubjective recognition in a new form. We argue that such moments of meeting shift the relational anticipations of each partner and allow new forms of agency and shared experience to be expressed and elaborated" (p. 1).

As noted earlier, Sander does not discuss at length how "awareness" occurs during such moments of fitted actions and intersubjective recognition. Likewise, in Chapter 1 we imply that some level of self-reflective awareness would be required for patient and therapist to mutually recognize and ratify between them that an important and new way of being together had been negotiated. Such moments of highly reflective mutual awareness do ratify some important moments of change in adult psychoanalytic treatments. However, these moments are relatively rare, may not occur at all, and when they do occur tend to mark unusually major reorganizations in the patient–therapist relationship. Therefore, as described, they may not characterize much of the day-to-day business of conducting psychoanalytically oriented treatment.

However, Sander makes clear that the concept of recognition process is derived from the study of biological processes and does not necessarily require recognition at the level of reflective awareness. In applying this construct to the process of the earliest parent–infant interaction, Sander also removes recognition process from the realm of self-reflective awareness. The level of self-reflective capacity expressed in the statement, "I know that you know that I know ... " is a level of explicit or conscious awareness that occurs well beyond the level of primary self-awareness characterizing even the second 18 months of life.

How then do we understand "recognition process" in terms congenial with both infant research and more ordinary moments of change in psychoanalytic treatment? Sander seems to imply that when applied to the organization of the dyad as a system, recognition process can operate at any of several levels of awareness, depending on the developmental levels of awareness available to the participants. While any given relational move may be the outcome of very abstract thought processes, most relational transactions rely heavily on a substrate of affective cues that give an evaluative valence or direction to each relational move. These relational moves are carried out at an implicit level of rapid cueing and response that occurs too rapidly for simultaneous verbal translation and conscious reflection. Therefore, the fittedness of a relational move to the joint goals of the dyad is probably more typically "sensed" or "apprehended" directly, rather than known reflectively in the moment.

Sander's linking of the sense of fittedness between partners to the creation of increased coherence in the system is an important additional contribution in that he suggests that human partners have an intrinsic ability to apprehend when more coherent fittedness of activity in the service of joint goals is achieved between them. In his view, this "fitting together" carries with it an experience of positive affective enhancement that he has termed "vitalization."

In this account, then, recognition process is most likely to occur at the level of relational moves that are unreflected upon and hence often unavailable to introspection. Recognition is then experienced as a direct apprehension of the increased fitting together of the two partners' behaviors in the service of jointly held (but often implicit) goals. Such "fitting together," if it can be reliably repeated, constitutes increased coherence or organization of the dyadic system as a whole.

How does this conception illuminate the process of the emergence of a dyadic system between two new partners? In Sander's view, as in the biological theorizing of Weiss (1947), the concept of recognition process provides the directional element to clinical or development encounters; it is how we feel our way along in unscripted relational transactions.

The process of regular encounters between the organization of the infant's and parent's relational moves, or of the patient's and therapist's relational moves, creates a field of tension between the two diverging organizations. The resolution of this tension requires a creative and improvisational process by which both parties make exploratory attempts to find accessible points of fitting together in the service of collaborative activity. In this improvisational field, all exchanges will alter the experience of the other and elaborate each person's implicit awareness of the other's available relational moves. This universe of possible moves is not finite, as in a rule-bound game like chess, however, but is varied by the creative and self-organizing properties of complex living systems in interaction with each other.

While the two partners might have some overarching goals for being together, the pathways for getting there and the series of more local goals that occur along the way are constructed dyadically out of the encounters of the moment. The sense of increased fittedness of actions between the two partners will guide their choices of moves to be repeated and those to be varied or discarded. This recognition by patient or therapist of the "fittedness" of the other's move is most often conveyed by a responding move on the part of the other partner, a move that builds on the previous move in a way that deepens the dialogue in the service of the therapeutic goals. The increased coherence or coordination of the dyad in the service of systems goals is apprehended or recognized through the recognition of the increased fittedness of the partner's response to the self's capacity for coordinated action. By apprehending how the partner's next move builds (recognizes) or fails to build on one's own prior initiative, each senses the current state of fit with the other. Both partners sense the fittedness of their actions to the relational potential of the other and hence to the achievement of more complex joint dyadic activity in the service of joint goals.

A brief example to illustrate these processes in the clinical encounter can be taken from a recent meeting with a self-destructively acting-out adolescent patient. For several months we had been struggling to build an alliance through a tumultuous early phase of anger and testing on her part. In one of her more alienated sessions when she was listing her disappointments in all her treatment providers, and rejecting all of my comments, she finally looked at me with a hard querying look and fell silent. I asked what she was thinking that made her lapse into silence. She said, "You never know what these people are thinking. I mean they're human. They're probably thinking about the errands they need to do, you know, go to the cleaners and things." I heard this partly as her reference to feeling unseen within her family as well as in her treatment with me. We had talked several times before about her pervasive sense that who she was went unrecognized by the people who were important to her. At this point, to reiterate this sense in relation to me felt sterile and abstract. She seemed rather to be challenging me to say who I was and what I was thinking at that moment as a way of probing whether I was going to be able both to deal with the intensity of her feelings and to invest in this work with her in a way that she felt recognized.

I also felt attacked and exhausted by the continuing intensity of her struggle with me as one of the "unseeing others" and was able to recognize in this feeling her own sense of being internally attacked and depleted. After I thought about these implications for a second, I said, "Would you like to know what I've been thinking about as I was listening to you?" She nodded and I continued, "I was thinking what a difficult adversary you are to yourself because you're very thoughtful and disciplined and insightful (all obvious traits in this excellent student) and right now all those strengths are being used against you rather than in the service of furthering your life." She then began to talk at a very meaningful level about her inner experience of feeling like an abused wife who couldn't separate from an abusive husband, the "husband" who was embodied in her self-destructive behavior, because she feared that he was the only one who could love her.

Although this was a verbal exchange and my response contained what might be called an interpretive side, my understanding of what had transpired between us had more in common with a theory of specific fittedness and recognition process than a theory of interpretation. She brought a central "way of being with" into the treatment room, which involved, in part, angry opposition to the "unseeing others," but opposition directed away from the important others in her life and toward herself. I improvised as best I could to respond to her indirect confrontation more directly. I was attempting implicitly to recognize and respond to a number of levels of her communications to me, while at the same time avoid overpowering her defenses against her rage or undermining her precarious self-esteem. Many, or even most, such therapeutic improvisations early in the treatment process are "misses" in that little perceptible intersubjective joining, or "fitting together" in Sander's terms, occurs. In this moment, however, a deepening of her willingness to share her inner world with me occurred that was perceptible to us both (although this exchange was not explicitly referred to until many sessions later).

In my experience of the moment, the recognition process that occurred between us was at a procedural or enactive level. One possible
narrative at the level of relational moves might read as follows: She
was aggressive and indirectly attacking. She lapsed into silence to inhibit a direct attack. I queried her silence to invite a more direct angry
engagement. She took the chance to move out of her silence and confront me indirectly around whether therapists were really listening. I
took up the challenge to respond to the implicit confrontation more directly. My direct response to her indirect confrontation encouraged her
to confront her tormenters (including myself) more directly. This occurred implicitly in that it was inherent in the structure of the dialogue,
whether or not her tendency to inhibit her aggression was part of the
explicit content of the conversation. She then built on the implicit invitation to be more direct by reflecting more collaboratively with me on
the internal forces that held her back. Thus each of us improvised step
by step into a new possibility, each was observed by the other, and each
of us sensed the expansion of the repertoire that became possible.

In Sander's conceptual framework, we constructed a series of specifically fitted responses that opened new possibilities for collaborative
therapeutic activity, accompanied by a sense of vitalization of the relationship that was palpable to us both. Although this happened through
a verbal exchange, the essential structure of the exchange itself was
never verbalized or even reflectively recognized in the sense that it
could be easily rendered in words. However, the procedural fit was apprehended by both of us through the apprehension of the fittedness of
the other's next relational move.

The flux of energy-infused interactions that culminate in new areas
of dyadic organization cannot be specified in advance and depend ex-
quisitely on the timing of their occurrence in relation to all the prior
movements of the relationship. The same therapist response earlier or
later in the treatment relationship might have no effect or have a dele-
terious effect because its relation to the overall state of the relationship
would be different. Recognition process requires a fittedness to the
overall gestalt of the relationship at many levels. Nevertheless, in the
fine structure of session-to-session work, as well as in the more encompassing organizational shifts that are observed in treatment after a period of months or years, those moments of recognizing and building

on the fittedness of each other's responses constitute the fulcrum of change to new and more complex levels of coordinated activity. While we might have some general representation of where we want to go therapeutically or developmentally, the pathways for arriving there are always indeterminate and created out of encounters of the moment. In the example above, my patient and I had gone through a series of microencounters with each other for several months in which signals of anger and question and confrontation were exchanged between us until a new and fuller fitting together began to emerge.

These microencounters with many nonverbal components are also the units out of which our ways of being with others are constructed developmentally. While language is increasingly incorporated into these encounters with development, the structure of the encounter itself may never be represented in words. It is simply enacted and grasped implicitly in its enacted form. Under positive developmental conditions, parent and child will elaborate an intersubjective repertoire of "what can be done together" that will function smoothly across many developmental and life challenges to maintain responsive communication and to regulate physiological arousal within an adaptive range (see Lyons-Ruth, 1999; Lyons-Ruth & Jacobvitz, 1999).

These moments of specific recognition and specifically coordinated action represent the goal states of dyadic collaboration. As achieved goal states of a dyadic system, they function as psychic organizers, as feedback to both parties that they are on the path toward achieving joint action. In psychoanalytic treatment, the overarching goal is to enhance the individual adaptation of the patient. Joint action in this context, then, means the collaboration of analyst and analysand toward increasing the flexibility, range, and effectiveness of the patient's adaptive capacities, along with the reduction of the experience of maladaptive behavior and dysphoric states.

Ed Tronick et al. (1998), in work with the BCPSG, elaborated on the enhanced inclusiveness, range, and adaptive potential that are inherent in the collaboration of two minds, or in "the dyadic expansion of consciousness." A second mind is brought to the task of solving the adaptive challenges faced by the first. Two heads are better than one, especially if the second has experience or training not shared by the first and vice versa. Here I would expand further on the concept of a dyadic expansion of consciousness to note that consciousness is not only expanded. When two minds attend to each other, something new and unique is created, namely, an intersubjective field. Only in an intersubjective field is one able to make initiatives to explore, to play with, to influence, and, ultimately, to carry out complex activities in collaboration with other minds. One requires a fluid medium for learning how to swim and one requires a joint psychological field for learning how to do things with other minds. The joint state is desirable not because it is an end in itself, but because of what the ability to achieve joint states allows the two of you to accomplish together, in therapy or in development more generally. The need for an intersubjective field in which to develop coordinated dyadic activity provides a powerful impetus for the achievement of intersubjective dyadic states.

## RECOGNITION PROCESS IN DYNAMIC BIOLOGICAL SYSTEMS

In addition to a consideration of how recognition processes occur in clinical encounters, Sander's broader systems approach to recognition process in biological context needs to be sketched out. Sander cites Paul Weiss regarding the two great mysteries in biology, namely: (a) How do organisms maintain stability of organization of the whole? and (b) What biological principle governs the formation of bonds that result in structure formation and maintenance? Weiss proposes that specific determining qualities are used as a means of recognition of one part of the system by another to achieve matching specificities or resonance between two systems or parts of systems, for example, specific properties of sound waves are matched by specific qualities of the ear; specific properties of nerve endings are matched or recognized by specific properties of tissue to be innervated; specific properties of light are matched or recognized by specific detectors in visual systems.

Drawing from Weiss's writings, Sander emphasizes that infant and caregiver form a new regulatory system that is distinct from either individual considered separately. Integrating Sander's writings with recent work on dynamic systems theory by Thelen and Smith (1994) and others, one can also propose that as energy is invested in a new complex dyadic interactive system, the system will give rise to spontaneous emergent properties. Emergent properties in dynamic systems terms are forms of organization that are not specified a priori but that emerge in the interaction between organism and environment, or, in the dyadic case, between two individuals. In Thelen and Smith's developmental example, for instance, there is no "walking center" or "walking icon" in the brain (or in the genes). Instead, walking is discovered or constructed de novo by each infant in interaction with his or her environment. When a "fit" is discovered between the properties of the infant's body, such as his weight, leg strength, and coordination, and properties of the environment, such as gravity and surface characteristics, the fit is exploited in the service of producing upright locomotion and elaborating more complex ways of moving in the world. In other examples of the individual and the environment as a single complex dynamic system with emergent properties, Sander cites examples such as the entrainment of the sandfly's biological rhythms to the rhythms of the tides that inundate it, and the entrainment of the infant's endogenous sleep cycles to the 24-hour day-night cycle.

However, dyadic psychological systems have certain qualities not shared with biological systems. The unique qualities of dyadic psychological systems can be obscured by analogies with biological systems or by examples based on interactions between the individual and the inanimate environment. At the level of dyadic psychological systems, the recognition process that creates and maintains relational organization requires the intersubjective coordination of complex psychological states rather than simply the coordination of verbal or physical acts per se. As in the above clinical example, these recognition processes may require extensive mutual negotiation, failure of recognition, and efforts at repair (see Lyons-Ruth, 1999; Tronick, 1989). This psychological recognition process links inner experiencing, and later reflective awareness of experience, with the experience of other minds, allowing complex coordination at the dyadic systems level.

Sander proposes that at the level of psychological or mental structure, psychological organization emerges and is maintained through a constant process of exchange with the environment, with an impetus toward coherence of mental structure that is generated and maintained through the exercise of agency or initiative. In Sander's model of development, agency or initiative is directed from the beginning toward achieving mutual adjustments of organism and environment (or self and other) that create and maintain both coherence of internal psychological structure and continuity of adapted coordination with other minds.

Unlike other organisms, who have brief infancies and who can exercise considerable self-regulatory agency from very early in life, human infants must exercise a great deal of early agency indirectly through influencing their caregivers' behaviors. Thus, the specificity of the recognition process through which the caregiver apprehends the infant's communications is particularly critical to the coherence of psychological organization that the infant is able to achieve. In Sander's view, this nonlinear, dynamic systems view of change and development is the background for the operation of recognition process in development.

## SELECTIONIST MODELS OF NEURAL AND BEHAVIORAL DEVELOPMENT

Current dynamic systems models also emphasize selectionist principles. For example, in developmental neuroscience, Edelman (1987) has described the process of "neural Darwinism" or neuronal group selection. In his dynamic systems model, some preexisting neuronal groupings are strengthened and elaborated by exposure to environments within the range of adaptive fittedness while others are not "matched" or "recognized" by available environmental inputs and are pruned away.

An important aspect of Edelman's theory is his resolution of the paradox between the unique, idiosyncratic, and redundant nature of the neural connections developed in all areas of the brain by a particular individual, and the highly reliable, species-typical adaptive behavioral capacities that result from such idiosyncratic neuronal groupings. Edelman uses the example of the frog's visual system, in which the underlying idiosyncratic neural connections characterizing the individual each result in the highly reliable visual capabilities typical of the species. Edelman introduces the concept of biological value to account for the uniformity of function that emerges from idiosyncrasy of structure. Once the goal (or value) of the neural system is set, for example, to distinguish dark from light, the system will recognize certain inputs as providing more specificity of fit to the requirements of the neural system. However, there are numerous overlapping sets of synaptic connections that can be selected or strengthened to achieve the same outcome.

At the level of behavior, similar principles apply. As in the examples of walking described by Thelen and Smith (1994), many redundant locomotor behaviors and behavioral adjustments are explored by the infant. Those that match the requirements of the environment are repeated, strengthened, and refined further.

Both Edelman's theory and current behavioral research converge on the joint propositions that there are many idiosyncratic pathways that may be functionally equivalent when individuals are exposed to average expectable environments. If the environment provided does not provide the range of stimulus characteristics "valued" or recognized by the system in question, however, the resulting neural or behavioral structures may develop abnormally or fail to develop altogether. For example, Martin, Spicer, Lewis, Gluck, and Cork (1991) have shown that compared to non-isolated monkeys, monkeys reared in social isolation for the first 9 months of life show structural abnormalities in neural dopamine tracts in the basal ganglia on autopsy 20 years later.

Two-person systems are also nonlinear, idiosyncratic, and unpredictable in that interaction is inherently improvisational and creative. In the past, the concept of "repetition compulsion" has captured the conservative aspects of our emotionally central ways of being with others and highlighted the recognizable outlines that recur in these patterns. However, closer inspection reveals that the microstructure is never an exact repetition of the past. Instead, every new rendition is a variation on the theme, colored in turn by all past "repetitions" or variations. Something is always changed in each variation, as recognized in such concepts as "repetition in the service of mastery." In the concept of repetition in the service of mastery, the possibility of finding a new "repetition" or variation that leads toward a new solution is made explicit. Thus, something is always changed. One can never fully "unregister" one's experience nor can one ever go back exactly to a prior organization of experience.

How two such directional but unique and not fully predictable psychological systems fit together to form enduring and coordinated developmental relationships has been Sander's central concern and his biologically grounded constructs offer the scaffolding of a new developmental base for psychoanalytic theory.

# Introduction to Chapter 4

THIS CHAPTER DEALS WITH THE MOMENT-TO-MOMENT LEVEL OF THERA-
peutic interaction, what we call the *local level*. In the first chapter it was
alluded to, but in insufficient detail. The essential problem of describing the local level raises the question of its structure; that is, what are
its basic units and its overarching units. This is the primary task for
any descriptive effort.

The material that we sought to describe is particular to the interactive context of two people being together and working toward more
or less shared goals. Recall that we were influenced by the study of
mother-infant interactions and by special moments that arose in psychotherapy sessions that seemed charged with significance. With this
in mind, the basic unit for describing interactive process was called the
*relational move*. The relational move is a unit of intentionality where the
intention can be conscious or non-conscious. It is any communicative
"gesture" directed toward another that may be apprehended, and it
expresses some intentionality from the communicator. It is any slice of
behavior from which an intention can be inferred. It can be a verbalization or a non-verbal communication, or an act or silence. This clarification is essential to avoid the common misunderstanding that our

descriptive system is geared toward and limited to the non-verbal. Verbalizations have implicit relational meaning as well as explicit meanings. These are not the same.

A relational move is short, lasting from a split second to many seconds, but not longer. Its duration is something we became familiar with from mother-infant interactions. It is the length of a full breathing cycle as well as most vocalizations, spoken phrases, actions, posture changes, pauses. It has a duration of roughly 1 to 10 seconds, which is not a magical time unit. The cognitive neurosciences have recognized this slice of time as having its own specificity and function—namely, to chunk together during that duration the multiple sensations received and integrate them into a single chunk, a whole, a gestalt. Without such a chunking process, the world would be an overwhelming assault of stimuli.

In thinking about the relational move, the crucial role of intentionality became more apparent. After all, the relational move has an interpersonal function. One could almost say that mutual intentionality or intentionalities were the two locomotives that pull the process forward.

It is obvious that relational moves run off in sequences. These sequences make up the moving-along process. This process is not linear. These often loosely connected sequences leave great room for slight or significant misunderstandings about intentions which may result in derailments that need repair or testing that requires reorientation.

In this process of moving along, there occur relational moves that are special in the sense that they feel as if something important has just happened, something that could alter the course of the following relational move for better or worse. Such moments or relational moves carry a sense of destiny about them that determine possibilities for relational moves in the future. Because they carry a strong emotional impact, we have also conceptualized them in terms of moments. Moments have the advantage of allowing easier description of the affective and tension shifts that occur during such moments. It must be remembered that a present moment as we describe it is no more than a relational move as seen from a subjective perspective. It should be noted that when we talk about *now moments* and *moments of meeting*, we are at the same time describing special relational moves.

Once again, the idea is to stay at the local level in identifying the working units of our model. Relational moves, present moments, and the sequences of moving along all remain in the domain of the local level.

## Chapter 4

# Explicating the Implicit: The Local Level and the Microprocess of Change in the Analytic Situation[1]

DESPITE RECENT INTEREST IN INTERACTIVE PROCESSES IN PSYCHOANA-lytic treatment, and recognition that important curative aspects reside within them, the study of such processes in the analytic situation has barely begun. Because of our experience with developmental research, we have thought it possible to study interaction in a way that is analo-gous to microanalytic studies of mother–infant interaction (Beebe et al., 2000; Sander, 1980; D. N. Stern, 1977; Trevarthen, 1979; Tronick, 1989). These studies focus on moment-to-moment activity, a level of analysis we have come to view as vitally important. We will refer to it as the *lo-cal level*. It is a domain that is organized, highly structured, and com-plex, yet our theories do not address it systematically. In this chapter we will offer a description and provide constructs and terminology for talking about therapeutic process at the local level.

Although our focus in this chapter will be on expanding awareness and description of the local level in the therapeutic process, we do not

[1]Originally published in the *International Journal of Psychoanalysis, 83*,1051–1062. Reprint-ed with permission by Blackwell.

wish the reader to bypass the importance of understanding the relation of the local level to the broader context. It will also be apparent that there are gaps in understanding as well as problems and questions that our efforts have raised. These include questions we intend to address as we continue our work, such as, how do we connect the narrative or declarative level with the enactive or procedural level? How do we conceptualize the relationship between sequences of relational moves and the goal toward which they are tending? What is the relationship between the local level and both transference and the dynamic past? What is the relationship between the local level and the "latent content"?

We asserted in previous publications that therapeutic change results from interactional, intersubjective processes between analyst and patient (D. N. Stern et al., 1998; Tronick et al., 1998). We claimed these processes act by producing changes in procedural knowing about relationships (how to be with) (Sander, 1997; D. N. Stern, 1983), which we called implicit relational knowing. We believe that such changes are an important dimension of therapeutic action, calling them the something more than interpretation. We also spelled out a view of how a change in relational procedures can be produced by what we called a moment of meeting. A moment of meeting was thought to occur when the intersubjective state of the dyad was altered by a fitting together of the initiatives of the interactants. Such fittedness, we reasoned, "gives shared direction and helps determine the nature and qualities of the properties that emerge," (BCPSG, 1998a, p. 907) meaning that it serves as feedback to the two partners that they can work successfully together in a particular way, and encourages further elaboration of those ways of being together. We will further define and discuss the concept of fittedness below.

We had begun the collaborative inquiry that led to these ideas by asking the clinicians in our group, could moments be identified where change had occurred or seemed possible or imminent? This organizing question initially led us to look at ongoing process as strings of moments that we encompassed with the term moving along. Our initial question biased our thinking toward an emphasis on high-intensity moments, a bias that we recognized as problematic. We and many other clinical observers could see that therapeutic change occurs during the quieter moments of clinical process as well as during moments of meeting. It was apparent that during these quieter moments, interactions could also lead to new forms of knowing and being together. We concluded that it was not only during charged moments that fittedness was at issue. We therefore felt it necessary to develop a fuller account of how change might occur during quieter moments, and this comprises the subject of the current chapter.

## MOVING ALONG: CLINICAL PROCESS AT THE LOCAL LEVEL

The usual way of discussing analytic material is in narratives reconstructed by the analyst from memory or with the aid of notes taken during the session. However, videotape observations reveal that these narratives fail to capture many of the microevents of the complex, multilayered interactive process. This detailed process constitutes what we call the *local level*. The split-second world of the local level is a level of small specific events, rather than a level of abstract meanings. In this chapter we will demonstrate that such a nonverbal implicit process exists and is organized into complex patterns that are possible to study. Moreover, our view is that this local level process is an important domain of therapeutic change, because it is the site of change in relational procedures. Parenthetically, events at the local level would be important in the timing and configuration of the "next" interpretation. As it is the substrate of interaction, its study requires us to focus on interaction itself.

How exactly do we study interaction? Indeed, what is it? The *Oxford English Dictionary* (1971) definition, "action or influence of persons on each other," begs the question of how such action or influence is exerted. Here, models and insights from developmental research and dynamic systems theory seemed particularly pertinent. The observational methods of developmental research, which rely on repeated viewing of videotaped interactions between infants and their mothers, have illuminated a wealth of detail in the split-second microprocess. The minutiae of interaction, body language, gestural and facial expressive elements, vocal rhythms, tonal elements, and timing can be observed and coded. For adult analytic patients, this meta-communicative or meta-content level is often also conveyed through the verbal medium, via nuances of word choice, timing, and prosody of speech.

It seemed to us that it would be potentially useful to put clinical process under the microanalytic lens in an analogous fashion. Perhaps this split-second world is critical to understanding change in therapy with adults as well. In infant observational studies, this split-second world is where relational life happens. Although the therapeutic medium is linguistic, the interactions we observe here and the patterns that emerge are largely implicit, in that much of what transpires does not enter reflective consciousness (Pally & Olds, 1998).

### Interaction Is Inevitable and Biologically Grounded

As living organisms, we are destined to interact/exchange with our environment. It is how we sustain life, self-regulate, and expand ourselves (Boston Change Process Study Group [BCPSG], 1998b). We view this process of exchange as a biologically grounded process that can be considered and observed ethologically (Tinbergen, in Schiller, 1957). If two animals are put in the same space, a complicated process of regulating the physical distance, of moving toward and away from each other, will occur. Equally postures and movements will shift to establish the nature of the engagement. These are the "kinesics" of the interaction. With humans, this process is largely mentalized, meaning that the exploration, regulation, and establishing of proper contours, boundaries, and temporal structures to the interaction will occur mainly in the intersubjective rather than in the physical space. But it occurs nonetheless. Such mentalization is under general cultural constraints, and in the analytic situation, in addition, a set of specific ones. It is a process of trying to get closer, or further away, or to avoid something happening, or to get something to happen, or to increase or decrease the state of arousal, or to shift the affective state, in relation to the other. These might be called "mentalized kinesics." It is on the basis of such back and forth that we arrive at the feeling of being "in sync" with another or are left with the feeling that the other is a million miles away. We know when we like or dislike someone, when we want to be liked or feel indifferent, when we yearn to be closer or wish to withdraw, when we want something to happen or to put a hold on the level of activation. This negotiation occurs in the implicit domain of interaction, even though it may be mediated through verbal exchange. As an example, a patient well acquainted with his problem in "showing up" began a session by saying, "Today is unusual in that I'm both here with you and also hidden behind my eyes."

Interactants have intersubjective goals, such as staying together or not, or not now, or not here, doing things together or not, or not now, or not here, and these intentions are always being enacted. In these enactments, the initiatives of the two partners may or may not become fitted. The intentions of the two interactants are being constructed moment by moment in the ongoing process through the continuous creation of gestalts of one's own and the other's intentions and states. In the example above, the patient's opening remark is an exploratory move, assessing where he is with his analyst that day. The analyst's response will further constrain how they might move toward a well-fitted interaction. There must be feedback mechanisms that are continuously operative, informing us as to whether we are moving closer to our goals or not, and if we are fitting together in our interactive initiatives so as to move toward those goals. Again, such information is usually implicit, in that it may reach consciousness but need not. Each interactant is concurrently acting in ways that convey intentions and inferring the intentions of the other. Each is engaged in an intersubjective quest to negotiate the best fit between one's own intentions and those of the other.

We consider this psychoethological level to be the local level of interaction and to be going on all the time when two people are interacting. Everything else will be contextualized by it. The integrity of the self as a unit, its self-organizing imperative, requires continual action/ reaction/interaction. This is the local level.

### *Interaction Is Spontaneous, Creative, and Co-Constructed*

Interaction is a complex aggregate of old and new elements. It cannot be completely novel, as the two interactants would not recognize each other or have a starting point for fitting together and carrying out joint activity. Nor is it utterly predictable. When it is stereotyped or contrived, we see it as unsatisfying, inauthentic, possibly disturbed. As it is unscripted, it must be spontaneous.

An example from an opening session of a videotaped child analysis will serve to illustrate some of these aspects of the local level (Harrison, 2001). Laura, a 5-year-old, is surveying the doll's house before rummaging around in the analyst's toy box to find objects to place within it. Although her mother is behind her, Laura appears to be monitoring her closely, while also avoiding eye contact and verbal exchange with the analyst, who is in the background to the child's left. Three minutes into the session Laura turns for the first time from her mother to the analyst, at which point the sequence can be said to begin. One possible commentary on the exchange is in italics.

### Sequence I

1.L: That's so no one can get in the room! (*I don't want you to approach me. Yet the words are at variance with the affect and prosody, which say, hmm, maybe at some point . . . )*

2.A: Yeah, that's a good idea! How about giving me something to do! Want to tell me something . . . I could do . . . with the . . . doll's house? (*The analyst's immediate goal is to make a connection with Laura, to try to insinuate herself into the child's play. This local level goal of establishing some kind of engagement with the child is nested within the ultimate goal of helping her change.)*

3.L: I . . . I don't know, yet. (*Backing off, but still maintaining tenuous contact.)*

4.A: Okay. I'll wait till you suggest something. (*Deferral and acceptance of Laura's reluctance to share initiative.)*

5.L: This room is going to be only beds! (*Initiative.)*

6.A: Only beds. (*Acceptance/ratifying, still trying to join.)*

7.L: I don't think that will work. That room only has beds and this room only has beds. (*Backing away.)*

8.A: Okay . . . Two rooms . . . and only beds. (*Again, acceptance/ratification of Laura's holding the initiative.)*

9.L: Yeah. Well, actually . . . that won't be a bedroom. This will be a bedroom. *(Backward/forward, repeat of enactment of polarity; this time a direction emerges.)*

10.A:   Okay. *(Stays with her.)*

11.L:   So it matches. *(Forward in the direction established. This direction is now seen to represent a move toward togetherness between the two of them—"matches.")*

12.L:   And there's only one way to get in. You have to hop in . . . and jump on the bed . . . like this. *(Access is strictly controlled to maintain a comfortable intersubjective distance. But things have moved from "no one can get in" to "there is one way.")*

In this brief sequence, the analyst is attempting to join the child. The child is hesitant about warming up too fast (line 3) and backs off in response to each of the analyst's initiatives to join her, with the analyst surrendering, inferring that Laura cannot share the initiative at this point. Laura goes through a process of her own (initiative, followed by complex partial retreat with each of the analyst's moves) as they are in fact doing something together. The child and analyst are negotiating the intersubjective space between them, each selecting her next move in response to what the other is doing.

### Sequence II (Begins 26 Seconds Later)

26.L:   (Hums.) Tons of blankets! *(Yes.)*

27.A:   Okay. . . . Don't forget, I'm waiting to be given orders. *(Can I join you yet?)*

28.L:   (Laughs.) Hmm. Always hard to find the blankets. *(She is searching in the toy box but appears to be unable to find what she is looking for. Deflection/hesitation, and avoiding direct interaction.)*

29.A:   The what kids? *(The analyst has misheard Laura, thinking she said "blank kids," and not understanding, asks for clarification and more direct communication.)*

30.L:   The Blankets!! *(More contact without connecting.)*

31.A:   Oh, the blankets. *(It's your show and, well, at least we're together on that.)*

32.L:   It's also hard to find the pillows. *(Laura repeats theme of not find-*

*ing something. Unable to find what she is looking for, she adapts by shifting to something else but must again shift course when her search bears no fruit. She is still keeping the engagement on hold, but adding little pieces of contact.)*

33.A:    Yes, some of the blankets and pillows might have gotten . . . sort of . . . something might have happened . . . to them. *(Analyst is searching for a way of keeping the connection going without adding content or direction. It is a placeholder, seeming successful as the child shifts to something else.)*

34.L:    Yeah, well . . . this is a table. . . . Only we'll need two of them. I know you have two. *(Yes/first mention of "we'll.")*

35.A:    Want me to look? *(Can I join you now, gain admission into your play room by offering something?)*

36.L:    Yeah . . . I found it! *(Yes, you can join me, offer me something. Wait! I accomplished my goal, help is not needed. The "not necessary" part is really of another, lesser order of significance, since everything has been building to the joining, and after three offers of help by the analyst as a way of trying to join, and two refusals by the child as a way of staying apart, Laura finally accepts a coming together.)*

37.A:    Good for you! *(I validate your success/I recognize your beginning willingness to let me join in with you. I like it!)*

Again, we can see a back and forth between the two, as they co-assemble their interaction, contingently responding to each other. We can see that at this level one does not know what will happen from moment to moment (what if Laura had found the blankets? Or if the analyst had correctly heard her say "blankets" (line 29) rather than "blank kids"?), and both must improvise even though one may have an overall sense of the direction. One does not know what the patient will say or how the analyst will respond. The interaction is always in the process of emerging and evolving, mostly ad-libbed. Goals continue to evolve and to shift as the interaction proceeds (e.g., shift from blankets to tables, while in the intersubjective field, shift from keeping the analyst excluded to Laura letting her guard down slightly). Therefore, at least at the local level, the process is characterized by unpredictability and uncertainty. As two people interact, their behaviors are assembled in the moment, in context, co-constructed, although the past, as a background, is brought to bear. Each influences and responds to the other in an ongoing improvisational process that involves continuous dynamic adjustment by each party. On what basis do they make these adjustments? It can only be based on their adaptive strategies, their implicit relational knowing, which is lived in the actions, including speech actions, and interactions of each individual. Intentionality, as inferenced from the interaction, of necessity generates meanings. And, as what transpires is assembled by the interactants as it is happening, it can only be a creative, spontaneous, co-created process. It is improvisational.

Examples from the psychoanalytic treatment of adult patients could also be viewed from the perspective of the local level. For example, consider what occurs when a patient lapses into silence. There is silence as long as both patient and analyst "agree to" the silence. But what does the silence consist of? Is it a demand of the other, a coercion, a conciliation, a breather, tense, peaceful, or playful? Do the two differ in their interpretations of the silence? Each will construct his or her own ongoing, evolving assessment of what is transpiring and what it feels like, based on his or her unique history. Let us say the analyst decides to say something after 2 minutes. Things will proceed from that. Were the analyst to have decided to say something after 15 seconds, the subsequent course would have been different. We could say there are many roads not taken. In this sense, the interactive process is always in the process of being created and is unpredictable, with intentions shifting as each makes continual microadjustments to the other. Where the interaction is going to go will only be known after it has gone there.

### Interaction Is a Sloppy Process

Each person is an independent center of initiative. Therefore, no two partners can ever remain perfectly aligned in their interaction, nor would that be necessarily desirable. Since interaction is unscripted, poorly fitted interactions are inevitable. The interactants will go past each other. They will go away, come back, pause, indicate they want things to continue or to change. The interactive process has many sources of "noise" or sloppiness that are part of the complexity of interaction. Recall Laura's shift from blankets to pillows (lines 26–32) and the analyst's mishearing her. Inevitable slippage, inefficiency, or sloppiness is contributed to by the multiple parallel mental systems that constitute each "mind," by the difficulties inherent in knowing another's mind, and by the fact that each individual will have somewhat different motivations and idiosyncratic interpretations. However, these inevitable interactive misses also open up the possibility of renegotiation, of connecting in a different way, of a change in direction. Viewed from this perspective, the sloppiness is also generative. As each partner generates multiple attempts to engage with the other, new possibilities for interaction emerge. In accord with the mutual regulation model, the critical feature will be the procedures for realigning (Gianino & Tronick, 1988).

The following clinical vignette (compressed for clarity) illustrates the misalignment and realignment of this regulatory process (Nahum, 1998).

The patient Jean says her colleague Cass is opinionated and wrongheaded, but "I just placate her and smooth things over."

A:   What is it you are smoothing over?

P:   That I feel contempt for her. She's an idiot! She always comes out with the wrong thing.

A:   What is wrong?

P:   And I'm wounded by her tone-deaf remarks!

A:   What feels wounding?

P:   . . . I feel I've lost the connection with you. There are so many things I want to say . . . and you keep asking questions!

A:   Oh?

P:   Here's Cass who gets on my nerves, and now you get on my nerves. I have to ask if the whole world gets on my nerves!

A:   Maybe feeling a person's direction is not aligned with your own gets on your nerves.

P:   Maybe, because I suddenly feel a loss of momentum. I've been feeling I want to tell you everything that's been upsetting me. Then it suddenly feels like, what's the point?

In the first part of this exchange, analyst and patient are missing each other's intentions, although the misalignment only surfaces when the patient, with irritation, points it out. Her attention to the misalignment, however, brings both parties to engage in a process of finding a better alignment. Both engage verbally in flagging the misalignment. It should be noted, however, that at other times, the process can occur at an implicit level, with automatic adjustments that are not in consciousness. Conceivably, an irritated tone could creep into the patient's voice, and the analyst, sensing that something is amiss, might back away from questioning quite so actively.

## RELATIONAL MOVES AND THE PROCESS OF INCREASED FITTEDNESS

We consider that self-organizing systems tend toward greater coherence (Sander, 1980). In the therapeutic situation, we view the process of moving toward increasing coherence as a progressive one that can happen quietly, step-by-step, implicitly. We experience the move toward greater coherence as a sense of increased fittedness in the dyad, producing a feeling of enhanced well-being while together. To discuss this process, however, we must consider a smaller interactive unit, which we will call the relational move. In considering the local level of what happens in the therapeutic engagement, we chose the term relational move to label the smallest slice of verbal or nonverbal action that could be parsed as an intersubjective intention. A central problem we encountered, however, was that while actions are observable, their associated intentions or meaning(s) must be inferred. But we would claim, along with Freeman (1995), that this process of inferring intentions through parsing of actions is central to how the brain works, to how we understand others. These inferences regarding the other's intentions are the raw material from which one's relational moves are constructed that guide interpersonal action.

The parsing of intentions is a critical issue facing any two interactants. The relation between the observed action and the inferred intention is loose. The parsing of action into intentions or meaning often requires reiteration and redundancy in interactive sequences so that potential alternative "readings" can be evaluated and ruled out. This inference and evaluation process is occurring all the time at an implicit level. The ongoing indefiniteness in the process of inferring intention or goal-directedness in the other's activity contributes inevitable sloppiness to the interactive process. This sloppiness in inferring intention from action is a source of corresponding sloppiness in the interactive process itself. Sloppiness is inherent in the nature of human subjectivity. Each partner is not only putting forth actions and inferring intentions, but having an effect on shaping the actions and intentions of the other as they emerge. Over time, out of a process of negotiation, the intentions of each may become recognized by the other. This is why a relational move is an aspect of process and cannot be predefined as a particular type or duration of action.

As intentions become more aligned, new, previously unforeseen joint activities can emerge. Each will be continually gauging, based on exploratory moves, "are we together?" and "is it where I want us to be?" The process of exploration and gauging fit is ongoing. In our view, fittedness is continually sensed through awareness of fit of the other's complementary actions in response to one's own initiative. This recognition need not be explicit, however; it does not require awareness at a conscious level. When achieved, fittedness produces a feeling of vitalization, or increased well-being, because there is increased coherence of the dyadic system as a whole. Fittedness of relational moves thus catalyzes changes in analyst–patient interaction, as it does in parent–infant interaction. Fittedness of relational moves, the emergence of more spontaneous, coherent, and collaborative forms of interaction will lead to changes in the moving along process. Each time there is a fit, even if minute, the dyad will be in a slightly different place. Recall that Laura and the analyst moved from "no one can get into the room" to "there is only one way to enter." This is the slightly different place. From the perspective of the implicit, local level, their working together shifted to a new context from which to proceed. The joint attentional intersubjective space they created moved the system to a more complex coherence. What has been created belongs to both, becoming part of the implicit relational knowing of each.

## A DYNAMIC SYSTEMS THEORY VIEW
## OF FITTEDNESS AND CHANGE

Along with developmental research, dynamic systems theory has provided an important set of principles regarding change processes (Stolorow, 1997; Thelen & Smith, 1994). The concepts of emergent properties and attractor states are particularly relevant to considering change processes in psychodynamic therapies. Emergent properties are changes in an organism that are not prespecified by the organism's design but evolve as an aspect of organism-context relationship. An attractor state is a stable pattern, and can be thought of as where the system "prefers" to reside, although it is not absolutely obliged to. In earlier publications (BCPSG 1998a, 1998b) we referred to a person's implicit relational knowing as an emergent property. One's implicit relational knowing will create the set of constraints that make up the attractor states in which that individual's inner and outer relational field(s) tend to exist, as such "knowing" governs what is relationally and internally possible for the person.

The analytic process inevitably involves working simultaneously at affective, cognitive, and enactive levels to deactivate old, more negatively toned procedures and meanings, while simultaneously constructing more integrated, flexible, and coherent ways of being together (Lyons-Ruth, 1999). Destabilization is necessary to move the system to a different way of being from its habitual one, but paradoxically, safety is its prerequisite (Stechler, 1999).

### Interactive Elements That Catalyze Change

It is apparent by now that we are placing great emphasis on what happens in interaction and at the local level. In a sense we have returned to where psychoanalysis began, where Freud (1895/1950) gave priority to the act. And after the introduction of the structural model, he implicitly returned to this position in saying that treatment must be developmental, and something must happen between patient and analyst (Greenberg, 1996). Our view is that fittedness, acting as a new context, creates the potential for further elaboration of new forms of shared experience. It alters the intersubjective field, shifting the implicit relational expectations of each partner. With such a shift, an opening for the elaboration of new initiatives (change) becomes possible. In the therapeutic engagement, variations can and will continue to be introduced into the interactive flow, creating possibilities for meetings or failures to meet. When there is meeting, or fitting together of initiatives, a greater inclusiveness is created, meaning that each has at that moment grasped something essential about the intentional state of the other (see BCPSG, 1998a). Implicit relational knowing is altered as is the direction of interactive flow. Where there is failure to meet, inclusiveness is potentially constricted or prevented. What we did not previously emphasize, as we confined our conceptualizations to charged moments, was that fittedness, or the recognition of complementary actions, is the central clinical notion that captures the tendency of systems toward greater coherence. Fittedness is being evaluated continually in the moving along process and concerns issues along a spectrum of import. Reaching fittedness leads to incremental changes in implicit relational knowing, which are experienced as "getting better."

## SUMMARY AND CONCLUSION

Although it has been a cornerstone of psychoanalytic theory that all behavior is motivated, it has never been considered at the level of intersubjective regulation in the domain of implicit knowledge at the local level. We believe this level is an important addition to concepts such as transference-countertransference and the unconscious. Our developmental orientation leads us to conclude that this is the level at which emotional procedures or implicit relational knowings are established and reorganized throughout life. It therefore requires our most careful scrutiny in attempting to understand this level of therapeutic action. Implicit relational knowing is permeated with affective "valuations" regarding how to proceed with others. It therefore organizes attentional focus, guiding both the inference-making process and the action. Through it, the past is carried along, engagement is regulated, and meaning generated.

We conclude with four points:

First, therapeutic change happens in small, less charged moments as well as occasionally in highly charged 'now' moments and moments of meeting; second, therapeutic change involves change in implicit relational knowing, and this change occurs in the ongoing flow of each partner's relational moves at the local level; third, change in implicit relational knowing comes about by achieving more coherent ways of being together, and finally, more coherent ways of being together come about through a process of recognition of specificity of fittedness between the two partners' initiatives.

# Introduction to Chapter 5

In Chapter 4, we began to develop a language to describe the implicit level of therapeutic interaction, which we believed captured what really goes on, or is going on, between the two interactants. As the local level came into clearer focus and we examined it in a way comparable to how one might examine a mother-infant interaction, certain features assumed special prominence. Again, the arrival of this idea was announced in the previous chapter, but here we develop it more fully.

In looking closely at the local level we realized how much sloppiness, fuzziness, indeterminacy, and incomprehensibility there was at the moment-to-moment level of exchange. Initially we were confounded by this, but it soon dawned on us that we might have noticed something critically important to the change process. We also realized the essential property of co-creativity was inherent to the direction of any exchange. We saw this level of analysis as augmenting, rather than replacing, more traditional psychodynamic descriptions at the macro level. The relationship of the traditional level of therapeutic description and the moment-to-moment level would be analogous to the anatomic versus the cell biological descriptions of an organ.

In this chapter we also spell out more fully the logic of our use of dynamic systems theory and describe how well suited it is to this level of analysis. We delineate how much of the data of development and the therapeutic exchange (for example, self-organizing properties, non-linear shifts, and unpredictability) lends itself to a dynamic systems theory explanation.

Another realization that took more specific shape after Chapter 4, which is elaborated in more detail here, is a deepening understanding of the profoundly two-person nature of what have heretofore been considered the intentional states or directions of the individual. In the previous chapter, the two therapeutic partners were viewed primarily as individuals with separate, person-centered intentional directions that need to be fitted together in the therapeutic interaction. In Chapter 5, as well as in the following chapters, we advance the more challenging view that many social intentional states are co-created out of the ongoing social communication process and are not rightly considered as properties of either separate individual in the interaction. Instead, contrary to the dominant way of thinking about intentional states as person-centered, we feel that many socially directed intentions emerge as shared directions or as properties of the dyad, rather than of the individual. In this regard, we apply a dynamic systems model not only to the broader sweep of therapeutic change, but also to the microprocesses through which the moment-to-moment shared directions of the dyad emerge.

An unelaborated implication of this realization is the need to reconsider the nature and limitations of psychic determinism, because randomness and the co-creative process *in the moment* require a shift in our assumptions about how change occurs in the individual. It could perhaps be said that there has been an inherent contradiction in the psychoanalytic conception of monadic psychic determinism and its idea of change possibilities, which this newer conceptualization resolves.

The second section of this chapter involves our reply to three critiques of the article that were published along with the original article. In our response, we address salient points, such as where does meaning reside, what is deep and what is superficial, and what is the role of language. These issues are all addressed in much greater detail in Chapter 6.

**Chapter 5**

---

# The "Something More" Than Interpretation Revisited: Sloppiness and Co-Creativity in the Psychoanalytic Encounter[1]

IN APPLYING DYNAMIC SYSTEMS THEORY TO PSYCHOANALYTIC PROCESS, we have come to the view that psychoanalytic therapeutic interaction is an inherently sloppy process (Boston Change Process Study Group [BCPSG], 2002). This sloppiness arises from the intrinsic indeterminacy of the co-creative process between two minds. Sloppiness here refers to the indeterminate, untidy, or approximate qualities of the exchange of meaning between patient and analyst. This chapter is an attempt to elaborate and explore this idea of indeterminacy, as well as its implications for the process of psychoanalysis. We will also ground this understanding of the sloppiness of moment-to-moment therapeutic process in observed features of a transcripted analytic session.

---

[1]Originally published in *Journal of the American Psychoanalytic Association*, 53(3): 693–729. Copyright © 2009 by American Psychoanalytic Association. Reprinted by permission of SAGE Publications, Inc. AND The Boston Change Process Study Group. (2005). Response to commentaries. *Journal of the American Psychoanalytic Association*, 53(3): 761–769. Copyright © 2009 by American Psychoanalytic Association. Reprinted by permission of SAGE Publications, Inc.

We will attempt to describe the process of psychoanalysis at what we have called the local level (BCPSG, 2002). The local level is the second-by-second interchange between patient and therapist consisting of relational moves (BCPSG, 2002) composed of nonverbal and verbal happenings such as spoken phrases, silences, gestures, and shifts in posture or topic. Each relational move at the local level is seen as revealing an intention to create, alter, or fine-tune the immediate nature of the therapeutic relationship. Any exchange will have a local level.

This approach permits a focus on what we think has been insufficiently recognized as happening in the therapeutic process. Many recent thinkers have been exploring interactive dimensions of the psychoanalytic process (e.g., Benjamin, 1995a; Hoffman, 1998; Mitchell, 1997; Ogden, 1997). However, most relational thinkers have been concerned with the larger sweep of psychodynamic meaning and have not focused systematically on the moment-to-moment level (but see Beebe & Lachmann, 2002). Examining process at the local level can be seen at this point as a converging lens for viewing psychoanalytic process, another level of analysis that does not replace traditional psychodynamic descriptions at the more macro level.

New conceptual and descriptive approaches often require new terminology to capture ideas specific to that approach. As we began to develop our views of the moment- to-moment dimension of psychoanalytic treatment, it became clear that most of the established psychoanalytic vocabulary included strong conceptual links to the dynamic unconscious and the tripartite theory of mind. Using the established vocabulary to refer to our somewhat different view of the varieties of unconscious processes proved confusing rather than clarifying. Therefore, we found it unavoidable to introduce new terms into our discussion.

While our findings may have implications for many important psychoanalytic issues such as the reach of the dynamic unconscious, the relation between the imprecision observed at the local level and its technical handling, or the relationship between what we are calling co-created spontaneous material and intrapsychic dynamic material from the past, such implications are beyond the scope of the present chapter.

For the moment our approach and the descriptions that come from it will occupy our attention.

Despite the negative connotations of the term *sloppiness*, we view sloppiness as pervasive, inescapable, and inherent to the moment-to-moment level of all dyadic interaction. And rather than seeing this sloppiness as problematic, we see it as critical to the generation of new possibilities for psychotherapeutic change. Our perspective is that, on the one hand, the sloppiness of the exchange of meaning introduces substantial uncertainty into the interaction, something that is usually viewed as errors or mishaps; but, paradoxically, it also introduces new possibilities for increasing the coherence of the interactive process between analyst and patient. Sloppiness is potentially creative. While dynamic systems models, which include the feature of sloppiness in one form or another, have contributed striking new insights in many areas of science (e.g., Edelman, 1992; Freeman, 1995; Prigogine, 1997; Thelen & Smith, 1994), few theorists have considered how these models might be applied to relational processes in psychotherapy (but see Beebe & Lachmann, 2002; Stolorow, 1997). In exploring the implications of developmental research for psychoanalytic therapies, we have taken aspects of the dyadic, relational, and intersubjective perspectives on analysis and integrated them into a developmentally based dynamic systems view of therapeutic process. Dynamic systems models are especially well suited to dealing with complex systems with many interdependent variables. Such systems have self-organizing properties, resulting in discontinuous, nonlinear shifts in organization that are largely unpredictable. These shifts lead to the unanticipated emergence of properties that did not exist before.

The characteristics of this dynamic systems framework include several features. First, the dynamic engine of the therapy lies in the self-organizing properties of analyst and patient together as a dyad. Second, analyst and patient contribute both individual tendencies and other-shaped input. These multiple variables can at times be in opposition, at other times congruent or complementary. Third, the trajectory that will emerge from the interaction of the two partners is unpredictable and includes emergent properties that pop up from the interaction of the many variables. Fourth, the emerging trajectory will be sensitive to and constrained by the initial conditions of the relationship, including the relational histories brought by both partners. Such a framework includes a strong role for both organization and constraint operating within the system.

In addition to a dynamic systems framework, developmental research has pointed to the importance of nonconscious, implicit, procedural forms of memory. We have recently called attention to the importance of such implicit forms of representation in the relational arena and have termed these "implicit relational knowings." Implicit relational knowing refers to representations of the ways individuals relate to each other that are outside both focal attention and conscious verbal experience (Chapter One and Lyons-Ruth, 1999).

We do not reject the concept of the dynamic unconscious. Rather we think in terms of a range of unconscious phenomena. Traditionally, the dynamic unconscious, which has a verbal or symbolic label, and is unconscious only by reason of repression, is the only one in psychoanalysis that is considered to be "psychodynamic," the locus of all affectively important representations. However, there is also implicit knowledge that is nonconscious, has no verbal/symbolic label, and does not require repression to remain unconscious (Chapter One). Because the implicit level represents goal-directed interpersonal action, with its strong affective valences and conflictual elements, this level is also rich in psychodynamic meaning, without necessarily being part of the dynamic unconscious (Lyons-Ruth, 1999). However, further teasing apart of the contributions of the implicit nonconscious and the repressed unconscious is beyond the scope of this chapter. Here our task is to direct attention to the existence of the implicit level.

We find that framing the contribution of the past to the present in terms of implicit relational knowing offers several advantages. It provides a description of the past-present relationship that is consistent with current developmental and neuroscientific knowledge (cf., Lyons-Ruth, 1999; Schore, 1994; Westen & Gabbard, 2002a). Cognitive neuroscience has repeatedly demonstrated the existence and separable functioning of two forms of memory, commonly labeled implicit and explicit, or procedural and semantic, memory. Developmental research has described the preverbal infant's capacity for representing and anticipating patterns of interaction with others before symbolic or explicit forms of memory are functioning and long before any symbolic description of the interaction structure could be formulated.

While previous psychoanalytic theory has tended to equate nonverbal forms of representation with the preverbal functioning of infancy, current neuroscience makes clear that implicit forms of representation are fundamental to complex adult functioning as well as to infant functioning (e.g., Jacoby & Dallas, 1981; Schachter & Moscovitch, 1984). In addition, complex new learning occurs in adulthood through implicit mechanisms. This new learning is not mediated by translation of implicit knowing into symbolic or conscious form, even though words or images may be involved as part of the learning that is implicitly represented. Indeed, many forms of implicit knowing are about how to do things with words. Because implicit forms of memory are not initially encoded in words, the verbal form is not how the mind usually functions.

In addition, the concept of implicit relational knowing maintains a view of the dynamic unconscious (repressed) and nonconscious processing as central to affective and relational life, while freeing us from a model of the dynamic unconscious as the necessary or only way to understand the intrapsychic domain. It also frees us from the expectation that change necessarily requires verbal understanding in the sense of making the unconscious conscious. While most relational theories explain change as the result of the shared verbal understanding of patient–analyst transactions achieved after the critical interactions have occurred, our model proposes that affectively rich implicit processes can bring about change in interactive capacities in the moment (see D. N. Stern, 2004). In some instances, these changes may not require that the interactants explicitly reflect on what has transpired.

We conceive of implicit relational knowing as a domain of relational memory that is constantly in the dynamic process of being reorganized with each new relational encounter. Though any two therapeutic partners have many intersubjective capacities, including capacities for interpreting relational intentions and the states of mind of the other, the capacity for creating shared implicit knowledge does not reside solely in either of them acting alone. Rather, as the therapeutic relationship moves along, shared implicit knowing and shared intentions emerge bit by bit from the co-creative relational overtures each provides the other. The dynamic dyadic system has emergent capacities for creating new and unpredictable forms of shared implicit knowing in the interactants as new ways of being together are co-created in the treatment.

In summary, we make the following assumptions: Most of the affectively meaningful life experiences that are relevant in psychotherapy are represented in the domain of nonconscious implicit knowledge. This also includes many manifestations of transference. Therefore, much of what happens at the local level is psychodynamically meaningful, though not necessarily repressed. The fact that the dynamically repressed unconscious can also be an active influence at the local level is not our focus. We are simply calling attention to a different level of process.

In elaborating this dynamic systems model of the emergence of new forms of implicit relational knowing, we have come to focus on the moment-to-moment activity of the patient and the analyst. In previous work, we began by grappling with memorable moments that were "lit up" for both patient and therapist (BCPSG, 1998a). In subsequent work, we expanded our focus to include the quieter everyday moments of engagement between the two therapeutic partners at the local level of moment-to-moment interactions (BCPSG, 2002). At this local level it became clear that change occurred in similar fashion in the small, apparently unremarkable moments, as well as in the "lit-up" moments of more noticeable therapeutic change. Because we believe that the local level is an important site of therapeutic action, we think that clarifying the processes and phenomena, including sloppiness, occurring at this level will help to illuminate additional facets of what actually happens in a psychoanalytic treatment.

Compared to the attention devoted to meta-theory, the moment-to-moment level of therapeutic process has received scant attention. We believe this level of therapeutic activity has its own complexity, structure, and organization. It is at this moment-to-moment level that implicit relational procedures are enacted and evolve. However, our focus on the local level is not intended to imply that the background and meta-theory of the psychoanalytic framework are not relevant as well. In fact, future work will need to focus on integrating the local level with the level of larger psychodynamic meanings and narratives.

## SLOPPINESS AND CO-CREATIVITY ARE
## INTRINSIC TO THE THERAPEUTIC PROCESS

A view of the therapeutic process as sloppy at the local level is a central observation of this chapter. It has far-reaching consequences. Sloppiness expands the possibilities and variability inherent in the psychoanalytic dyad. And co-creation is the process by which sloppiness is capitalized upon to generate order or shared direction in the interaction.

The analyst typically enters the treatment process with only a general and fairly abstract notion of where he or she might like to see the patient progress in relation to the resolution of conflict, the enlarging of areas of effective functioning, the reduction of anxiety, or the flexible expression of affect. The patient also enters with only very general ideas of where he or she might like to end up. Neither analyst nor patient can know in any specific detail what the two of them will need to do together to reach their goals. Indeed, both analyst and patient can only grapple with the immediate dilemma of what to do to take the next step in the interactive process. This grappling is, of course, the point at which all of the analyst's dynamic training and humanity come into play. It is here that the analyst's grasp of some healing direction, some selection of what to "recognize" in the patient's words and actions, will be operationalized. But this indeterminacy of the "how to" of therapy is inescapable, regardless of technical stance, and emerges necessarily from the irreducible fact that both patient and analyst are sources of independent agency and subjectivity and at the same time are constantly influencing each other.

The sloppiness of a therapeutic dyadic system emerges in part from a core feature of therapeutic interaction that we will refer to as *fuzzy intentionalizing*. When any two creative and independent agencies interact, a central problem they encounter is that while actions are observable, their associated intentions or meanings must be inferred. We would claim, along with Freeman (1995), and in line with current infant studies (Carpenter, Akhtar, & Tomasello, 1998; Meltzoff, 1995) that this process of inferring intentions through parsing of actions is central to how the brain works, to how we understand others. These inferences regarding the other's intentions are the raw materials from which one's own relational moves are partially crafted.

The inferring of intention, or motivational direction, is a critical issue facing any two people interacting, but looms particularly large in a psychoanalytic treatment because of the primary focus on motivational directions. When we use the term *intention* here, we use it in both the narrow sense of "What is the other trying to do now with that comment?" and in the broader sense of "What are the larger meanings or goal directions that contribute to the act or comment?" However, the relation between the observed action—usually a verbal action in the analytic setting—and the inferred intention is necessarily loose. The parsing and translating of action into intentions or meaning often requires reiteration and redundancy in interactive sequences so that potential alternative "readings" can be evaluated and ruled out. This inference and evaluation process is occurring all the time primarily at an implicit level, outside of consciousness.

### *Sloppiness and Intentionality*

The ongoing indefiniteness in the process of inferring intention or goal-directedness in the other's activity contributes inevitable sloppiness to the interactive process. Each partner is not only putting forth actions and inferring intentions; these actions and inferences of intention have an effect on shaping the actions and intentions of the other as they emerge.

This sloppiness in apprehending intentions is one source of corresponding sloppiness in the interactive process itself. Sloppiness is inherent in the nature of human subjectivity. Over time, out of a process of negotiation, the intentions of each may become "recognized" by the other at an implicit level.

This ongoing process of fuzzy intentionalizing involves a great deal of variability and redundancy at the heart of the therapeutic process. This is necessary to allow the two partners to find fitted responses to each other that lead to the emergence of a joint direction in the treatment. The recognition process at the core of our view of therapeutic change capitalizes on sloppiness with its variability, unpredictability, and redundancy to achieve special moments of meeting that contribute to the emergence of a new shared direction for the dyad. We have discussed this implicit recognition process in previous papers (BCPSG, 1998a, 1998b, 2002) and will return to it in more detail in the final sections of this chapter.

### Sloppiness and Co-Creativity

Because we find that sloppiness is intrinsic to moment-to-moment relating, we needed to grapple with how it might contribute to the generation of change. It is here that the concept of co-creativity comes into play. We think of co-creation as a self-organizing process of two minds acting together that takes advantage of the sloppiness inherent in the interaction to create something psychologically new. What comes into being did not exist before and could not be fully predicted by either partner. The multiple sources of confusion and surprise in any interaction contain multiple potentials for unpredictable elements to emerge and to be elaborated in the dyad. Nonlinear dynamic systems as seen in dyadic interaction, by their nature reassemble, interpersonal and mental events in ways that are not predictable and that emerge spontaneously as a function of the interaction. Therefore, interactive processes make nonlinear leaps or qualitative shifts. For this reason, new intentions, feelings, and meanings are some of the creative products of interest in a nonlinear dyadic system. Although meanings, feelings, and intentions are not usually thought of as created products that pop up unexpectedly from a dyadic process, they are arguably the most important and complex products that emerge from human interaction.

We use the term *co-creativity* rather than *co-construction* for several reasons. Co-construction carries implied meaning that is inconsistent with a dynamic systems model. The word *construction* implies a directed process in which preformed elements are brought together according to an a priori plan. In contrast, with co-creativity there is no assembly blueprint. Instead, the elements assembled are themselves formed during the process of the interchange.

This creativity at the heart of the microprocess of therapeutic interaction is easy to overlook. At times it may even appear that nothing much is happening. However, at the subjective level there is a sustained experience of uncertainty and unpredictability, as the therapist and patient attempt to mutually apprehend and align their emerging intentions and initiatives in the service of a sustained shared direction in the interaction. Parenthetically it must be mentioned that not every direction that could be co-created would be healing or constructive for the patient. But this is a matter of technique and conception of therapeutic efficacy, beyond the scope of this chapter.

## CO-CREATIVITY AND SLOPPINESS IN
## AN ANALYTIC SESSION

We will illustrate these features of relational systems and their essential role in generating therapeutic change by looking very closely at the line-by-line process of an analytic session, using excerpted material from three successive portions of a transcript of an audiotaped session of an analysis conducted by one of our members. The full transcript appears in the Appendix at the end of this chapter. Because implicit relational knowing has often been misunderstood as referring entirely to the nonverbal aspects of the interaction, we felt it important to illustrate that these sloppy features of the communication are not confined to a nonverbal domain but are evident at the implicit procedural, or process, level of the verbal exchange itself. What an exclusively verbal transcript leaves out is that there are multiple verbal and nonverbal levels of communication occurring simultaneously in any two-person exchange, and the coherence of these communications within and across levels is critical to their impact on the therapeutic partner.

Despite the psychodynamically rich nature of the themes presented by the patient in these excerpts and our belief that the local level is connected to the level of psychodynamic meanings, we will not discuss these dynamics. While any therapeutic interaction could lend itself to discussion of psychodynamics, it also has an organization at the local level, regardless of the particular analytic technique adopted. The negotiation of intention and direction will look quite different with different techniques, but such negotiation of direction will always be present. And the reality of the features we are describing is not apparent unless one looks very closely at this moment-to-moment level. In fact it is lost at the narrative level. So, we will demonstrate what we mean by sloppiness in the co-creative process as it occurs at the local level, relational move by relational move. We will illustrate the process of fuzzy intentionalizing, with its associated need for variability and redundancy. We will also comment on how these features of sloppiness are intrinsic to the creation of shared meaning.

To summarize the case history, the patient had come for analysis 4 years earlier for recurrent thoughts of suicide as her only way to assert herself in the aftermath of a history of familial sexual abuse. The Monday session to be described followed an extra session the preceding Friday that the analyst had proposed, having sensed increased distress in the patient during the preceding meeting. In the extra session, the analyst suggested that the patient might have felt coerced to come, but the patient had disagreed.

In the Monday session, the patient reported two dreams she'd had since their extra meeting. They then used these dreams to enter territory that was new for the two of them. The first dream occurred on Friday night: The patient was in a group therapy meeting that reminded her of a sexual abuse group she had actually attended. That group had disturbed her because, by emphasizing her victimization, it made her feel worse, not better. The second dream occurred the night before, Sunday, and contained somewhat humorous material in which imperfections of the analyst made him seem more human and normally fallible, not someone totally in control of his life. Here the patient felt the analyst, unlike her previous notions, now was much more like she was. The next day, the patient began by sitting up rather than lying down and said that, uncharacteristically, she felt she had an agenda of her own. In fact, later in the appointment they began for the first time to talk about termination in a way that felt realistic and reasonable to them both.

How did they arrive at this new territory from having begun at a point of distress? Obviously the answer lies in the full history of both analyst and patient and their previous encounters, and is not attributable only to the current exchange. However, we will confine our attention to the line by line of the transcript rather than attempting to have the analyst explain and clarify in retrospect his internal process. Our concepts will be used to highlight aspects of the change process that occur at the local level of the interaction and that give rise to the more visible, macro-level changes experienced by this analytic dyad.

## CO-CREATION OF INTENTIONS IN
## THE THERAPEUTIC PROCESS

In the first excerpt, we will focus on the co-creative process and fuzzy intentionalizing in the therapeutic interaction. We will use an example from early in the analytic session in which the analyst and patient had been discussing the first dream of the disturbing group therapy session. On Saturday morning she thought of telephoning the analyst to say that she felt differently about him than she had in the therapy group. However, she decided that she could wait until the next meeting to tell him. Below, she describes the second dream (concerning the analyst's imperfections and her feeling more like him) as a contrast to that first dream of the disturbing group therapy session. As you will see, the analyst does not stay with her talk about the Sunday night dream but directs her back to the idea of calling him after the dream concerning the group therapy.

### First Transcript Excerpt:
### *"What dream are we going to talk about and why?"*

(Appendix lines 1 to 37)

P:   So there are two completely different . . . the dream that I had last night left me feeling really connected to you, and you know it made me feel—I don't know, I guess closer to you, that you would tell me you were not perfect.

(She has presented two dreams with some discussion and analysis, but at this point she proceeds with the second one. Why? While there may have been many reasons for her choice [defensiveness, closeness in time, etc.], this is an example of the indeterminacy in communication regarding the direction the person intends to take, what we refer to as *fuzzy intentionalizing*. Was there more to learn from the first dream? We don't know, because what she talks about, the feeling of closeness in the second dream, is where she has taken us. And even within the choice she has made, she introduces some minor uncertainties ["—I don't know, I guess . . . "]. These declarifications could be resistances, reluctances, or a real question about what she was saying. In any case, they add to the fuzzy intentionality, or indeterminacy, in inferring where the patient wants to go.)

A:   Uh-huh.

(This may "mean" go ahead, but in a number of different possible ways: Because I'm trying to be with you. Because I have not yet understood enough and need to hear more. Because I don't have anything to say yet. Because I don't even know where you're headed. Because I need more time, maybe the other dream is more important. Any and perhaps all of these intentions could be in operation, making for a fuzzy mix. She gets the general idea because of convention and their past history of working together. Fuzziness is present but not too broad or important here, yet.)

P:   Um. I'm not sure where I'm going to go with this either. Or if I do know where, I'm not sure I will go there. It's starting to feel like I'll need some help. (He does help in the next line.)

A:   You actually thought about calling me on Saturday about this other dream?

(Here, we have the first surprise, an example of the unpredictability in the sloppiness. The therapist exercises his own initiative and shifts the discussion to the other dream. In fact, not even to the dream but to what she thought of doing after the dream. Why? He seems to have radically altered the direction of things. Did he know why at the moment of doing it? The word "actually" stands out. It is either a request for clarification that she really did, indeed, think about calling him. Or a statement of his own surprise that she did. Or related to his concern that he had coerced her into accepting an extra hour. In any case his intentions are probably multiple, and not yet well formed. It turned out fine, but that does not mean he knew what he was doing at the time. The analyst's shift and abandonment of the second dream [from Sunday night] is also surprising because the second dream appears to contain hotter transference material.)

P:  Yeah!

    (She works through some of the fuzziness by focusing on only one piece of unclarity. Yes, she really did think of calling him up.)

A:  Which would have been, uh, and the reason you were thinking of that, that kind of very real connection, was what?

    (He is struggling here to find his way. He makes four incomplete and rapidly abandoned different sorties to find and express his intention, an example of redundancy within his thinking. In so doing, he comes up with, or rather returns to, a different orientation to the words "real connection," which she had used in her first statement about the second dream. He has recontexualized the term. He could be seen as starting to make a small and tentative bridge between the two dreams, or he might be talking about the reality of the connection between them. This intention still remains fuzzy. But the term "real connection" is starting to become an enriched co-created notion that will later help organize the session. The enrichment of this notion is a joint product of the sloppiness and of the attempts to find a joint direction and point of meeting in mutual understanding.)

P:  What are you referring to, the calling?

A:  Yeah, the calling.

    (They trade attempts to reduce the uncertainty and discover/create less fuzzy intentions. Here, we also see redundancy and variations to lock home clarifications.)

P:  Well, because I had seen you on Friday and felt there was like a thread of consciousness that had flowed into that dream.

    (She also vaguely senses some relationship between the two dreams. Their fuzzy intentions are starting to converge. The sloppiness between them concerning which dream to discuss and the switching between dreams has made the relation between the two dreams emerge as a theme. However, this was neither A's nor P's original intention. It emerged from their collaborative attempts to clear up some of the indeterminacy.)

A:  Yeah.

P:  It seemed kind of confusing to me that—I don't know how to say this exactly. It's like a throwback or something. To be dreaming about GT (the group therapist) and feeling that kind of pressure.

(Unsteadily, she goes back to the other dream, the first dream. There is a disjunctive going back and forth, another example of redundancy. In this context, the feeling of "pressure" emerges. It rises up as a new interesting element, still fuzzy but well marked.)

A:  Yeah.

P:  Is what I don't quite get—I mean I think—
    (She is stumbling forward, here.)

A:  The pressure is there, isn't it? Here we come into the issue of coercion, being made to do something. And in this dream you really are being pressured to say something more. And I guess I wonder how did it, uh, connect to the fact that we had that extra session on Friday.

    (He interrupts. Is he feeling a pressure too, but with a different and as yet unclear intentionality? Improvisation enters here as he goes from the idea of pressure to that of coercion. They now have to work through the fuzzy intentions that will compose and clarify this notion. The coercion of the extra session has apparently been on his mind, contributing to his, not necessarily her, sense of pressure. He is testing to see if there is a fit of intentions here.)

P:  —what it seems like to me is that—the dream was more connected to the idea of me feeling I have to measure up, come up with the right stuff.

    (She says the fit with his idea of coercion was not good. The analyst was partly right and partly wrong. For patient, the connection to the extra session was less important and is not picked up. What is more important at this moment is that she is clarifying what pressure means, namely "to come up with the right stuff." The emergence of this crucial precision on her part was facilitated by analyst's misunderstanding, another harvest from sloppiness. Note again the repeated variations necessary to move to greater mutual clarity.)

A:  Uh-huh.

    (Having been put back on her path, he is watching and encouraging this unexpected unfolding.)

P:  than the feeling of coerced into coming here. Somehow there is a difference somehow in there from sort of making a link with

*(She is refining the precision and stumbling forward. The level of sloppiness seems to have momentarily increased again. She is alone, with another, and out of this sloppiness they are co-creating something novel and something with greater clarity.)*

A:  Yeah, uh-huh.

*(He is urging her to continue to find her way, their way).*

P:  feeling coerced to coming here on Friday, which I didn't feel, at least consciously. Because what I was feeling had more to do with their (the group's) asking me—it was like I had to be sicker than I felt.—And I think that's frequently a part of what my mind-set is when I come here, that there is some sick part of my mind that I have to access.

A:  Uh-huh.


Progressively they have co-created islands of intentional fittedness and shared direction from the sloppiness. Through the same process of using the co-creativity of sloppiness, these islands then coalesced to make larger spaces of shared implicit knowing. In this way they stumble forward from her feeling that she had to be sicker than she was, the feeling that emerged from the dream of the group therapy. This is a way station toward her greater sense of agency, which was most clearly seen the following day when she began the session sitting up.

To sum up our understanding of this set of transactions, at the level of implicit process, the patient has recently articulated her recognition of the need to claim her agency. She decides not to call her analyst Saturday morning. Then she brings two dreams—one in which she is connected to another person through her sexually abused, sick self, and the other through her competent, equal-to-the-analyst self. In the ensuing dialogue with the analyst they discuss the dreams and patient's associations to them from the point of view of symbolic meaning. Also, however, on the local level they are simultaneously working on the development of the patient's agency through the implicit, moment-to-moment interactions we call co-creativity. (The analyst's contribution to this task is to give the patient the opportunity to clarify what is her own experience, to not merely accept his direction, an illustration of technique in the scaffolding of the patient's agency). In a sloppy process of trying to find a fit with each other, they negotiate shared intentional directions and local level meanings. Although this might be viewed as merely facilitating the patient's developing agency, our view is that such facilitation is part of the co-creative process that leads to changes in her sense of agency.

Out of this activity, more complex symbolic meaning and intentionality emerge. These more complex meanings that emerge include that of the patient being connected to another person through a positive sense of self—"equal"—while at the same time being aware of angry, helpless self experience—"the sick part of me"—that she is still struggling to manage. The intentions that emerge include the beginnings of her own "agenda" and the confidence to assert it.

How does the co-creative, sloppy nature of the local level process operate in this segment to contribute to change? Here we can see that rather than change in symbolic meaning leading the way through mutual understanding of patient's dreams and associations, it is in the implicit jockeying back and forth, checking out at each step how much each can contribute and respond to the emergence of a new shared direction, that a new shared meaning is co-created. As patient and analyst search for a fit with each other, while at the same time referencing their own agendas, they are co-creating a shared intention. This new, potential shared intention reorganizes and recontextualizes each of the old agendas in the process of its emergence (see Freeman, 1995, for related data on the recontextualization of previous perceptual experience by new experience).

It should be noted, however, that the problem of arriving at a shared direction is more complex than simply decoding the ambiguous communications of the other. The deeply relational nature of the human mind means that an intention or motivational direction is not simply a thing in one person's mind that is conveyed to the other (Bruner, 1990; Dilthey, 1976; Husserl, 1930/1989; Lakoff & Johnson, 1980; D. N. Stern, 1985; Vygotsky, 1934/1962). Instead, joint intentions or directions for the next steps in the relationship are co-created, negotiated between partners on a moment-to-moment basis. What we usually think of as solely within the person is not internal and fixed but is continually co-created in interaction with another person. Each partner is both putting forth actions and inferring intentions, which have an effect on shaping the actions and intentions of the other as they emerge. Not only is the communication of intention by each partner ambiguous but those communications are constantly shifting and adjusting based on the feedback of the partner and the possibilities sensed by each of finding a shared direction for their exchanges. The expression of a relational intention, then, is not a simple one-person act but an emergent property of the interaction itself. Finally, the mental complexity and agency of each of the participants introduces inevitable unpredictable and improvisational elements into how any joint direction will be worked out. The essence of the therapeutic interaction can be seen to be this joint negotiation and co-creation of intent or direction.

## SLOPPY PROCESSES AND
## UNPREDICTABILITY AND VARIABILITY

We have also noted above that co-creativity is the upshot of an unpredictable, improvisational process and that fuzzy intentionalizing depends on variability and redundancy. We do not intend to imply that everything that transpires in a session is unpredictable. Rather we emphasize that the interplay of two subjectivities inevitably throws up unpredictable and surprising phenomena at the local level.

Let us look again at the clinical material in light of these multiple sources of new elements in the interaction. The patient has been talking about the second dream, in which the analyst seemed more like her. In this segment there are two extended silences, one for 83 seconds and one for 68 seconds. What is notable in relation to our current focus is that the outcome of each is unpredictable, variable. One cannot know how long each will last, who will end it, what will happen.

*Second Transcript Excerpt: "How do we know where we are going?"*

(Appendix lines 117–144)

P:  In the dream, it made me feel stronger.
A:  Yeah!
    (He seconds her thought.)

P:   It made me feel more . . . equal to you . . . (83+ sec)

A:   Is that something that's happened nowadays? . . .

(After the long pause, is there something about the idea of her being equal that gives both of them pause? Or is it A's recognition that it is P's moment to take the initiative that sets the stage for the long pause?)

P:   Uhh. . . . I think to some extent . . . my feeling is beginning to change about . . . about that. I wouldn't say that. . . . I don't think it's a done deal (chuckles). . . . Umm . . . One of the things that I was thinking about on Saturday as I was thinking about calling you was that I . . . I was convinced in my own mind that I could call you and that I could tell you about that dream and it would be okay So somehow that made me feel like I didn't have to do it.

(She is saying that she now recognizes that she had the agency and didn't have to prove it.)

A:   Uh-huh . . .

(She shifts in a way that the analyst couldn't have predicted—to focus on the thought of a Saturday call.)

P:   You know I didn't have to prove anything so . . . so I didn't do it.

A:   Uh-huh.

P:   You know it was enough to acknowledge to myself that I knew I could pick up the phone and tell you about it and that could be interesting, but I could also (brief chuckle) tell you about it today.

A:   Uh-huh.

P:   And I mean there's something in my viewing it that way, my viewing that it was okay to call you that makes me feel we're more equal,

A:   Uh-huh (concurrently with the patient's words)

P:   than unequal.

A:   Uh-huh . . . (68-second pause)

P:   In the dream, um, the dream last night, I was feeling like, um . . . I don't know . . . how to say it exactly . . . the word acceptance keeps coming into my

(She breaks the silence with the new idea of acceptance. While it relates to and expands on connection, it introduces a variation)

A:   Uh-huh

(concurrently with the patient's words)

P:    . . . head. It was like I was feeling accepted. . . . the way I am, and . . .

    (She repeats the idea of acceptance, after the analyst's assenting *uh-huh*, in a second initiative that underscores her interest in moving in this direction.)

When the patient introduces the idea of acceptance, a shift in the intersubjective field has occurred that could not have been predicted as an outcome of the silence. One can see that there is no consistent narrative structure at the local level, and no way to tell what would follow any of the relational moves. Even the most insightful therapist cannot know what the patient will say in her very next sentence. And even if he does know the general topic, he cannot predict the exact form it will take. Yet the exact form of what he says will create the context and thus influence what happens next. This important feature of what actually happens in the therapeutic process is not revealed by focusing on dynamic unconscious meanings.

To take this unpredictability into account, one need only attempt to consider that what did happen is not what had to happen. Many things could have happened. At any point, guided by the meaning the moment had for either, the patient or the analyst could have made a different relational move that would have changed the path of their actual interactional flow. The presence of co-creativity and fuzzy intentionalizing in the therapeutic interaction means that any particular relational move could have been different. There are many equally valid and effective pathways for the dyad, many of which would arrive at roughly the same destination. In biology and developmental psychology, this equivalence of diverse and idiosyncratic pathways has been termed the principle of equifinality.

## SLOPPY PROCESSES ARE REDUNDANT

Despite this unpredictability in the precise path to be taken in the therapeutic interaction, analyst and patient convey meanings, develop implicit knowledge of how to be together, negotiate mutual directions, and feel connected with each other. With the conveying and inferring of intentions being such a fuzzy, unpredictable, and variable process, how does any individual come to know what meaning was being expressed? We felt the key to this puzzle lay in the recurrence and redundancy that characterizes interactions. To state the case more strongly, an enormous amount of time in treatment will necessarily be spent in repetitions, variations on a theme, restatings, so that intentions will be optimally inferred and collaborative directions can emerge.

We have noted that sloppiness which is intrinsic to intentionalizing is both variable and redundant. This reiterative process characterizes the bit-by-bit exchange and negotiation of meaning. We see this again near the end of the first excerpt where they discuss which dream they were talking about. At this point the patient is talking about the "part of her mind that is sick and that she had felt pressured" to discuss.

### Third Excerpt: "We need to do this in many different ways."

(Appendix lines 29–66)

P:   feeling coerced to coming here on Friday, which I didn't feel at least consciously. Because what I was feeling had more to do with their (the therapy group) asking me—it was like I had to be sicker than I felt . . . And I think that's frequently a part of what my mind-set is when I come here, that there's some sick part of my mind that I have to access.

A:   Uh-huh.

P:   in order to be talking about the right thing. You know, there's some pathological thing in my head that I have to be able to

   (She reiterates the sense of having to talk about the sick part of her mind.)

A:   Yeah, and that is something that you feel here sometimes.

   (He agrees with her with emphasis about the experience between them.)

P:   Yeah.

   (She says, *yes, you're getting it.*)

A:   So the dream is also about coming here, the pressure to get this sick part of your brain out in the open.

   (By strengthening and clarifying in her own mind through the exchange what she had meant by pressure, the patient has helped the analyst get the idea that the pressure is about discussing the sick part of her, not about feeling coerced into the Friday appointment. His getting it has strengthened her sense that her initiative can enable her to make herself understood.)

P: The thing that is really confusing to me is that when I was in that group with GT the thing that was so impossible for me was to feel convinced that my experience was somehow . . . comparable to the other people in the group.

(She's repeating the sense of feeling pressured about the "sick part of her mind," this time by saying she felt differently from the other group members, who were more inclined to focus on their victimization and who seemed to feel more damaged by their abuse experiences.)

A: Yeah.

P: and I just could not feel that . . . I first of all didn't understand why anybody would want me to think that. What good does it do me to think that?

A: Huh?

P: I don't know. I get confused. You know, when I came to see you what I wanted you to tell me that I was sicker than I thought I was and that it was okay for me to be here.

(Now she directs their attention to the way she and the analyst talked about the "sick part of her" in their first meetings: to be connected, one must be sick. Therefore, she had to exaggerate her "sickness," an earlier manifestation of the sense of pressure. She is indirectly referring to her sense that in those early meetings the analyst had also helped her retain focus on the positive parts of her self-experience.)

A: Uh-huh.

P: And then, with that group and with GT it was like, oh yes, you're very sick. (chuckles) You've got this really horrible thing wrong with you. And I'm thinking it's not really that bad! It was like two very opposite experiences.

(Now she takes the focus back to her experience in the group, in effect coming back to the topic of the first dream, feeling pressured.)

A:  Uh–huh.

P:  . . . And I think there is still some issue for me in my own perception of myself, about whether I want to be sick or not. I mean I
can't, I haven't quite figured out how to make that scar fit in to my
image of myself. . . . And because of that, every time I come here I
feel like I have to come with that wound, that gaping wound being
the most visible thing. If I'm actually feeling in touch with the way
my life is now (i.e., without such a sense of a gaping wound), then
I don't know what to say to you, there's nothing to talk about. You
know, you'll ask me why I'm here.

   (She's not sure, but it's becoming clearer that they are discussing to what extent her "perception of herself" contains only that
"sick" part of her. From the beginning of this excerpt, the two of
them have been looping around her feeling of pressure to focus on
the "sick" part of her and have expanded the issue of the "sick part
of her." She wonders: Can they be connected with her not being
sick? Within a few minutes, they have moved to talking more
about the second dream and her feeling "stronger" and "more
equal.") How in this brief exchange did they come to "agree to"
what their shared intention was? It was not explicitly articulated.
The key to this joint accomplishment lies in the recurrences in the
patient's and analyst's statements. These recurrences are not redundant in the sense of being unnecessary or boring. The cycling
of their recurrent turn taking is critical to how they co-create a
shared relational intention. It is a mutual bootstrapping, an exploratory process of slow, incremental steps toward co-creation of
shared meaning and shared direction.

There are several reasons why this redundancy of relational moves
is necessary. The objective behaviors making up the relational moves
during each turn-taking step can only partially convey each partner's
emerging apprehension of the joint direction. The behaviors do not
map the intention in a one-to-one fashion. The mapping is sloppy. We
also see in this vignette how the same intention can be conveyed in an
infinite number of ways.

In addition to the inherent variability of the expressive and receptive processes, here we can see that intentions are most often not fully

formed and therefore are often tentatively expressed. The recipient's comprehension of the emerging intention is similarly partial and hesitant. Therefore, implicit questions are communicated between the partners in forms like, "I want to talk about X, but do you? And can we talk about it, given the way we are together? And what shape will the intention take as we begin to jointly articulate it?" This expression of a relational intention is not simply a "yes" or "no." Rather it demands a series of responses from the other person as the two continue to negotiate and form the intention. In turn, each response is not simply a go-ahead "yes" or "no," because it too demands a response ("Yes, I do, but do you, really," or "I am not sure I get what you want," or "Is this the sort of thing you had in mind?") The first person needs to respond again, and so on, recurrently. Out of the recurrence in their exchange, the mutual intent emerges. This view of a sloppy, redundant, co-creative process gives us a way of modeling more specifically how relational intentions are created by dyadic systems. When the analyst "got" what the patient meant by pressure, she also became clearer about it herself and moved on to say how she felt differently with the analyst than she had with the group. The change in the analyst catalyzed a change in the patient. Her being able to facilitate the analyst's understanding heightened her own sense of communicative competence, an altered sense of self.

Redundancy overcomes the inherent variability of the expression and reception of a relational intent. It is a bit-by-bit process that not only clarifies each individual's sense of the emerging intention of the other person but also catalyzes the creation and consolidation of each partner's own intention. When recurrence is successful, a co-created shared intention or direction of interaction emerges. Although we view the individual as a source of primary activity, organization, and intentional direction, the emergent directions of the individual are continually selected, reassembled, recontextualized, and redirected by the relational context. Functionally speaking then, the relational unit is the crucible in which "individual" intentions are forged, as part of participating in a joint direction with another. Paradoxically, the only way to become yourself is through participating in shared intentional directions with others.

## SLOPPINESS, CO-CREATIVITY, AND
## THE ROLE OF THE PAST

Although we speak of intentions as mutually created, we do not mean to imply that they are being created de novo. De novo creation denies the past and the carrying forward of the past to relational possibilities available to each individual. The influence of the past on the present has been framed in several ways. For example, in earlier theory, the past was viewed through the lens of representations or meanings that were formed at the time of the events themselves. In one set of more contemporary views, the past is viewed as a narrative construction of the patient that is subject to change as a function of the therapy (Schafer, 1992). In our view as well, the organization derived from the past is, while influencing the present, also continually being updated. The current conceptualization departs from the narrative approach in most other aspects, however. The narrative approach operates at the explicit level of conscious, reflective dialogue and change occurs through the dialogue in the therapeutic session. In contrast, we do not conceptualize the updating of the past as operating primarily through explicit narrative processes. Instead, in keeping with current models of brain function (e.g., Edelman, 1992; Freeman, 1995), we view implicit relational knowing as being automatically or implicitly updated in small ways with each relational encounter rather than as operating primarily through explicit narrative exchanges. Each time aspects of older internalized models are accessed in the treatment, those past organizations are subtly reorganized by the present context of interaction between patient and therapist. In our view, the accumulation of many small changes in implicit relational knowing in this new context, these subtly shifting organizations, would influence behavior outside the treatment situation. The recontextualization and reorganization process occurring at the local level is subtle and occurs in tiny shifts that would not be easily visible until they have cumulated in the treatment.

The creative process we delineate at the level of primary moment-by-moment interaction does not vitiate the influence of the past on the present interaction; instead the past configures the present moment through the constraints contained in the implicit relational knowings that both partners bring to the encounter, that is, the transference and countertransference. As noted earlier, these knowings include expectancies derived from the individual pasts of the two participants and expectancies derived from their joint history of encounters together. Thus, the co-created parsing of a highly variable flow of behaviors into mutually recognized relational intentions is contextualized, and in part made possible, by the dyad's already created implicit relational knowings, knowings that in turn draw on each participant's past outside the dyad.

This implicit relational knowing includes implicit knowing of how analyst and patient have been together in the past and their short- and long-term implicit and explicit goals. An illustration of how their history together can be seen in the material is in the following example (Appendix lines 120–123):

A:  Is that something that's happened nowadays? . . .
P:  Uhh. . . . I think to some extent . . . my feeling is beginning to change about . . . about that. I wouldn't say that . . . I don't think it's a done deal (chuckles). . . . Umm . . .

     (moving along, following the chuckle she says) one of the things that I was thinking about on Saturday as I was thinking about calling you was that I . . . I was convinced in my own mind that I could call you and that I could tell you about that dream (about the disturbing group session) and it would be okay so somehow that made me feel like I didn't have to do it.

     (Despite reassurances calling between sessions was something she felt she shouldn't do, and had done only on one occasion.)
A:  Uh-huh . . .
P:  You know I didn't have to prove anything so . . . so I didn't do it.
A:  Uh-huh.
P:  You know it was enough, it was enough to acknowledge to myself that I knew I could pick up the phone and tell you about it and that would be interesting, but I could also (brief chuckle) tell you about it today.

Aside from the fact that the telephoning between sessions had a mutual meaning for this patient and analyst, P's chuckle also communicated mutually shared knowledge—for example, the way they both frequently used humor, often of this mildly self-deprecating kind, to ease tension. When she chuckled, they both knew implicitly that he would understand that she was trying to ease tension. This shared awareness affects the analytic interventions—whether to interpret the turning away from negative affect, or whether to appreciate P's self-regulatory activity as having the goal of continuing to explore challenging issues in the hour. Another instance of this kind of shared implicit knowing from their mutual past is the way the analyst's "um-huhs" were understood by both of them as him saying "yeah, go on—"

However, even though we view each individual as having a past and as bringing a set of potential ways of relating into the new encounter, we see the dyadic situation as dominating the past events. In our view the way the past of the two participants influences their interactions is the way transference and countertransference expressions present themselves in this model. It is the present interactions of the participants that recontextualize the transferential manifestations of the past. The current dyadic direction will continually select from the past of each person those elements that will be used to fashion a joint direction in the dyad. And those elements will be rapidly recombined into new jointly created elements of process between the two parties. The creative elements of the therapy will often overshadow the static elements that depend on the past to the extent that the two parties begin to construct a joint direction. We feel that the center of gravity lies in the process of interaction between two parties, not in the individual pasts of each person. Similar to current views of memory, we feel that the present moment contextualizes what will be remembered but also transforms that memory as it is recontextualized in light of the present interaction (Edelman, 1992; Freeman, 1995).

## CO-CREATIVITY REQUIRES
## A RECOGNITION PROCESS

Some obvious questions arise about so sloppy and variable a dyadic system. How does it arrive at adequate resolution to move on? What is the punctuation of the relational exchange? How do the patient and therapist sense when they have successfully joined in an intentional direction? How is it that some relational initiatives between patient and analyst are selected to be repeated, followed up on, and elaborated and others are not? Here Sander's work on recognition process served as our guide. He has repeatedly examined the problem of accounting for directionality in human growth and development and he sees both biological and psychological organization as directed toward increased coherence of adaptive organization (1997).

By recognition process, we mean the sensing by both parties that a specific fitting together has occurred in their responses to each other in the service of moving toward mutually held goals. Sander (1997) has pointed out that the essential characteristic of these moments is that there is a specific recognition of the other's subjective reality, or intentional direction, at multiple simultaneous levels. Each partner grasps and ratifies a similar version of "what is happening now, between us," by providing a specifically fitted response to the other's initiative (Chapter one and BCPSG, 1998a [Stern et al., 1998]).

Sander's view of recognition process at the level of self-awareness can be extended to encompass this kind of specific fittedness at an implicit, nonarticulated level, with no implication of awareness or consciousness. For example, in Sander's classic frame-by-frame film analysis of the father and the infant, the infant falls asleep in the father's arms at the moment of a specific fittedness between the father's actions and the self-organized sleep processes of the infant (Sander, 1997). The implicit recognition that comes with specific fittedness serves the same function for the patient and the analyst. When a fittedness of intention is achieved, a coherent shared state of intersubjectivity emerges and there is a mutual sense of a shared direction. Recognition process is the joint apprehension of this dyadic state.

This recognition of the "fittedness" of one person's initiative is most often conveyed by a responsive move on the part of the other partner, a move that, when successful, builds on the previous move in a way that deepens the dialogue in the service of the collaborative goals. Both partners sense the fittedness of their actions to the relational potential of the other and hence to the potential achievement of more complex and more collaborative ways of being together. Recognition process in this sense is the directional element of developmental and clinical process; it is how we feel our way along in unscripted relational encounters.

Sufficient fittedness is most easily defined in terms of what happens next. Has it permitted a change in direction, a shift in felt coherence, a vitalization? This functional definition raises the problem of intrinsic and extrinsic criteria for knowing when fittedness is achieved. The actual criteria of sufficient fittedness are so fluctuant, so relativistic to past such happenings, that it is a constantly moving set point.

Two illustrations of how fittedness and recognition are mutually ratified are seen in the transcript. The first comes toward the end of the first session of the week, after the patient talks of the uneasiness she feels with the feeling of acceptance (transcript lines 144–153).

P:   It was like I was feeling accepted . . . the way I am and . . . there's something about the feelings that go along with that, that make me afraid, and I start to feel afraid of being hurt, when I notice that I'm letting my guard down, or something, . . . and, you know, one of the things that is disturbing to me is that I'll wake up with that feeling of being accepted and then as soon as I'm conscious of the fact that it's a dream I start to feel afraid of the feeling. It's like I don't really want to feel that with you.

A:   Huh! . . . something's scary.

P:   Yeah.

A:   Yeah.

When the two echo each other with "Yeah" and "Yeah," we see the mutual acknowledgment of their shared state.

Another example of the recognition process can be seen at the beginning of the second session of the week, after the excerpted session. It began extraordinarily differently, with the patient wanting to sit rather than lie on the couch. For the first time, she began talking while sitting up on the couch and looking at the analyst (transcript lines 160–171).

P:   Today I somehow don't want to lie down right away.

A:   Well, that's a change!! Can you say what's happening?

P:   I'm not exactly sure, but somehow I feel like I'm more aware of what I want for myself. It's like I have my own agenda.

Shortly after that, she lay down and continued to talk about this feeling of being in a new state with her analyst.

P:    Today it feels a lot more connected here . . . because it feels like I'm opening up something to you . . . in a voluntary way. It's like, you know, I'm in control of what we're talking about, in a way that I don't usually feel. It's like I have an agenda today.

A:    (wryly) It's hard to have agendas other days?

P:    Yeah!

The two then burst into loud mutual laughter.

When the two burst into mutual laughter after talking of the patient's novel discovery of her feeling of having her own agenda, they enact a mutual sense of shared fittedness of initiatives. This shared recognition of fittedness is the period, or sometimes the exclamation point, that marks the creation of a new joint intention that contextualizes the interaction. When this recognition occurs, a new phase of exploration can begin. In fact, it did later in the session when the two began to realistically discuss termination for the first time.

THE SLOPPY PROCESS OF THE
LOCAL LEVEL AND OTHER VIEWS OF
PSYCHOANALYTIC PROCESS

Of course, the clinical material presented can be considered from many different perspectives. Our goal in viewing the material here was to examine the local level of interaction, where the process of negotiating a shared intention comes into center focus. Other theories, where the focus is on the narrative level, might find in it the unfolding of a preexisting narrative, or unconscious fantasy about ambition, or conflicts about aggression, or the exchange contributing to the emergence of a sense of self. They might focus on the transference meaning of these developing themes in the therapeutic relationship. They might understand the intensification of affect in the analytic process in terms of an underlying fear of aggression that free association has revealed. Then they might identify insight as the mechanism through which the conflict is resolved and fear is diminished. In addition, the analyst who has integrated these many alternative readings of possible intentional directions for the patient–analyst interaction may have more possibilities for helping the patient. However, we feel that the analyst's openness to the sloppiness of the therapeutic process and the need to join directions with the patient through a process of dialogue and negotiation are also necessary to the successful emergence of a shared direction and therefore to a successful analysis. The local level of the patient–analyst dialogue is the critical matrix for this co-creation and recognition process.

We could also consider alternative paths from the point of view of the analyst's activity. The analyst might have chosen to give priority to free association and to not interrupt the free associative process with his comment early on about the patient's thoughts of telephoning him. Similarly, he might have analyzed the patient's defensive departure from free association in the long pauses, for example, by inquiring about what happened just at the point she fell silent. Alternatively he might have chosen to return to the dream to analyze transference issues such as conflicts about dependent longings, sexuality, and aggression. Or, he might have chosen to further elaborate her fantasy of being "very sick" as an avenue into intense affect in relation to a self-representation as sexual and aggressive, bad, and damaged. Finally, but not exclusively, he might have worked in displacement to explore transference reactions, such as through a focus on GT and the therapy group. All the above approaches may inform the analyst's work. Whatever the approach, however, it is inescapable that every analyst is simultaneously interacting with the patient at the microlevel. And any approach will have implications at this level. It cannot be ignored in any view of treatment, whatever the orientation. It has changed our clinical sensibilities.

## SUMMARY AND CONCLUSION

This chapter explores sloppiness that is an inherent property of the two-person intersubjective dialogue at the local level. We find it to be an enormously interesting and productive aspect of a dynamic systems model of psychoanalytic treatment. It is also an essential element of the co-creative process that leads to greater intersubjective coherence. We view sloppiness, not as errors or mishaps in the dialogue, but rather as a generator of potentially creative elements that may alter the direction of the dyad's evolution in unexpected, even previously unimaginable, ways.

Where do the novel elements come from in the analytic process that make it such a surprisingly specific journey? One could say that sloppiness is to a two-person psychology what free association is to a one-person psychology. They each add the unexpected specific details. They create the surprise discoveries that push the dyad to its uniqueness. However, there is also an important difference. Free associations are assumed to lead to and from preexisting networks of meanings. Sloppiness, on the other hand, is not part of any prior organization, even though it, too, is influenced by the past.

Sloppiness, like free association or other unanticipated "pop-up" events, has potential creativity only when it is framed and used within a well-established therapeutic system or within a well-functioning dyad. Without the direction and constraints of those dyadic systems, the improvisational elements can veer toward chaos.

We have demonstrated with audiotaped transcripts of two analytic sessions several examples of sloppiness and its associated features, and we have suggested how these features may advance the co-creative process of psychotherapy. This view contributes to the emergence of a relational theory of psychoanalysis based on a dynamic systems model and provides descriptions of how such sloppy dyadic processes work to create psychoanalytic change.

## FURTHER COMMENTS ON ISSUES RAISED
## IN THE PRECEDING MATERIAL

When this material was originally published, three commentaries were included in the same journal issue: (House and Portugues, 2005; Litowitz, 2005; Mayes, 2005) to which we replied, and we reproduce our response below.

We appreciate the thoughtful consideration given by the three commentators to the somewhat new and unfamiliar directions taken in our paper. From varied perspectives, each author raises numerous points for further dialogue regarding the fundamental assumptions underlying a view that privileges the implicit process between analyst and patient. While it is tempting to try to have a further exchange concerning all of the points raised, we will confine our closing comments to the points we consider most salient and critical to the theoretical framework we are proposing here.

First, we should briefly clarify that we do not view sloppiness per se as the something more than interpretation that leads to change. Rather, we describe sloppiness as an inescapable feature of therapeutic exchanges (at the local level) that is used in the service of co-creating new ways of fitting together. "Sloppiness" encompasses the spontaneous, improvisational, unexpected interpersonal events that "pop up" in interaction and then can be captured to catalyze intersubjective moments of meeting and bring about change. House and Portugues (2005) translate sloppiness and fuzzy intentionalizing into "the complexity and difficulty of communication between two people," whereas we find that conceptualization of sloppiness and fuzzy intentionalizing moves us toward elucidating this "difficulty."

## MEANING: SIGNS, SYMBOLS, AND
## INTRINSIC MEANING

We will begin by addressing Litowitz's (2005) elegant description of the psychoanalytic endeavor from the point of view of semiotics, because we find our viewpoint both closely aligned with hers regarding the social origins of meaning, yet deeply divergent from hers, as well as that offered by House and Portuges, in our view of the processes that give rise to such meanings.

We find many points of agreement with Litowitz in her description of the process of communication as co-created, as needing constant disambiguation between partners, and as the process through which meanings emerge. We are also in agreement with her regarding the positions she depicted of Quine (1960) and Bahktin (1981) that underneath the generalized meanings of words are a history of "past communicational exchanges [that] cling to our words." Hobson (2002) has similarly noted that "every word has a hidden glow of feeling," accrued from the specific relational encounters in which it has been embedded. Litowitz's citing of Rommetveit (1974) reveals further similarities in our thinking about the fuzziness of communication, that is, "anticipatory comprehension that sets up expectations of understanding that often turn out to be misunderstandings." Further underscoring this point, Litowitz also notes that "every sign is always inherently vague." However, Litowitz also includes affective cues in her list of signs, and herein lies the origin of our deep differences in perspective. Affective cues, as well as intention cues, exude meaning but are not accurately viewed as symbols or as signs, either in the most usual sense of those terms or in the view from developmental research. Instead, affective cues have an inherent, biologically wired meaning or valence or valuation (value in Edelman's terms) from birth onward.

So where does meaning reside if these cues are not signs? Affect cues (as well as intention cues) are mainly movements composing facial expressions, gestures, and positions. Using facial expressions as an example, certain expressions can be conventionalized by a society and thus become signs that have a referent beyond its own performance (e.g., a disgust face when referring to last night's dinner). But how are we to consider a disgust expression while eating something disgusting? It is not true to say that it refers to something else, such as the inner feeling of disgust, because the facial expression is biologically part of the inner feeling. This can even be true for many conventionalized facial behaviors, such as a smile. It can be a sign, but it is also a performance with a specificity that carries it beyond the conventional sign. It is this specificity of performance that carries the authenticity of the affect compared to its sign value. It refers to itself only, so to speak.

Others, Darwin included, point out that facial expressions can act as signals to other members of the species (not to eat what disgusted one member). But even in this case, the status of a sign is questionable because recent findings on mirror neurons and other forms of "other-centered participation," make the facial expression not a signal or a means of referencing but the initiator of resonance or contagion. So we are left with authentic affective cues that refer to themselves only, where the communication is in the performance.

Infants understand the basic valence of such cues from the beginning, so they are not arbitrary. Not at the beginning of life nor thereafter are they pointers or signifiers of something else. They have inherent meaning as positive or negative communications in and of themselves. These communicative signals form the basis for the elaborate face-to face-exchanges of affect that are one of the uniquely human features of early communication (see Hobson, 2002; Jaffe, Beebe, Feldstein, Crown, & Jasnow, 2001; D. N. Stern, 1985; Tomasello, 1999). Most of what we are talking about in the affective flow between mother and infant or therapist and patient consists of sequences of acts that have intrinsic meaning. These, of course are mixed with true signs and symbols.

So the infant certainly does create meanings prior to the use of symbols, and meaning need not be symbol connected. Viewing videotapes of mother–infant interactions leaves no one questioning that the mother's actions mean something to the infant and that the infant's responses reflect the meanings generated within him. We view this implicit (non-symbolic) understanding of relationships (implicit relational knowing) as foundational to our meaning systems, and as a necessary substrate to the subsequent mapping of more arbitrary signs and symbols onto the already acquired implicit meanings of lived experience. Peter Hobson (2002), in his book, *The Cradle of Thought,* lays out this argument and the wide-ranging evidence for it in eloquent detail.

In sum, affect and intention cues have inherent meaning from a biological standpoint that is not arbitrary or vague. And this difference is important to any theory of the emergence of meaning. Therefore, approaches that fail to distinguish between affect cues and other more arbitrary semiotic systems will contribute to confusion rather than clarification of how meaning is co-created developmentally and therapeutically. Consistent with current scientific views of mind and brain function, we therefore advance the view that implicit relational knowing is a separate form of representation from language-based explicit knowledge. Implicit relational knowing does not change with the acquisition of language, nor is it transformed into language when language arrives. It is a separate domain of represented experience that continues to develop throughout the life span just as explicit semantic knowledge develops. Implicit relational knowing is not confined to anticipations of relational actions alone, but includes their associated feelings and intention cues. The richness of implicit knowing is one of the most important findings of the last decades of infant observation and attachment research. These findings have made it clear that implicit relational knowing is one vehicle through which the past is carried into the present. Implicit relational knowing cannot express anything but the past (as personally experienced) and the present moment contains everything from the past that organizes the person's response "now."

Analysts must consider the possibility that the most important levels of psychodynamic meaning can be carried, enacted, and expressed through nonsymbolizing processes. Perhaps the confusion that this assertion generates stems from a belief that meaning can only be generated through symbolization. Michael Basch defined meaning as "a dispositional effect on action" (1975). This applies to both explicit and implicit meanings, but is a particularly good description of implicit forms of meaning. The relationally imbedded meanings that are exchanged through rapid affective communications during lived experiences are the ones that most fundamentally organize one's directions and these are central to psychoanalysis. Therefore, we dispute the statement that "each human seeks meaning through the mediation of semiotic systems shared with other humans." (Litowitz, 2005, p. 752) While semiotic systems are unquestionably important, they are merely a part of a much more inclusive intersubjective system that begins with the sharing of affective and intentional orientations toward one another and toward the world, and such sharing of orientations is at the heart of interpersonal exchange and the generation of meaning. We believe it is a fundamental error that has been carried forward in psychoanalytic thinking to base meaning (and mediation) in semantic meaning. Language and abstract forms of thought build on earlier modes of making and representing meaning, but these earlier modes are not symbolic, nor are they superseded by the symbolic. A variety of work proves that both complex rule learning and the learning of affective valence can occur in the absence of the capacity for explicit, declarative forms of memory. To quote the review of Lewicki, Hill, and Czyzewska, "nonconscious information-acquisition processes are not only much faster but are also structurally more sophisticated, in that they are capable of efficient processing of multidimensional and interactive relations . . . knowledge that is indispensable for . . . encoding and interpretation of stimuli and the triggering of emotional reactions" (1992, p. 796) (Knowlton, Ramus, & Squire, 1992; Lewicki et al., 1992; Tranel & Damasio, 1993).

Although the infant innately is biologically prepared to develop the ability to use symbols, a large cognitive and neuroscience literature supports the view that the kinds of generalized expectations that the infant elaborates, as well as the generalized perceptual prototypes that emerge from repeated experiences with different exemplars of objects, are not to be equated with their eventual symbolic representations. We would not agree, then, with the House and Portuges argument that the processes through which "a rich discriminated set of experiences come to be remembered and expected" are symbolic or proto-symbolic. Instead, they rest on different cognitive and perceptual capacities than those that support symbolic functioning (e.g., see Sabbagh, 2004, for the dual neural sites involved in representing the thoughts and feelings of others). Indeed, symbolic functioning does not become available until the middle of the second year. This does not mean that the infant is not thinking. Thought and symbol use are not synonymous, nor are they isomorphic.

## WHERE DO PSYCHODYNAMIC PROCESSES RESIDE?

Litowitz also raises a critical question when she asks how the notion of a dynamic unconscious can be included in our model of implicit processes and further asks, "Isn't some notion of defense required for a 'dynamic' unconscious?" Although she agrees that defense does not need to be tied to repression (as an example she cites the avoidant attachment patterns observed among infants at the end of the first year of life) as in Freud's original model, and that unconscious mentation does not need to be tied to verbal knowledge, she has not taken this to the conclusion we have reached (and that House and Portuges seem to find so problematic): namely, that conflict, defense, and what is referred to as unconscious fantasy reside in the implicit domain, rather than as part of the repressed. House and Portuges needlessly fear that our theorizing is an attempt to do away with the dynamic unconscious and "risks abandoning the individual's personal culture." We, however, do not locate such personal culture as primarily within "language and the repressed." We are trying to bring greater attention to the implicit domain as a vast and clinically important part of the nonconscious, and to emphasize how much of what is "psychodynamic" is nonconscious not because of repression, but because it is organized implicitly.

As we have elaborated in a previous paper (Lyons-Ruth, 1999), defensive infant behaviors around attachment needs are precisely the evidence we need to locate the onset of defensive processes in implicit (nonreflective, nonsymbolic) affective processes available prior to the mediation of semiotic systems. (See also recent evidence for the relation of early forms of dialogue to later dissociative processes: Lyons-Ruth, 2003; Ogawa, Sroufe, Weinfeld, Carlson, & Egeland, 1997). In our view, nonconflicted affective exchanges, as well as the more conflicted defensive stances that may be a part of those exchanges, are grounded in implicit or procedural forms of representation of lived experiences with others. While, with development, verbal exchanges increasingly become a part of interactions with others, the "rules" governing those interactions are negotiated through affect cues from the beginning of life and are rarely raised to the level of conscious verbal description. Instead, they remain a part of our implicit relational knowing. Such "rules" for interaction include expectations about what forms of affective relatedness can be expressed openly in the relationship and what forms need to be expressed only in "defensive" ways, that is, in distorted or displaced forms. Like the syntax governing language use, we begin deriving and using these rules from very early in life, as part of our procedural knowledge, long before we're capable of generating any conscious verbal description of what such rules are like.

## WHAT IS DEEP AND WHAT IS SURFACE?

These comments should begin to make clear that our most profound difference with Litowitz's view, as well as that of House and Portuges, is around the issue of what should be considered the level of deep versus superficial "meaning." In our view, previous work in psychoanalysis has conceptually reversed what should be considered the deeper level of meaning and what should be considered the more superficial. The deepest level of meaning, from which all later forms of meaning emerge and refer, is the level of lived engagement with others around central developmental needs, as these engagements are represented in implicit, procedural forms of memory. Litowitz wants to equate observing the structure of affectively rich lived experience with the reductionist methodologies of an earlier behaviorally oriented scientific era. She, House, and Portuges feel that we are not dealing with the "deep" material. For example, Litowitz conflates "local," meaning moment-to-moment, and "surface," stating that we are speaking of "the local surface." A few sentences later she speaks of our "staying with surface phenomena." However, the central implication of what we are saying is that the traditional view of what is "profound" or "deep" and what is "superficial" must be turned on its head. Our suggestion is that conflict, defense, and unconscious fantasy originate in the implicit knowing of lived interactions. We consider the local level to provide the raw material, the foundation, for the grasping of the psychodynamics that then will be responded to implicitly and rendered interpretively by the analyst. It is here that the past is carried forward into the present. The concepts of conflict, defense, and so on, as explicated in language, are useful abstractions that arise from the lived experiencing of conflict and defense in the interaction that is encoded in the implicit. It is in this sense that these abstractions are secondary. One of the reasons for this misunderstanding is that in analysis, one talks about these issues many times over, so that one loses sight of the fact that the explicit version comes from an original implicit experience.

Although relational transactions have been considered the "surface" level of meaning in previous analytic theorizing, this level of enactive representation encodes the most profound aspects of human experience, including their elements of conflict, defense, and affective resistance. Therefore, this level can no longer be considered "surface" or superficial.

## LANGUAGE: OLD AND NEW

Our use of dynamic systems theory was questioned by Mayes, who was uncertain about its utility. She (2005, p. 749) noted that "it is important to ask what does the self-ordering complex system point of view offer to their central argument that is either unique or cannot be found in other, perhaps more accessible, points of view." In our view, the dynamic systems perspective offers at least two things. First, it offers a new explanatory framework for the unpredictability of what happens when we are in the thick of a session, and second, it changes our tolerance and utilization of what may, at first thought, look like errors but which may also be considered indications of flux and new emergent properties taking shape in the dyad.

Mayes also would like to put our description back into the more usual language of "understanding the patient." However, reverting to the usual language means that we revert to a language that has not made many of the distinctions we feel are needed to carry our understanding forward. "Understanding the patient" is a global description that privileges the analyst's perspective. It is not a two-person conception of the complex process that is occurring as the two therapeutic partners negotiate the therapeutic encounter. Such "understanding" is also usually conceived as something that is conveyed to the patient via the explicit content of what the analyst says to the patient. We searched for a different language in order to begin to distinguish more clearly between that which is conveyed explicitly (through the semiotic vehicles that Litowitz emphasizes) and the more implicit level at which the patient recognizes the therapist's adjustment to the most important level of meaning she is trying to convey. The therapist's adjustment may have no semantic content and no explicit verbal level: It could be a silence, an emphatic rise in voice tone, or any other of an infinite variety of subtle adjustments, such as what is left uncommented on versus what is taken up next.

We think that "understanding" is communicated at this implicit level of how the therapist's next relational move feels fitted or not fitted. This understanding or fittedness is constantly negotiated by small moves between the two parties, as we tried to illustrate in chapter 4 as well as in this chapter. Therefore, we feel that reverting to the more usual language leaves us without the more fine-grained descriptive terms we need. A new language is needed to open up and explore these complex elements of the exchange.

As we explicate in this chapter, interpretation by the therapist that the patient needs to claim her agency or that "to be connected, one must be sick" is an after-the-fact, abstract summary of what has already played out in the interaction between them. However, as this new level of agency was in the process of being negotiated, no such after-the-fact summary was available of the pattern that would emerge. Instead, the patient and therapist had to mutually feel out the interactive path and wait to see what kind of organization would emerge in their mutual encounters. It is at this primary level of negotiating a new path in the moment-to moment therapeutic interaction that we locate Litowitz's "ends (i.e., for what purpose)" we engage in therapeutic work. Fitting the direction of the work to an abstract verbal summary will always be derivative of, and secondary to, the accomplishing of the new direction in the moment-to-moment therapeutic interchange itself.

One of the central challenges for science will always be to find the level of description of a phenomenon that leads to generative insights regarding fundamental processes. We feel that observing the moment-to-moment exchange of meaning and relatedness in the two-person therapeutic exchange is such a rich and generative level of inquiry.

## APPENDIX: SESSION TRANSCRIPT

### Day # 1: Monday

*Patient:    So there are 2 completely different . . . the dream that I had last night left me feeling really connected to you, and you know it made feel . . . I don't know, I guess closer to you, that you would tell me that you were not perfect.*

*Analyst:    Uh-huh.*

*P:    Um.*

*A: You actually thought about calling me on Saturday about this other dream.*

*P: Yeah!*

*A: Which would have been, uh, and the reason you were thinking of that, that kind of very real connection, was what?*

*P: . . . What are you referring to, the calling?*

*A: Yeah, the calling.*

*P: Well, because I had seen you on Friday and felt there was like a thread of consciousness that had flowed into that dream.*

*A: Yeah*

*P: It seemed kind of confusing to me that . . . I don't know to say this exactly. It's like a throwback or something. To be dreaming about GT* (the group therapist) *and feeling that kind of pressure.*

*A: Yeah.*

*P: Is what I don't quite get . . . I mean, I think.*

*A: The pressure is there, isn't it? Here we come into the issue of coercion, being made to do something. And in this dream you really are being pressured to say something more. And I guess I wonder how it did, uh, connect to the fact that we had that extra session on Friday.*

*P: . . . What it seems like to me is that . . . the dream was more connected to the idea of me feeling I have to measure up, come up with the right stuff.*

*A: Uh-huh.*

*P: Than the feeling of coerced into coming here. Somehow there's a difference somehow in there from sort of making a link with.*

*A: Yeah, uh-huh* (concurrently with the patient's words)

*P: feeling coerced to coming here on Friday, which I didn't feel at least consciously. Because what I was feeling had more to do with their asking me— it was like I had to be sicker than I felt.*

*. . . And I think that's frequently a part of what my mindset is when I come here, that there's some sick part of my mind that I have to access.*

*A: Uh-huh.*

*P: In order to be talking about the right thing. You know, there's some pathological thing in my head that I have to be able to.*

*A: Yeah, and that is something that you feel here sometimes.*

*P: Yeah.*

*A: So the dream is also about coming here, the pressure to get this sick part of your brain out in the open.*

P:   *The thing that is really confusing to me is that when I was in that group with GT the thing that was so impossible for me was to feel convinced that my experience was somehow . . . comparable to the other people in the group.*

A:   *Yeah.*

P:   *And I just could not feel that . . . I first of all didn't understand why anybody would want me to think that. What good does it do me to think that?*

A:   *Huh.*

P:   *I don't know. I get confused. You know, when I came to see you what I wanted you to tell me that I was sicker than I thought I was and that it was ok for me to be here.*

A:   *Uh-huh.*

P:   *And then, with that group and with GT it was like, oh yes, you're very sick. (chuckles) You've got this really horrible thing wrong with you. And I'm thinking it's not really that bad! It was like two very opposite experiences.*

A:   *Uh-huh.*

P:   *. . . And I think there is still some issue for me in my own perception of my self, about whether I want to be sick or not. I mean I can't, I haven't quite figured out how to make that scar fit in to my image of myself . . . And because of that every time I come here I feel like I have to come with that wound, that gaping wound being the most visible thing. If I'm actually feeling in touch with the way my life is now, then I don't know what to say to you, there's nothing to talk about. You know, you'll ask me why I'm here . . .*

A:   *Huh . . . If you don't come with the gaping wound?*

P:   *Uh-huh. Yeah, if I don't present myself in the proper damaged state, then I'm not going to get—taken seriously, or something. It's like I'm not in my proper role . . .*

A:   *And that is in the dream Friday night, that you feel that I'm sort of trying to get you to be in this proper role of a damaged person. And it is like in the second dream too, that and the issue is how damaged are you. On the one hand you're pressured into being more damaged and on the other you're being told you're not so bad, sounds like.*

P:   *Yeah, I mean the issue.*

A:   *That's the issue you're not sure how bad.*

P:   *Well, my feeling in the dream last night was that the reason I was allowed to see your children and your wife was that I was ok.*

A:   *Uh-huh.*

P:   *That somehow that was ok, that you were trying to convince me
that . . . I guess that I was like everybody else* [i.e., normal].

(Some lines of transcript deleted here.)

P:   *One of the books that I picked up while I was out at the Bookfair was—I
mean I went out there for one specific thing and I found it immediately and so
then I made the mistake of starting to roam around. And I found this book
completely by accident, called, um,* How To Go To Pieces Without Falling
Apart.

A:   *Hum.*

P:   *Hum. It's written by a psychiatrist in New York who is also a Bud-
dhist. And I just was flipping through it while I was waiting for you. He was
quoting Freud's disciple, Sandor Ferenz, or whatever his name is.*

A:   *Uh-huh.*

P:   *And Ferenz said it's not the free association itself that is the cure. It is
that if you* can *free associate, you're cured.* (chuckles)

A:   *Uh-huh.*

P:   *And I thought you know that really struck me as relevant to what you
and I have been talking about.*

A:   *Yeah, uh-huh, how specifically about you and me?*

P:   *Well, that you know my problem seems to be that I'm still way too
much in control of what I'm aware of thinking.*

A:   *Uh-huh.*

(Some lines of transcript deleted here.)

Then somewhat later in the session the issues about the first dream
come back into discussion.

P:   *It* [talking with the group therapist] *makes me feel too vulnerable,
and it makes me feel something I don't feel I can afford to feel . . . Ya' know, I
would rather . . . I would rather focus on . . . I don't know, the part of me that
feels strong, than to be in touch with the part of me that felt like I was going to
be stabbed to death* [a reference to some of the sex play that occurred in her familial sexual abuse] *. . . It just makes me think I could never, I couldn't have
tolerated doing therapy with her or something like her because that really
would make me fall apart, and it feels like I would be disintegrating in such a*

*way I could never reconstruct myself. I would be too, like I'd have no confidence in myself at all, as opposed to the way my relationship with you has always been. You and I both know that there is a part of me that is strong . . . I don't know where any of this is going, but.*

A:    *Well, where, I, I mean I guess I was thinking, do you feel that in the second dream this, are you, how strong are you vis-a-vis me? You told me how strong I am raising these children and yet . . . I tell you that, you know.*

P:    *In the dream, it made me feel stronger..*

A:    *Yeh!*

P:    *It made me feel more . . . equal to you . . . (83± sec).*

A:    *Is that something that's happened nowadays? . . .*

P:    *Uh . . . I think to some extent . . . my feeling is beginning to change about . . . about that. I wouldn't say that . . . I don't think it's a done deal (chuckles) . . . Umm . . . One of the things that I was thinking about on Saturday as I was thinking about calling you was that I . . . I was convinced in my own mind that I could call you and that I could tell you about that dream and it would be okay. So somehow that made me feel like I didn't have to do it.*

A:    *Uh-huh . . .*

P:    *You know I didn't have to prove anything so . . . so I didn't do it.*

A:    *Uh-huh.*

P:    *You know it was enough it was enough to acknowledge to myself that I knew I could pick up the phone and tell you about it and that would be interesting, but I could also (brief chuckle) tell you about it today.*

A:    *Uh-huh . . .*

P:    *And I mean there's something in my viewing it that way, my viewing that it was ok to call you that makes me feel we're more equal*

A:    *Uh-huh* (concurrently with the patient's words*)*

P:    *than unequal.*

A:    *Uh-huh . . . (68 sec).*

P:    *In the dream, um, the dream last night, I was feeling like, um . . . I don't know how to say It was exactly, the word acceptance, keeps coming into my—*

A:    *Um-huh* (concurrently with the patient's words).

P:    *head. It was like I was feeling accepted . . . the way I am and . . . there's something about the feelings that go along with that, that make me afraid, and I start to feel afraid of being hurt, when I notice that I'm letting my guard down, or something . . . and, you know, one of the things that is disturbing to me is that I'll wake up with that feeling of being accepted and then as soon as I'm conscious of the fact that it's a dream I start to feel afraid of the feeling. It's like I don't really want to feel that with you.*

A:   *Huh! . . . somethin's scary.*

P:   *Yeah.*

A:   *Yeah.*

P:   *And I don't know whether it's because I know I have to tell you about the dream* (chuckles) *and I'm, you know, afraid of your reaction when I tell you that, or if I'm afraid of the reality of trying to have the relationship feel that way, or maybe that's the same thing. I don't know . . .*

(The session ended with the patient and analyst exploring more of what was scary to the patient about feeling "accepted.")

### Day # 1: Monday

The following day began extraordinarily differently in that the patient wanted to sit rather than lie on the couch. The transcript of that session the next day follows:

P:   *Today I somehow don't want to lie down right away.*

A:   *Well, that's a change!! Can you say what's happening?*

P:   *I'm not exactly sure, but somehow I feel like I'm more aware of what I want for myself. It's like I have my own agenda.*

(Shortly after that she lay down and continued to talk about this feeling of being in a new state with her analyst.)

P:   *Today it feels a lot more connected here . . . because it feels like I'm opening up something to you . . . in a voluntary way. It's like, you know, I'm in control of what we're talking about, in a way that I don't usually feel. It's like I have an agenda today.*

A:   (wryly) *It's hard to have agendas other days?*

P:   *Yeah!*

The two then burst into loud mutual laughter.

# Introduction to Chapter 6

THE CONTROVERSY REGARDING WHERE MEANING RESIDES, REPRESENTED by the critiques included as part of Chapter 5, stems from a deep division within the field of psychoanalysis. The question of where meaning resides has also been raised in regard to our writing from the beginning. Because of this controversy over the sources of meaning, we were impelled to articulate in more detail our view that affective valuation is a primary source of meaning, separable from the semiotic function. Affective valuation is also intrinsically linked to intentionality, because affect is the value-laden component of the intentional direction or goal.

Another frequent critique of our work is that we have omitted the psychodynamic level of meaning, focusing on the level of interaction, a level that has heretofore been considered superficial. In this chapter, we make clear that we have not omitted the level of psychodynamic meaning; rather, we have relocated it. In what follows, we elaborate the view that psychodynamic meaning, which includes psychoanalytic conflict and defense, originates and resides in the implicit domain of affect and intentionality, not primarily in a dynamic unconscious as traditionally formulated—which in its conceptualization relies on higher order representational processes and their repression.

Therefore, we would replace the idea of conflict between tripartite structures with a more interpersonal view of conflict. In this model, complex patterns of conflict arise between the intentional directions of the self and the intentional directions of important others. These conflicts are represented at the implicit level of affective evaluation and intentional direction, rather than at the level of semiotic processes.

These dynamic features of affect and intentionality can also be brought up to the verbal reflective level and worked on explicitly, but that is not where they originate. Rather, they originate in the implicit domain.

**Chapter 6**

# The Foundational Level of Psychodynamic Meaning: Implicit Process in Relation to Conflict, Defense, and the Dynamic Unconscious[1]

INCREASINGLY, PSYCHOANALYSIS HAS BEEN GRAPPLING WITH THE IN-teractive, intersubjective aspects of the psychoanalytic situation. For several decades clinical writers from a variety of perspectives have de-scribed the intersubjective aspects of the patient–therapist treatment situation. Relational analysts (e.g., Aron, 1991; Beebe & Lachmann, 2002; Benjamin, 1988, 1995b, 2004; Ehrenberg, 1992; Knoblauch, 2000; Mitchell, 1998) have recently been at the forefront of these efforts. Sev-eral of these thinkers have brought a developmental orientation to their perspectives. Those analysts (who have as their intellectual mentors Sullivan, and later Mitchell) have understood the importance of the in-teractive in the creation of the intrapsychic, as have others such as Renik. However, a more encompassing theoretical foundation for grounding this clinical thinking in development has not yet emerged.

[1]Originally published in the *International Journal of Psychoanalysis, 88*, 1–16. Reprinted with permission by Blackwell.

Relational transactions involving action and interaction have been considered the "surface" level of meaning in previous analytic theorizing. However, the level of implicit relational knowing encodes the most profound aspects of human experience, including their elements of conflict, defense, and affective resistance, and this level can no longer be considered "surface" or superficial. What has arisen from the previous upside-down view of the mind is a privileging of abstraction over interaction and a privileging of the symbolic/semantic over the affective/interactive. The effect on the way psychoanalysis has been conceptualized and practiced cannot be overstated.

We will describe here how we see conflict and defense, which are affect-based, as both constituted and revealed at the local level of action and interaction in early development. As we get closer to the specifics of the process of therapeutic interaction and draw on the now extensive body of developmental research, an altered view of psychoanalytic process emerges. The "deep" level, as depicted in our interpretations, is in fact derived from the "surface" level of moment-to-moment exchange. In this framework we assert that the local level, where implicit relational knowing is enacted, is the foundational level of psychic life. It is where psychodynamic happenings, including affect, conflict, and defense, originate.

## IMPLICIT RELATIONAL KNOWING
## AS A FORM OF REPRESENTATION

The question of what constitutes a representation remains unresolved. Traditionally a representation referred to something stored in a verbal/ symbolic or imagistic form. The concept seemed to lack a process dimension that infant research began to supply. Infant research has shown that much is stored, or represented, in some form of memory that does not involve words or images. Sander (1985) showed that as early as eight postnatal days, the infant had stored (represented) a gestalt of a feeding sequence that was violated when mothers donned a ski mask, generating upset and feeding disruption in the infants. Such memories could be considered precursors to, or early forms of, implicit relational knowing.

Implicit relational knowing is thus a form of representation. In using the word *knowing*, we do not imply a symbolic process. It is the represented sense, based on one's history, of how to be with another. It concerns knowledge and representation that is not language based, so that studies of preverbal infants provide an unencumbered field for its study. In brief, implicit relational knowing is based in affect and action rather than in word and symbol. It is also nonconscious, but not under repression. Accordingly, it can be brought to consciousness and verbalized, but usually with much difficulty. Further, the complexity of the phenomena as enactively stored will never constitute a perfect or perhaps even good fit with its linguistic and narrated version. What has been most surprising is to realize that compared to explicit knowledge that is language based, the implicit domain is exceedingly rich and elaborated, containing greater nuancing than language and instantiating a primary relational meaning system, as we will elaborate below. By design, everything that the preverbal infant knows about interactions with others is contained in his implicit relational knowing. Implicit relational knowing also makes up the majority of what we, as adults, know about social interaction, including transference.

Let us give two quite different illustrations of implicit processes, the first from fiction, and the second from developmental studies. An excerpt from *The Master*, a novel by Colm Tóibín (2004), serves as an illustration: "She knew that everyone around them wished to hear what she was saying and thus she alternated between a raised voice and a whisper. She nodded to some people and spoke briefly to others, but she stopped for nobody. Instead she proceeded through the throng to their box, making it clear from the manner of her gaze that no one was free to join them." What Tóibín manages to capture in his verbal description of this woman's actions and expressions is how she positions herself in relation to others. This is a clear demonstration of implicit relational knowing, in her actions as well as in how these are "interpreted" by others. She does not have to say to others, to put into words, that they are not free to join her. She has said it with the entire range of expressive possibilities available to an embodied human being. It is worth noting that it would be such "actions" that would lead the psychoanalyst to interpret her conflicts, defenses, and desires.

Such interpersonal meanings are embedded in interactions from the beginning of life. For example, in a videotaped home observation of a young depressed mother and her 18-month-old toddler, the mother is sitting on the couch and her son is also on the couch sitting a foot or two away from her drinking from his bottle. She is sitting stiffly in the far corner of the sofa staring into space, smoking a cigarette with one hand and resting her other arm along the back of the couch in the direction of her son. Her toddler finishes his bottle and stands up on the couch, bouncing up and down for a minute or two. Then he pauses before flopping over onto his mother's lap. At this point, without moving her stiff and remote arms, she jerks her head toward him and barks, "I told you not to jump on the couch!"

Given the timing of her attack, her distaste did not have to do with his standing on or bouncing on the couch but with his making playful physical contact with her. In other sequences on the same videotape, we see her son walk up to her and reach out his hand toward her knee, only to pull it away suddenly before actually touching her. His mother's aversion to affectionate touch appears to have led him to inhibit his own initiatives around seeking physical contact with his mother. As this pattern is repeated over time, it is being preserved as part of his implicit relational knowing and is likely to color later interactions with others.

One can plainly see in the mother the intense affects accompanying her attempts to shut down certain forms of dialogue with her infant (e.g., affectionate physical contact), which the infant then incorporates as a part of his own attempts to shut down those same forms of discourse within. This is quite different from Fonagy's idea that the infant of a borderline mother actively inhibits his ability to reflect on the parent's affect because of the unbearable content of the representation of the parent's hate (Fonagy, 1991). The alternative view is that the parent's hate is expressed through particular processes in the parent–infant exchange, such as stepping away from the infant's approach for comfort, or repeatedly interrupting and overriding the infant's attempts to exercise initiative. These maternal actions are implicit and become internalized by the infant in their process form (not their content form) as hate for attachment bids and profound resistance to reaching out to others for help.

Developmental findings have made it clear that experiences that are stored implicitly are not impoverished events limited to sensorimotor experiences or to the impersonal realms of procedural memory discussed in the cognitive research literature. Rather they can involve highly complicated knowledge involving affective responses, expectations, and thoughts. Implicit knowledge is also not necessarily more primitive. It is not replaced when language appears, nor is it necessarily transformed into language later in development (Chapter 2, this volume; Lyons-Ruth, 1999). Rather, the implicit domain continues to grow in breadth and elaboration with age. Implicit knowledge is a far larger domain of knowing about human behavior than explicit knowledge at all ages, not just in infancy. Even more importantly, in development, language and symbolic forms of meaning are intrinsically grounded in these early forms of implicitly represented relational experience (see Hobson, 2002, for a detailed developmental account). Appreciating the scope, sophistication, and affective dimensions of implicit relational knowing is important because it changes how one views the unconscious, as we will elaborate.

## INTENTIONS AS ORGANIZERS
## OF RELATIONAL MEANING AT
## THE IMPLICIT LEVEL

There exists a basic level of experience organized around intention. Viewed from the outside, it consists of reading affects and actions in terms of intentions. This goes on from the outset of postnatal life. There is an innate mental tendency to parse or chunk human behavior into intentions and motives (Carpenter, Akhtar, & Tomasello, 1998; Meltzoff, 1995; Trevarthen, 1979) inherited from our primate ancestors (Tomasello, Carpenter, Call, Behne, & Moll, 2005). As such, the intention forms a basic psychic unit of implicit meaning. It is an expression of motivated activity that is grasped implicitly. The concept of intention does not imply self-reflective thought.

Intention units include not only the desire and idea to act but also the action, the object of the action, and the goal. It is relevant that brain imaging observations have identified "intention detection centers" in the brain that get activated in a subject when he observes behaviors in another that lead him to infer an intention (Ruby & Decety, 2001). In addition, studies of mirror neuron systems now demonstrate that one participates in the intentional states of the other at a neuronal level by activating the motor neurons corresponding to the intentional actions observed in the other, but without having to imitate the other's actions (Decety & Chaminade, 2003; Gallese, 2001). Accordingly, this foundational structure of perceiving human behavior in intentional units belongs to the nonverbal, implicit, local level.

The claim that an intention unit exists at the implicit level, and that the process leading to its formation is a mental given, is supported by the fact that intention units are found in preverbal infants, where all experience is implicit. Recent developmental observations suggest that even for preverbal infants the primary task when watching human behavior is to grasp the intention that makes the seen acts coherent and meaningful. For instance, a preverbal infant watches an experimenter try to drop an object into a bowl, but miss. At first, the object is dropped before it is above the bowl. Then it is dropped after it has passed beyond the bowl. The infant never sees it being dropped into the bowl. Later, when the infant is given the bowl and object with the invitation to imitate what he saw, he immediately drops the object directly into the bowl and seems contented with himself. The infant grasped the intention of the experimenter even though he never saw it successfully realized. He gives priority to the intention he has inferred over an action he has seen (Meltzoff, 1995; Meltzoff & Gopnik, 1993).

Another experiment also shows how goal directedness is prioritized. The infant watches an experimenter try to pull the spheres off the ends of a dumbbell-like object but fail. Later when the infant is given the object, he immediately pulls the spheres off and seems to feel good about what he has done. The control experiment consists of a robot who, like the experimenter, tries to pull the ball-like ends off, and also fails. However, when infants are given the dumbbell-like object after they watched the robot fail, they do not try to pull the ends off. These infants have implicitly understood that robots do not have intentions (Meltzoff, 1995). There are many other observations bearing out this general priority of intention over action (Gergely & Csibra, 1997; Gergely, Nadsasdy, Csibra, & Biro, 1995; Rochat, 1999). Moreover, the act must seem meaningful in order to capture the infant's attention.

Decety and Chaminade (2003) showed that an infant who would imitate a mother putting a doll to bed would not imitate her putting a toy car to bed.

Subjectively, intentions are felt to have a thrust or a leaning forward of the intention itself toward its felt or to be discovered goal. There is an implicit agent. There is a line of dramatic tension made up of feelings and affects as the intention fulfills its destiny. All of this occurs in a span of time with a temporal architecture that accommodates this unfolding structure. That is to say, it is temporally dynamic (D. N. Stern, 2004).

In short, we claim that the parsing of motivated human behavior into intentions is a fundamental property of mind/brain; this results in a basic structure, the intention unit, which is implicitly grasped and represented nonsymbolically. Thus, intentions are the elemental psychodynamic units at the level of perception and interaction and from these, other psychic structures are composed.

All presentations of intention, whether in action, in words, or in stories, are based on intentions at the local level; accordingly, a large degree of continuity in meaning is assured across the levels of the implicit, explicit and narrative. The intentions of most interest to the psychoanalytic endeavor are those intentions to make and adjust the state of the relationship.

## RELATIONAL "KNOWINGS" AS
## IMPLICIT FORMS OF MEANING

Thought is not synonymous with verbal language and symbols. A primary source of confusion in previous theory stems from the equating of thinking and the generation of meaning with symbolic functioning. Analysts must now consider the possibility that the most important levels of psychodynamic meaning are carried, enacted, and expressed through nonsymbolizing processes. Perhaps the confusion surrounding this assertion stems from a belief that meaning can only be generated through symbolization, and that a being (the infant) incapable of reflecting on its actions cannot act meaningfully.

However, the example regarding the mother's response to her infant's playful contact illustrates that the infant does indeed create meanings before the advent of a symbolic capacity. We therefore assert that meaning need not be symbol-connected. Viewing videotapes of mother–infant interactions leaves no one questioning that the mother's actions mean something to the infant and that the infant's responses reflect the meanings generated within him. That is not to say the infant is reflecting upon the meanings he is creating, only that he is acting on them, something we are all too familiar with in clinical work with adults. In fact, in agreement with Hobson (2002), we claim that primary apprehension of relationships is foundational to our meaning systems, to our subjectivity.

Even more fundamentally than cognitive meanings, affectively relevant and relationally imbedded meanings that organize one's directions are central to psychoanalysis. Many psychoanalysts find this assertion problematic—not because they do not work with relationally embedded meanings, but because the theory of the "talking cure" has not been conceptualized in this way. It was assumed that the flow and exchange of words was where therapeutic action was contained, that is, "making the unconscious conscious." With this has come an implicit assumption that meaning inheres in symbolization and reflection (e.g., Litowitz, 2005). Infant observation, and the attendant illumination of implicit forms of meaning, has highlighted some of the problems with the older thinking. Interestingly, these studies have also buttressed some of the central tenets of relational psychoanalysis (Aron, 1991; Benjamin, 2004; Ehrenberg, 1992; Fosshage, 2005; Mitchell, 1997; Stolorow, 2005).

Given that this is not an entirely familiar way of thinking, it is worth elaborating further how defense, conflict, and the psychodynamic unconscious are all conveyed and transacted in implicitly represented relational processes. It is from this level that analysts extract and attempt to translate into words general patterns of thought, feeling, and relationship that are termed dynamic processes. However, these processes are initially conveyed and grasped through implicit, local-level phenomena. Psychoanalytic observers have been mapping out this implicit level of experience for over a century. The error has been to equate what was observed in relational interaction with the superficial, while reserving the idea of a deeper level for more abstract, generalized, experience-distant verbal renderings of those patterns.

## PSYCHODYNAMIC CONFLICT AND DEFENSE ORIGINATE AND RESIDE IN IMPLICIT FORMS OF MEANING

### *Conflict and Implicit Meaning*

The ideas of conflict and defense must be introduced into our consideration of implicit forms of meaning for this concept to have psychodynamic implications. As we have said, it is in the realm of immediate relational transactions at the local level that conflict and defense become initially structured.

In early life, psychodynamically relevant events are easily observable in relational contexts. Observations of 12-month-old infants reveal the presence of defensive stances at the level of enacted relationships. When parents leave their infants in an unfamiliar room and return after a brief interval, infants show different patterns of attachment behavior toward the parent, some of which are termed "insecure." Infants who display an avoidant pattern of attachment behavior toward the parent do not look to mother or greet her on reunion, as do "securely" attached infants. Rather they ignore her and seem to act as though her leaving and returning were not important. Physiological indices of stress belie this impression, however (Spangler & Grossmann, 1999).

In this situation, they are, in fact, in conflict and behaving defensively. They have implicitly learned that seeking to be comforted by their mother will probably elicit some subtle discomfort or rebuff. They compromise by suppressing attachment overtures, such as sharing pleasure at reunion or seeking contact with her, and seem to ignore her. A large body of research supports the inference that they have come to "know" that if they do not approach her for comfort, she will respond less aversively to them. These year-old infants have put into effect a coping (defensive) strategy to maximize their security and proximity to their mothers.

This avoidant strategy operates completely at the implicit or local level, takes only a few seconds, and is made up of very few relational moves. Yet, the strategy clearly conveys psychodynamic meaning that eventually might become an analyst's clinical focus as he tries to find ways to address with his patient an avoidance of intimacy and tendency to dismiss the significance of attachment relationships.

More serious forms of conflict are seen among infants with disorganized attachment strategies. In one videotaped example, after his mother has left him in the laboratory room with a lab assistant, an 18-month-old boy is standing at the door, ignoring the lab assistant's overture, calling for his mother and banging and kicking at the closed door through which she has left. When she returns, he is still at the door, but immediately on seeing her, he wrenches his torso around and begins to dash in the opposite direction, away from his mother. In spite of his attempt to escape, she reaches for him and grasps him awkwardly under the arms to pick him up, keeping him at a significant distance from her body. He protests by pushing away from her shoulders and screaming his resistance. His mother smiles over his screaming in a strained, mask-like way, but she eventually complies and puts him down. He then backs away from her to the far wall of the room and drops his head and shoulders in a slumped, defeated posture. The striking shift in this toddler's responses is dramatic, from the prolonged banging at the door and calling for his mother to running away from her as soon as she appears. It is difficult to explain this behavior without invoking notions of conflict.

These examples of conflict behavior toward attachment figures by the end of the first year of life have been extensively replicated. However, conflict is also observable earlier in the first year. For example, in a clinical consultation with a mother and her 2-month-old son, mother and baby are interacting, with the child in an infant seat in front of his mother. His mother is very active, very emotionally expressive, and a little too intense for the baby. Her voice is too loud, her timing is too fast, her transitions in expressions are too abrupt. The baby looks at her with widened eyes and a tense body, alternating his expressions for an extended period between pleasure and distress. The baby is in conflict. On the one hand, he wants to join her in the interaction; on the other hand, the interaction is too intense for him and he is on the edge of turning away from his mother and falling into a distress state. D. N.

Stern (1971, 1977), and Beebe et al. (2000) have also described conflict behaviors early in the first year of life.

As has been elaborated in a previous paper (Lyons-Ruth, 1999), defensive infant behaviors around attachment needs are precisely the evidence we need to locate the onset of defensive processes in implicit, nonverbalized interactions. In our view, both nonconflicted affective exchanges and more conflicted defensive stances are grounded in lived experiences with others and do not originate in primarily intrapsychic phenomena.

Although words are used for the first time in the service of relating to others during toddlerhood, the embedding of words into already meaningful actions does not make the meaning of these actions available to reflective thought or symbolic representation. The 3-year-old may be able to use the terms "good" and "bad," but he cannot represent consciously (or verbally) that he inhibits his impulse to reach out for comfort to his father because his father's physical withdrawal and cold voice tone communicate disapproval of comfort-seeking. Most relational behavior remains nonconscious and implicit even though the child's new words and understandings may be incorporated into these implicit relational procedures.

While we are describing here the earliest manifestations of conflict in the domain of the implicit, it is crucial not to equate the implicit with the nonverbal or the preverbal (Lyons-Ruth, 1999). The implicit can be revealed through verbal as well as nonverbal forms of interaction. However, the implicit aspects of meaning are not in the content of the words themselves. The implicit meaning exists, so to speak, between the lines, as the earlier quote from *The Master* makes clear. There are also forms of conflict that are transmitted implicitly through verbal interaction, as well as through nonverbal forms of interaction. While, with development, verbal exchanges increasingly become a part of interactions with others, the "rules," or syntax, underlying interactions are negotiated through affect and intention cues from the beginning of life and are rarely raised to the level of conscious verbal description. Instead, they remain a part of our implicit relational knowing.

Such "rules" for interaction include expectations about what forms of affective relatedness can be expressed openly in the relationship and what forms need to be expressed only in "defensive" ways, that is, in distorted or displaced forms. Like the syntax governing language use, we begin deriving and using these rules, rules that structure our conflicts and defenses, as part of our relational procedural knowledge, long before we are capable of generating any conscious verbal description of what such rules prescribe.

Reserving the more developmentally complex and relationally meaningful aspects of experience for verbally rendered forms of meaning is an example of the upside-down error of current theory. This version of theory is not now congruent with current understanding of the critical role of implicit meaning as foundational for verbal forms of meaning and thought, (e.g., Hobson, 2002; D. N. Stern, 2004), as discussed in more detail in the next chapter.

## *Defense and Implicit Meaning*

We argue that the established defenses that we see in the clinical situation often have deep roots in problematic internalized ways of being with others that are a part of the implicit domain. These defensive interpersonal adaptations are the essence of clinical dynamic material. They have always been considered "intrapsychic."

However, attachment studies have demonstrated that many defensive strategies are not best viewed as resulting from a particular intrapsychic conflict or an interpersonal perturbation confined to a specific developmental epoch. Instead, defensive strategies are likely to constitute one component of a much broader interpersonal arrangement that has endured over a significant period of the patient's life. Developmental research has revealed, for example, that a child's tendency to suppress vulnerable feelings of anger or distress and to displace attention away from relationships and onto impersonal activities should not be viewed as an obsessional defense resulting from control struggles in toddlerhood. Rather, for a sizeable number of children, such behavior is reliably evident by 12 months of age and is related to particular forms of parent–child affective dialogue over the first year of life, including parental suppressed anger and discomfort with close physical contact (Main, Tomasini, & Tolan, 1979) and parental mock surprise expressions to infant anger (Malatesta, Culver, Tesman, & Shepard, 1989).

Such restrictions in the parent–child affective dialogue are foreshadowed by the parent's style of discussing attachment experiences in interviews prior to the child's birth and they remain evident in the parent's organization of thinking about attachment-related topics long after infancy (van IJzendoorn, 1995; for meta-analytic review, Main, Kaplan, & Cassidy, 1985).

Attachment researchers have demonstrated more dramatically than any other group the contribution of enduring patterns of relatedness to the deletions and distortions in thinking commonly thought of as defensive. If negative affects, particularly hateful ones, produce hostile attack, intense devaluation, shaming, or withdrawal by the parent, they may be excluded from further dialogue and thought. Exclusion of negative affects from interaction also excludes those affects from the integrated developmental elaboration and understanding of anger-related behaviors, affects, and experiences that might come from more balanced inclusion in interaction.

Attachment research has consistently grounded defensive maneuvers in infancy, such as infant avoidance of affect, not only in temperamental qualities of the infant, but in the behavioral and affective responses of caregivers, responses based on the caregiver's own implicit models of relationships. This literature demonstrates that much that has been viewed as intrapsychic emerges from the interactive matrix and comes to constitute the intrapsychic domain. There is no other separate intrapsychic domain (see also Lyons-Ruth, 2003; Ogawa, Sroufe, Weinfield, Carlson, & Egeland, 1997).

Currently, mutual reflection on "enactments" in the therapy is seen as a rich source of insight about both participants' implicit procedural knowings, with their associated conflicted and defensive aspects. Developmental research further establishes that many of the defensive deletions and distortions evident in enactments have "two-person" origins. With this rich new view of all that happens in interactive and affective life, we would replace the idea of conflict between tripartite structures with this more dyadic view of complex patterns of conflict between the intentional directions of the self and the intentional directions of important others, conflicts that are represented at the implicit level.

## IMPLICIT MEANING AND THE PSYCHOANALYTIC CONCEPTS OF ACTION AND REPRESSION

### *Action and the Process of Interaction Embody Implicit Forms of Meaning*

Freud was Cartesian in separating the mental from the physical. He conceived of thought as a derivative of (secondary to) inhibited action. One often forgets that action was primary for him. His classic example was a hungry baby who could not engage in the "specific action" of the drive (sucking to satisfy the desire) because mother was not present. Accordingly, the psychic energy normally directed to the motor and sensory functions of the mouth was redirected and channeled to the perceptual part of the mind to create a hallucination of sucking-drinking. Inhibited action turns into a derivative product, mental phenomena. Similarly the technique of the couch and the prohibition against "acting in or out" were to force psychic energy into expression via thought, where it could be followed with free association and the "talking cure." The result, as D. N. Stern (1995) points out, is a strong intellectual current and "many modern strains in psychoanalysis (that) privilege the narration or interpretation that stands behind . . . an act rather than the act itself."

The technical and theoretical prohibitions against action, especially acting in, were also originally put in place by psychoanalysis to contain and redirect toward the mental potentially disruptive enactments of transference and countertransference. How, then, are we to view the fact that we now see therapy, even psychoanalysis, as based on action in the implicit domain, even when we are just speaking and listening?

Part of the resolution of this paradox lies in illuminating a false dichotomy or "misconception." "Freud's starting point, the fundamental assumption that the word and the act are dichotomously alternate modes of expression, is flawed. We now know that words do not restrain or substitute for action: they are action. . . . For each of us, what we say and how we say it is an extremely important part of our repertoire of actions" (Greenberg, 1996, p. 201).

From Freud's idea followed the view that action and verbalization were discrete and separable phenomena. It also followed that the technique of psychoanalysis was to pare down the possibilities for interaction to the verbal domain, with the goal of moving the verbal interaction to the level of reflective (interpretive) understanding. Once these parameters of technique were in place, the analyst's task became one of extracting the history of the patient's interaction patterns (the patient's object relations) from the highly filtered medium of the almost purely verbal exchange between patient and analyst. However, this ignores much of what makes participating in the psychoanalytic endeavor a rich and highly affectively colored exchange between two people, where the relevant patterns of relatedness are revealed more clearly and the process of understanding the more abstract patterns or "motives" guiding those patterns of relatedness are greatly facilitated.

At the level of directly observed interaction what one sees are not unconscious fantasies and Oedipal wishes but particular kinds of relational moves in the here and now, such as attempts to override the direction of the other, attempts to avoid sharing or responding to central affects expressed by the other, becoming fragmented or disoriented around some topics of conversation such as sexuality, and so on. From these experienced moves, psychoanalytic interpretations are drawn.

As an example, in a recent family evaluation by one of the authors, an 18-year-old boy and his father were discussing work possibilities. The father was saying how important it was for his son to decide for himself what he would like to do for after-school work to have the added independence of his own income. The son spoke of how he would like to work at a particular gas station where he knows some of the people and enjoys tinkering with the cars. His father immediately suggested he should start up his own swimming pool cleaning business in order to make his own hours and not have to work under others.

The father reiterates a pattern as he almost pleadingly emphasizes the importance of autonomy and independence in speaking to his inhibited son; but with each assertion of initiative on the son's part, the father has a countersuggestion. So his explicit emphasis on the importance of being one's own person is accompanied by his immediate dismissals of his son's attempts to take an independent direction. These contradictory layers of interactive processes, though expressed through verbal interaction, will be represented by father and son in an implicit procedural form. Such internalized experiences of important others are understood to be the stuff of the transference relationship that is then played out with the analyst.

Are we giving action (or joint action) precedence over thought? Yes and no. Such a question makes no sense from the contemporary perspective of an embodied mind and the capacity for other-centered participation. The recent paradigm shift in the cognitive sciences proposes a mind that is not an independent disembodied entity. Rather, thinking itself requires and depends upon feelings emanating from the body, as well as upon movements and actions (see Clark, 1997; Damasio, 1999; Hobson, 2002; Lakoff & Johnson, 2000; Sheets-Johnstone, 1999; Varela, Thompson, & Rosch, 1993). Intersubjective meetings involve people with embodied minds who act and react physically as well as mentally.

### Implicit Meaning as a Part of the Unconscious

To conceptualize the domain of the unconscious adequately, it is necessary to make clear distinctions among types of unconscious processes. LaPlanche and Pontalis gave us this succinct statement: "In Freud's writings, 'dynamic' is employed in particular to characterize the unconscious, in so far as a permanent pressure is maintained there which necessitates a contrary force—operating on an equally permanent basis—to stop it from reaching consciousness. On a clinical level, this dynamic character is borne out both by the fact that a resistance is encountered when attempts are made to reach the unconscious, and by the repeated production of derivatives of repressed material" (1967/1988, p. 126). They continued, "Freud himself noted that, 'we do not derive the psychical splitting from an innate incapacity for synthesis on the part of the mental apparatus; we explain it dynamically, from the conflict of opposing mental forces, and recognise it as the outcome of an active struggling on the part of the two psychical groupings against each other." Very importantly, in Freud's concept, before material could be repressed, it had to be in the explicit domain, that is, in the preconscious or conscious domains.

While Freud clearly equated the dynamic unconscious with the process of repression, many now use the term to refer to a broader array of psychodynamic processes, processes that are not necessarily considered part of the repressed. These processes would include all aspects of early object relations that are reenacted in treatment, as well as all areas of mental process that are out of awareness, in some way unintegrated with other aspects of thinking, and for which there is affective resistance to including those areas in exchange with self or other. Psychoanalytic usage must now move away from a narrow equation of the dynamic unconscious with the repressed to reflect this altered landscape.

Our argument is that the interactions that come to constitute implicit relational knowing are psychodynamic. They are about deeply held feelings, conflicts, and defenses. These phenomena have history, have motivational force, and are clearly psychologically meaningful, as well as being out of awareness, but not by virtue of having been repressed. We believe that the concept of the dynamic unconscious, and of psychodynamics in general, must now encompass this broader array of mental phenomena, including implicit relational knowing. The 18-month-old bouncing boy referred to earlier "knows" that his mother is aversive to affectionate physical contact, not to his bouncing on the couch, and he has clearly begun to represent and internalize that aversion with its attendant conflicts and inhibitions. His thwarted yearnings would be the upshot of the history of such depriving relational encounters. They would certainly be considered psychodynamically meaningful to any analyst. Such behaviors are the pithy essence of what we deal with every day with our patients. In our view, such behaviors demonstrate the psychodynamic centrality of implicit processes. These processes constitute the domain where the heart of analytic work occurs.

## CONCLUSION

The major point of this chapter has been to delineate the upside-down relationship between the supposedly "superficial" layer of immediate interaction and the supposedly profound layer of intrapsychic entities such as conflict and defense. Traditionally, the intrapsychic entities were assumed to determine what happened at the interactive level.

The interactive level was seen merely as the instantiation of deeper forces. We suggest, instead, that the interactive process itself is primary and generates the raw material from which we draw the generalized abstractions that we term conflicts, defenses, and fantasy. From these relational moves as experienced in the interaction, psychoanalytic interpretations are drawn. It follows that conflicts and defenses are born and reside in the domain of implicitly represented interactions, and that this relational living out is the emotionally deep layer of experience, while the abstractions that we use to describe the repetitive aspects of these relational strategies, such as conflict and defense, are secondary descriptors of this deep level, but not the level itself, and these abstract entities exist further from the lived experience.

# Introduction to Chapter 7

In Chapter 6, we explored what is deep meaning in psychoanalysis, and what is superficial. We suggested that operations such as conflict, defense, and interpretations are in fact abstractions of what is truly profound. They are derived secondarily. We asserted that the deepest, primary level is that of lived interaction or experience. The lived level of experience is primary, given that it is here that the intentions of the participants are revealed. These intentions, in turn, show the implicit relational knowing of the interactants.

Having been moved into a discussion of what constitutes meaning, we began to formulate more clearly how much meaning was constituted in relational forms. Here we show how relational meaning begins at the implicit level, which later gives rise to the reflective-verbal level. We then discuss how these two domains relate to each other in the formation of meaning.

## Chapter 7

# Forms of Relational Meaning: Issues in the Relations Between the Implicit and Reflective-Verbal Domains[1]

THE RELATIONS BETWEEN THE IMPLICIT AND THE REFLECTIVE-VERBAL domains have become crucial in thinking about psychotherapy. This is largely because of the growing awareness of the large domain of implicit knowing, both in infant observations and in adult therapy, as well as new importance given to enactments, which are usually seen as implicit. To make the dialogue more productive between clinicians and theorists, it becomes necessary to delineate as clearly as possible the differences, similarities, connections, and boundaries between these two domains. Stated differently, we wish to examine whether the two domains are best seen as: separate, interwoven, grounded one upon the other, or even fused. As the reader will note, we are comparing implicit with reflective-verbal rather than with explicit, as it is closer to what clinicians mean when they use the term "explicit."

Here we will examine the relevant issues that may help us think

---

[1]Originally published in 2008, *Psychoanalytic Dialogues, 18*, pp. 125–148 and pp. 197–202. Copyright Taylor & Francis Group, LLC. Reprinted with permission. See www.informatorld.com.

about the relations between these two domains. This is with the belief that greater clarity about the issues at stake is needed for the field of psychoanalysis to develop a coherent set of theoretical concepts. In addition, the issues raised here may be of interest to neuroscientists in planning research strategies that address the brain processes underlying the functioning of the mind.

## DEFINITIONS

The first problem is, what do we mean by meaning or experiencing or thinking or reflecting or implicit? Since our main focus is on relational psychological events, we will give working definitions for terms and concepts that we find useful or necessary in dealing with relational phenomena. These include especially: meaning, thinking, experiencing, reflecting, and the implicit.

### *Meaning*

We will not tackle the entire field of meaning. Rather we will make some basic distinctions that permit us to think more clearly about meaning across the different relational domains of the implicit, and the reflective-verbal, including narrations. We will start with dictionary definitions.

The first (and archaic) dictionary entry for "meaning" reads, "That which exists in the mind, view, or contemplation or settled aim or purpose; that which is meant or intended to be done" (*Webster's New Twentieth Century Dictionary*, 1977). In this version, while intention is crucial, the role of language is neither clear nor essential. The secondary entry for meaning adds language. The intention can remain unformed or amorphously latent "until it is retaken up" in the verbal domain where it acquires a meaning or signification. This sense of meaning is addressed below under reflection.

The *Oxford English Dictionary* (1991) presents us with the same dilemma. In the primary citation for meaning, a linguistic role is not essential, but more "to intend, to have in mind, to show forth." But again language seems to slip in secondarily: "to signify, to make known." Of note in these definitions, "contemplation" or "having in mind" are both present without necessary allusion to language or consciousness.

### *Thinking*

Most dictionaries maintain a creative ambiguity about this key word that we all assume to know what it means. Most dictionaries give as a primary meaning of thinking, "to form or hold in mind or to exercise the mental capacities so as to form ideas" (*Webster's College*, 1999). This leads us to run up against the definitions of "ideas." A quite unusual, but very pertinent notion of "ideas" is presented by the novelist Alessandro Barrico (2002):

> Ideas are like galaxies of little intuitions, a confused thing . . . which is continually changing . . . they are beautiful. But they are a mess . . . in their pure state they are a marvelous mess. They are provisional apparitions of infinity. Clear and distinct ideas are an invention of Descartes, are a fraud, clear ideas do not exist, ideas are obscure by definition, if you have a clear idea it is not an idea. . . . Here's the trouble. . . . When you express an idea you give it a coherence that it did not originally possess. Somehow you have to give it a form that is organized and concise, and comprehensible to others. As long as you limit yourself to thinking it, the idea can remain the marvelous mess that it is. But when you decide to express it (in words) you begin to discard one thing, to summarize something else, to simplify this and cut that, to put it in order by imposing a certain logic: you work on it a bit, and in the end you have something that people can understand. A "clear and distinct" idea. At first you try to do this in a responsible way: you try not to throw too much away, you'd like to preserve the whole infinity of the idea you had in your head. You try. But they don't give you time, they are on you, they want to know. (2002, p. 202)

What is clear is that thinking may or may not include verbal thought, nor linguistic manipulation, nor need it be conscious or reflective. But it can be all of these. Abstract reasoning is probably a very special kind of thinking that need not concern us here.

## *Reflection*

The dictionary definition is: "to bring back an experience, to throw it back, to reproduce it, mirror it, or bend the experience back." In a relational context, it means to reexperience a relational happening but in a different context and time such that the experience is reorganized. It is important to note that not every use of words includes reflection and not every reflection includes the use of words. The relations one is capable of reflecting on, as well as how one reflects, is a developmental issue. For example, there are many levels of reflection in general and many increasingly abstract levels of reflection on the self that have been described developmentally. Delineating these levels is beyond the scope of this paper, but is often a source of confusion in conversations between developmentalists and clinicians. In clinical discussions, use of words often gets equated with the most abstract level of reflection on the self's patterns of relations with others. However, much of therapy is conducted at rather noncomplex levels of reflection. Much of what transpires in therapy involves the use of words in other pragmatic, narrative, or reflective ways that do not involve reflection on the relational patterns of the self.

## *Experience*

The Oxford and Encarta dictionaries variously define experiencing as "involvement in an activity over time that leads to an increase in knowledge or skill." From philosophy, "experience" involves knowledge from observation acquired through the senses and not through abstract reasoning.

The definition of relational experiencing that we will use is involvement in relational transactions, real or imagined, lived through in time, informed by sensory/emotional processes as well as processes of thought (not including abstract reasoning) that builds to accumulate relational knowing.

## *Implicit Relational Knowing*

In defining implicit relational knowing, we have drawn on distinctions made by Kihlstrom and Cantor (1983) and other cognitive psychologists, but have adapted them to apply to the relational domain (Boston

Change Process Study Group [BCPSG], 2002). We view implicit relational knowing as one variety of procedural representation. Procedural representations in cognitive psychology are representations of how to proceed, of how to do things. Such representations, like knowing how to ride a bicycle, for example, may never become symbolically coded. More pertinent here than bicycle riding, however, is the domain of knowing how to do things with others, how to be with them ("ways of being with," D. N. Stern, 1985). Much of this relational knowing is also procedural, such as knowing how to joke around, express affection, make friends. Knowing about how to be with another we have termed "implicit relational knowing." In using the term, we wanted to differentiate implicit relational knowing from other forms of procedural knowledge and to emphasize that such "knowings" are as much affective and interactive as they are cognitive.

In addition, we view implicit relational knowing as typically operating outside focal attention and conscious experience, without translation into language. Language is certainly used in the service of relational knowing, but the implicit knowings governing intimate interactions are not primarily language-based and are not routinely translated into symbolic form. Implicit relational knowing is also not necessarily dynamically unconscious in the sense of being defensively excluded from awareness, that is to say, split off or repressed. Instead, it is part of our nonconscious processing, including "unformulated experience" (D. B. Stern, 1997) that has never been put into words, has never had to be, or never could be,

Non-language-based knowing is the only form of knowing in infancy by developmental default. But even after the acquisition of language this implicit domain continues to grow, as does the verbal domain. Each domain enlarges, elaborates, and creates associations within itself. The two domains grow and coexist throughout the life span.

## COMMONALITIES BETWEEN THE IMPLICIT
## AND REFLECTIVE-VERBAL DOMAINS

### Commonality No. 1: Intentions as the Basic Unit
### of Psychological Meaning

We assume that to intend is to mean. (See the dictionary definition above.) Further, we assume that the intention is the fundamental psychological meaning. Sequences of intentions give motivated human behavior its psychological existence, its coherence, and finally its meaning (Sander, 1995a, 1995b). This sense of intention is broader than is commonly used. Intentions fit into the larger movements of orientation and directionality given by motivational systems, or the long-term goals of a psychotherapy. Our use of intention is coextensive with many notions of idea units, or motives or wishes. It is also meant to include all the phases of an intention: its pre-execution phase while it is forming, its execution, and its aim. Taken together, we will call this the "intention unfolding process." The intention unfolding process arises from a fundamental psychological process that chunks the flow of motivated human behavior into intentions. The mental process of parsing human behavior into intentions and motives is considered a mental primitive, in the sense that it appears to be an innate mental tendency necessary for adaptation in a social world of other motivated beings. This chunking occurs when intentional behavior is perceived in others or felt in oneself. The intention unfolding process is a nonsymbolic process representation of motivated experience that is grasped implicitly. Studies of preverbal infants, cited below (or higher animals) support this idea. Accordingly, this foundational process belongs to both the small-grained, nonverbal, implicit, local level and also to the level of language. It arises in both because they share the same grasp of intentionality.

We propose that the intention unfolding process acts as the referent to identify and give meaning to intentions whether they are encountered in actions, or presented in linguistic or narrative form, creating a common coinage across levels. One way to think about an intention unfolding process is to ask, how can we know, or even more difficult, how can we infer the presence of an intention? How would we pluck it out of the flow of behavior, in all its variability, if there were no process by which to detect it? It is relevant that brain imaging observations have identified "intention detection centers" in the brain that get activated in a subject when he observes behaviors that lead him to infer an intention in another person (Ruby & Decety, 2001).

The intention unfolding process is the form that permits intentions and motives to emerge into awareness and take on meaning. The foundational role for this process makes it possible for intentions, regardless of their presentation, to flow from the same source and be comprehensible. Accordingly, some continuity of meaning from one level to another is not simply facilitated but is assured. What observations and ideas exist to support this view?

We need to deepen the definition of intention given above. Intentionality refers to the subjective sense of pulling or being pulled, or pushing or being pushed toward a goal or end state—or inferring another being so pulled or pushed. It is coextensive with Freud's notion of the wish or the desire; with the ethologists' notion of motivational activation and goal states; with the cognitive science view of value; and with the lay, legal notion of a motive. All of these provide the engine, direction, means, and goals for motivated behavior, thus making it coherent. It also includes the mental "reaching" for an image or idea to bring it onto the mental stage (Brentano, 1874/1973).

The basic idea of an intention unfolding process is not new. Most phenomenological philosophers agree that even pre-reflective or lived experience is structured around intentions. Further, this (implicit) experience is made of differentiated parts and has a temporal architecture (e.g., Husserl, 1962, 1930/1989). In other words, some fundamental (nonverbal) process structure, like an intention that unfolds in real time, must exist.

In the same light, current psychologists, like Jerome Bruner (1986, 1990, 2002) have suggested that motives (the why of a story) are the basic mental units we use to parse human behavior. It is a universal tendency to search for intentions and motives in human behavior resulting in intention-driven narratives for understanding the social world.

Recent developmental observations suggest that even for preverbal infants (until approximately 18 months) where experience is, by default, implicit and not conscious nor reflected upon—the primary task when watching human behavior is to grasp the intention ("behind" the acts). The intention makes the seen acts coherent and meaningful. For instance, a preverbal infant watches an experimenter try to drop an object into a bowl, but he misses the bowl. The object and bowl are both novel. At first, the object is dropped as it is approaching yet before it is above the bowl. Then it is dropped after it has passed beyond the lip of the bowl. The infant never sees it being dropped into the bowl. Later, when the infant is given the bowl and object to manipulate by himself, he immediately drops the object directly into the bowl and seems contented with himself. The infant grasps the intention and then imitates it, even though he has never seen it successfully realized. He gives priority to the intention he has inferred over an action he has seen (Meltzoff, 1995; Meltzoff & Gopnik, 1993).

In another experiment, the infant watches an experimenter try to pull the spheres off the ends of a dumbbell-like object. He tries but fails. Later when the infant is given the dumbbell-like object, he immediately pulls the spheres off and seems contented. The control experiment, with different infants, consists of a robot who, like the experimenter, tries to pull the ball-like ends off, and also fails. However, when these infants are given the dumbbell-like object after they watched the robot fail, they do not try to pull the ends off. For the infant, robots do not have intentions. (Gopnik & Meltzoff, 1998; Meltzoff, 1995). There are many other observations bearing out this general priority of the inferred intention over the seen action (Gergely & Csibra, 1997; Gergely, Nadsasdy, Csibra, & Biro, 1995; Rochat, 1999).

Subjectively, intentions are felt to have a thrust or a leaning forward toward their goal. There is an implicit agent. There is a line of dramatic tension as the intention fulfills or fails to fulfill its destiny as it becomes revealed. And all of this occurs in a span of time with a temporal architecture that accommodates this unfolding process. From events of short to long duration, the temporal parameters of the intention unfolding process are scaled. It is crucial to appreciate that it is temporally dynamic. It is these features that permit us to call it an "intention unfolding process."

In short, the intention unfolding process underlies the formation of all presentations of intention, whether in action, in words, or in stories. The domains have in common the sharing of the same intuitive grasp of the intention that makes behavior coherent and meaningful.

### Commonality No. 2: Sharing the Same Microforms Across Domains

The implicit and reflective-verbal domains share a similar microstructure. It has been suggested that the basic microunit underlying subjective experience is the "present moment" (D. N. Stern, 2004). This is the moment of "now" when an experience is lived, in any of the domains.

D. N. Stern suggests that the subjective present moment is also organized around intentions and is embedded in an emotional, lived story with a narrative-like format that is grasped intuitively while it is unfolding, even though it lasts only between 1 and 10 seconds. The experience of "now" is thus structured in form and temporal profile. He sees this as a fundamental process in our comprehending human behavior as coherent at all scales of its presentation: from the seconds during which an implicit experience endures; to the temporal unfolding of a spoken phrase; to the building blocks of a narrative. Across all domains the currency of temporally dynamic experience does not change.

### Commonality No. 3 : Mirror Neurons and the Parallel Activation of the Language Centers Along with Separate Motor and Perceptual Centers

Recent experiments suggest that concepts with verbal labels are not only processed in the language center but also in motor and perceptual areas related to the modality of the concept. For example, the words "digs, climbs, walks" are stored in speech centers, but also in specific regions of the brain where such motor operations usually originate. Similarly, words like "squeals, howls, sings" are stored in specific auditory regions of the brain, as well as in the speech center (James & Gautier, 2003). It appears that the word and the perceptual/motor experience are both being activated in parallel to create a whole experience.

This way of linking language to physical experience, action, and feeling may be explained by recent findings on "mirror neurons," which provide possible neurobiological mechanisms for understanding the following phenomena: reading other people's states of mind, especially intentions; resonating with another's emotion; experiencing what someone else is experiencing; capturing an observed action (vocal as well as visible) so one can imitate it; in short, sympathizing with another and establishing intersubjective contact (Gallese, 2001; Rizzolatti, Fogassi, & Gallese, 2001).

Mirror neurons sit adjacent to motor neurons. They fire in an observer who is doing nothing but watching another person behave (e.g., reaching for a glass). And the pattern of firing in the observer mimics the exact pattern that the observer would use if he were reaching for that glass himself. In brief, the visual information received when watching another act gets mapped onto equivalent representation in our own brain by the activity of these mirror neurons. It permits us to directly participate, virtually, in another's actions, without having to imitate them. We experience the other as if we were executing the same action, or feeling the same emotion. These "as if" mechanisms have been described by Damasio (1999) and Gallese (2001). Braten (1998) describes this as "altero-centric participation." This "participation" in another's mental life creates a sense of feeling/sharing with/understanding them, and in particular their intentions and feelings. We are purposely using the term "feelings" instead of "affects" so as to include sentiments, internal sensory sensations, motor sensations, "background feelings" (Damasio, 1999) and "vitality affects" (D. N. Stern, 1985; D. N. Stern, Hofer, Haft, & Dore, 1984), along with classical Darwinian affects.

What is true for visible movements, like reaching for a glass, is also true for vocalizations including words. Mirror neurons, presumably representing vocal chord, mouth, and tongue action, fire centrally when we hear someone speak. We know what the experience of making that kind of sound is like. (This is one of the reasons someone's act of clearing their throat can evoke a throat sensation in us. It is also probably why neonates can imitate a tongue protrusion). The elements of spoken sounds that are transmitted in this way include: the tension, effort, intensity, restraint, melody, rhythm, and other paralinguistic features of the sound, all that is the essential audible feeling-context for the heard word.

It has recently been suggested (Gallese, personal communication, June 5, 2005) that the mirror neuron system ties the word to the movement. That is, when words are being spoken, they may trigger the mirror neurons appropriate to the actions and movements verbally described. Whether or not they do this directly remains to be seen. However, words can discharge motor or visual areas. The suggestion is that mirror neurons may provide a different neural pathway for linking word and motor experience with different psychological implications. In these senses words are not disincarnated symbols, but are also pathways into direct embodied experience that function implicitly, and vice versa. This may help explain the evocative power of words and stories. We live them virtually.

## THE REFLECTIVE-VERBAL DOMAIN
## EMERGES FROM THE IMPLICIT DOMAIN

Foundational to the ideas in this section are two concepts. The first is the notion of the embodied mind. The second concept is dynamic systems theory. In the past 30 years a radically new point of view has arisen. It is captured by the notion of an "Embodied Mind." The prevailing Cartesian view is being replaced by this new view (Damasio, 1999; McNeill, 2005; Merleau-Ponty, 1945/1962, 1964/2000; Sheets-Johnstone, 1999; Thelen & Smith, 1994; Tomasello, 1999; Varela, Lachaux, Rodrigues, & Martinerie, 2001; Varela, Thompson, & Rosch, 1993; among many others). This implies that movement and language (while different modes) are largely integrated during evolution and ontogeny. One cannot think or feel or imagine or have sensations without the direct participation of one's body. Conversely, to move or to act is inherently an expression of a mental intention.

Some thinkers of the past century, even working in a Cartesian tradition, were aware of the need for an embodied mind. Heidegger believed lived experience is structured around intentionality, and that this organization is intuited. It is this structuring that makes primary experience ultimately interpretable at the reflective and linguistic level. Husserl (1962, 1930/1989) assumed that primary experience has a morphological form with internal differentiations and a temporal structure. Reflection can only accentuate or intensify the lived experience. Sartre (1943/1976) concurs with this, in saying that reflection does not reveal anything new. It only discloses and thematizes what is already familiar in the originary, pre-reflective, lived experience. The presence of an embodied mind is implicit in these reflections, as is the notion of an emergent grafting of the reflective-verbal onto implicit knowing.

The aspect of dynamic systems theory that interests us most is the fact that in complex systems with multiple variables (such as human interaction) new properties emerge that were neither predicted nor expected. A new and qualitatively different system emerges (the reflective-verbal process) from the encounter of implicit knowing with other minds (which includes language and culture).

In this section we will discuss four ways that the reflective-verbal emerges from the implicit.

### 1. "The Primary Metaphor"

Recent work from the perspective of the embodied mind suggests that a large number of the ideas we use in thinking and speaking spring from the fundamental sensorimotor experiences of our own bodies, acting in the world, and being acted upon, to generate "primary metaphors" (Lakoff & Johnson, 1980). These primary metaphors are fundamental implicit notions about ourselves, others, and the world. Primary metaphors are seen as basic sensorimotor ways of experiencing the world and conceptualizing it, in the form of nonverbal mental models. Primary metaphor in this perspective is not a "figure of speech," it is a nonverbal, implicit concept. For instance, Lakoff and Johnson suggest that the concept of "more" is related to the body position of "up." A subjective judgment of quantity is conceptualized in terms of the sensorimotor experience of verticality, that is, of having to raise your eyes or head to see something really big. "More is up" is a primary metaphor that springs from sensorimotor experience. The basic body concept can be used in language as in "prices rose" or "stocks plummeted." While language uses the primary metaphor, it is not linguistically based. Furthermore, the bodily experience that underlies the linguistic usage is neither arbitrary nor a dead metaphor (where the link from experience to word is only historical). The link still exists. The bodily concept is activated when words are used, or words can be activated when the sensorimotor schemas are experienced. Any use of a primary metaphor in the domain of speech will carry with it an activation of the sensorimotor system that constitutes the primary nonverbal experience. Therefore, our experience when we talk with primary metaphors is a bodily event as well as a verbal one.

Lakoff and Johnson provide a panorama of such primary metaphors (embodied mental models), each derived from sensorimotor experience of being in a real world, with real people with inferable intentions. The following are examples from Lakoff and Johnson:

- Relationships are journeys. Primary experience: moving through space. Example: "Our relationship only went so far, then it stopped advancing and we went our separate ways."
- Help is physical support. Primary experience: observing that some entities and people require physical support to continue standing and functioning. Example: "Support your local charities."
- Time is motion. Primary experience: experiencing the passage of time as one moves in space or observes motion. Example: Time flies. Time stopped dead in its tracks.
- States are locations. Primary experience: being in a bounded region of space and experiencing a certain state as correlated with a certain location (e.g., being cool under a tree, feeling secure in bed). Example: "I'm close to being in a depression and the next thing that goes wrong will send me over the edge."
- Actions are self-propelled motions. Primary experience: the common action of moving your body through space (even in the early years). Example: "I'm moving right along on the project."
- Purposes are destinations. Primary experience: physically reaching a destination. Example: "He'll ultimately be successful, but he isn't there yet."
- Causes are physical forces. Primary experience: achieving results by exerting forces on physical objects to move or change them. Example: "They pushed the bill through Congress" (1980, pp. 52–53).

These primary metaphors permeate our thinking and language extensively. Their use in normal, nontechnical discourse, especially about ourselves and others and our relationships, is ubiquitous. While usually nonconscious, primary metaphors not only give rise to the verbal concepts. They also remain the activated substrate from which many of our thoughts and language spring. Viewed this way, the obvious descriptive boundaries between pre-symbolic and symbolic, between nonverbal and verbal, between implicit and explicit do not exactly fade away. But it becomes clearer that they share the same root origins in common body experience, that is, the same embodied mental model.

In any event, while the actual form/sound of the word may be arbitrary (as a symbolic system requires), the embodied concepts that entwine experience with words are not at all arbitrary. They are determined by our morphology, our innate movement patterns, and the real external world of people and things.

## 2. Kinesthetic Concepts

Sheets-Johnstone (1999) takes this line of thought further. In arguing for the "primacy of movement," she suggests that we discover ourselves and the world via our own movement. She proposes that the "foundational phenomenon of animation" implies a corporeal consciousness and leads to corporeal concepts and representations as well as kinesthetic concepts. She documents Husserl's statement that "movement is the mother of all cognition" (Husserl, 1962, 1930/1989). The list of corporeal concepts is vast, such as: inside/outside, heavy/light, open/closed, up/down, sequencing, contingency, agency, and so on.

Here, again, we are confronted with a view of experience that sheds a different light on of some of our basic categories. The work of Lakoff and Johnson as well of that of Sheets-Johnstone is in the current tradition of repairing the Cartesian split between mind and body and binding them together again with the idea of "embodied cognition." In other words, when we speak, the corporeal or kinesthetic concepts, as well as the primary metaphor, are activated. Thus, we are doing much more than just making words. We are embodying our words, and mentally inhabiting our spatiotemporal movements. A dialogue between body and mind is in process and it is this that carries the full message to others and ourselves.

## 3. "Image/Gesture" as an Embodied Mental Model

Why does spontaneous spoken language sound human, compared to that of a robot? First, there are the paralinguistics (melody, stress, volume, etc.), which are the most common explanation. Secondly, there is the motive to talk. The listener feels the ongoing action of the motivation. Third, and related to the second, there is a kind of sloppy work to find the "right" words to communicate what one wishes. This sloppy work is visible or hearable by the listener.

In spontaneous speech, there is something in mind that wants expressing. Let us call this "something in mind" an image, in the broadest sense of the term. The image can be an idea, a movement, a gesture, an affect, a vitality affect, a background feeling. None of these are presently in verbal form. Now comes the messy work, especially in spontaneous dialogue. There is an intention (with its goal and structure) to link the image to words. For almost each phrase, the intention enters into a dynamic process with the existent repertoire of pieces of language to find the best fits. This is the "intention unfolding process." Emergent properties form. New linkages are created, tentatively accepted, revised, rejected, reintroduced in a different form, and mixed with all the other creative products of the intention unfolding process. This process, which usually takes several seconds, is dynamic, unpredictable, very messy, widely distributed in the body, and usually involves all analogous conscious and unconscious bodily happenings. This nonlinear dynamic process is perhaps what makes us most human. It would include how the word search gets performed, with what deliberation or rising excitement, with what burst of enthusiasm or calm when it "catches" a word. It is a process that can rush forward, hesitate, stop, restart gently, and so on. And even after the word is chosen and out there in public space, it can be partially taken back, and be revised or deleted as the talker stumbles forward with more or less grace, fluidity, and coherence. (Note, it doesn't matter if there is a "right" fit. None such exists. It only has to be good enough for effective communication.) It is these dynamic qualities that give the impression of an "inhabited body"—that is alive, now. Without these features of the intention unfolding process we would not experience a human being behind the words.

This body/mind dialogue of implicit experiencing and reflective-verbal processing makes it possible for a psychoanalyst and patient on the couch, not seeing each other, to know so much of the implicit and to share an intersubjective space.

It is in this light that David McNeill (2005) suggests that Johnson and Lakoff's (1999) model of "primary metaphors" be extended further. To evaluate how much further, recall that Johnson and Lakoff's basic idea of a primary metaphor concerned sensorimotor-kinetic experiences (such as walking, or looking up, or being held, i.e., things that normally are experienced when development encounters the world). These nonlinguistic primary metaphors provide the foundation (the nonverbal concepts) for aspects of language. In this view, movement is the mother of language. And, indeed, movement is the source of many linguistic concepts (Goldin-Meadow, 2003).

McNeill (2005) introduces the concept of the image/gesture to refer to all the bodily shapings of spoken thought. He sees spoken language as consisting of two components of equal generativity and importance. First, there is language, which is usually conceived of as a more or less static structure. Second, there is a dynamic process that he calls the image-gesture process. Superficially, this dynamic process consists of the gesticulations that are synchronous with speech. He points out that spoken speech is inhabited by the body moving in time, including facial expressions. Similarly, while gestures have their own isolated morphology, in real speech they become shaped by imagery and intention. Live speech and movement/gesture are forcibly synchronous. Even conditions such as stuttering or delayed auditory feedback do not break apart their synchronicity.

McNeil (2005) further elaborates "image/gesture" to include nonconscious, very short lived processes that emerge during the formation and execution of a thought or a phrase (the intentional unfolding process). If you are not reading a text, or have not memorized it, but are in the process of spontaneous discourse, each idea and spoken phrase is formed as it, or just before it, comes out. You don't know exactly what you are going to say until it you say it. During this intention unfolding process, the idea is still being worked on and aligned with pieces of language, well before the word(s) pop out, or the idea takes on its final form. McNeill garners much evidence to call it image/gesture. However, he is fully aware that gesture and imagery are not the only artisans of thought and language while it is being fashioned. All that is nonverbal plays this role: the affects; "the background feelings" from the body; the "vitality affects"; physical discomfort; mood; the state of subconscious motivational systems (hunger, sleep, sex); ambient sensations, immediate past history, and so on. All of these are meant to be assumed under the term image/gesture.

How do the forming ideas and the more or less right words find each other? After all, the intention unfolding process takes only seconds. It is a short and fast journey to tie the needed pieces of language to the image/gesture. McNeill, in Vygotsky's tradition (1934/1986), has the interesting suggestion that the dynamic, analogical image/gesture is paired with its opposite, the categorical, static word. The two are thrown together in a classical dialectic process where opposites are resolved and brought together through fusion. The verbal and nonverbal have not only been brought together but they have become one thing.

Without recourse to a dialectical theory, it seems simpler to imagine that as the dynamic intentional process works its way along, it is encountering words, phrases, and sounds. From these encounters unexpected emergent properties pop up joining together the intention to communicate, the image/gesture, and language. Thus the forming idea links with language as an emergent property. Here a dynamic systems theory description seems more commodious than a dialectical one. The idea of bringing together intentions and language in a dynamic system makes a particularly rich mix for emergent properties. The dynamic interplay of intention and word has similarities to choreography or music where inchoate intentions meet concrete positions, steps, and notes.

### 4. Nonverbal Contexts for Language

Words take their meaning in context. (For example, "I am content" vs. "the content of the package" or "I'm sorry, it was an oversight" vs. the oversight committee or "I cleave to you" vs. "I cleave the meat"). There is the context of the previously uttered words and phrases and there is the context of what is happening in the relationship at the moment of utterance. This is especially true for unscripted dialogue. What is happening importantly includes the implicit relatedness as well as the implicit knowledge between speaker and listener at the moment of speaking. In therapy this would include the moment-to-moment microshifts in the transference-countertransference relationship. There is most often a fluctuating context that determines what can be said, when, and how. In this sense, the ongoing language flow is sculpted moment by moment by implicit relational knowing, which provides a large part of the meaning.

## DISJUNCTIONS INTRODUCED WHEN THE REFLECTIVE-VERBAL EMERGES FROM THE IMPLICIT

### 1. Overview of Previous Points of Views

Until recently our worldview in the psychologies remained Cartesian. Descartes' notion that the psychic and somatic were separate and of different natures held sway. These domains were perhaps partially relatable but not integratable. The basic Cartesian view holds that language and nonverbal experience are quite distinct. They may act together so as to be complementary, or correlated, or scaffolding each other, but they always remain separate and independent phenomena. This position is a continuation of the long tradition of a mind/body split.

This presumed "gap" (Knoblauch, 2005) between implicit and reflective-verbal has presented two central questions for psychology and philosophy. First, does implicitly grasped, lived experience have any "meaning" in itself, as it is happening? Or is all meaning given after the experience in the act of reflection and verbalization? And second, to what extent does the act of reflection and verbalization distort experience that is implicitly lived?

What happens during the passage from implicit to explicit is the subject of a long-standing debate in phenomenological philosophy over the past century. Zahavi discusses the essence of these debates (1999, 2003). To summarize, at one pole of the classical view are those who think that the act of reflection distorts the implicit pre-reflective experience. They argue that the act of reflection turns implicit self-experience into an object and in so doing acts as a falsifying mirror of something that was originally subjective (Natorp, 1912). Heidegger (1982) agrees, to the extent that when lived experience is looked at during reflection it is no longer "lived-through" and is no longer subjective. Sartre (1943/1976) distinguishes a disrupted transformation that occurs when going from primary experience to reflection. Derrida (1967) goes further, and argues that there is an inherent fracture that creates a distortion between primary experience and reflected experience. He also ties reflection to language, as do many psychoanalysts. Some go further and suggest that (clinically speaking) there is no originary experience (implicit meaning) until it is given existence (psychological meaning) via reflection and verbalization, as if verbalizing creates our only experiential reality.

Knoblauch (2005) draws attention to the "gap" between words and the experiences that the words are meant to represent, as seen in the writings of Lacan (1977), and one of us, D. N. Stern, in an earlier writing. He cites Stern: "Language (for a child who is just learning it) is a double edged sword. It . . . makes some part of our experience less shareable with ourselves and others. It drives a wedge between two simultaneous forms of interpersonal experience: as it is lived and as it is verbally represented. . . . Language causes a split in the experience of the self (1985, pp. 162–163). (Stern's position has evolved since 1985.)

Lacan sees the same gap from a more dire perspective: "The symbol manifests in itself first of all as the murder of the thing" (1977, p. 104).

Knoblauch and others, while assuming that the gap can never be fully bridged, take a more positive view. Rather than letting the word and the direct experience undermine each other or just live their separate lives, he points out that in clinical practice each creates the immediate context for the other such that a duet, in two different voices, interacts to help make meanings of clinical pertinence more whole. He proposes an interrelationship between language and implicit experience that is rich and nuanced, where they interact in a continuous dialogue and create a duet. Still, they are viewed as two separate players in distinct domains but together producing a whole (Knoblauch, 2000).

Recently, Knoblauch (2005) has presented a most sensitive look at how language and nonlanguage play with each other, in speech and music. How they can compliment, trick, modulate, augment, recall each other. Or, each can select parts of the other for emphasis, or augmentation or irony or surprise or memory. His material is invaluable, yet it is written with a lingering whiff of Descartes in the air. Language and gesture do these wonderful things together, but remain separate voices, two unintegratable modes.

## 2. Our Position on Disjunctions Between the Implicit
## and Reflective-Verbal Domains

In contradistinction to these views, our position is informed by a dynamic systems model, which provides a description that goes beyond the paradox of two separate instruments (voices) that together can make music.

First, the verbal is grounded in the implicit and has to be "familiar." It has to refer to and play off the implicit intentional state. This is clear from our previous discussions of the embodied mind, of primary metaphor, and of the fact that language is rooted in the conveying of bodily experience developmentally and phenomenologically. A quote from Merleau-Ponty aptly states the case for the embodied mind: "The meaning is not on the phrase like the butter on the bread, like a second layer of 'psychic reality' spread over the sound; it is the totality of what is said, the integral of all the differentiations of the verbal chain; it is given with the words for those who have ears to hear. And conversely the whole landscape is overrun with words" (1964/2000, p. 155).[2]

In this sense then, it is not a duet of separate instruments. Instead one voice emerges from and is derivative of the other. Both are anchored in the same mental material and ambient culture. If one speaks in terms of a gap, why is it that the gap is not a chasm? Why are the two meanings (verbal and implicit) known and recognizable to each other, while divergent? Why cannot the two drift or be driven too far apart?

The familiarity resides in the fact that the words and lived experience are inherently related. This relatedness is achieved in development and in cultural usage. Thus the introduction of the verbal dimension adds not simply another strand to the symphony, but another element that is interpreted by each in relation to the intrinsic connection that is directly experienced between mind and body.

Second, while closely related developmentally, the implicit and the reflective-verbal are not isomorphic. We agree with previous writers that there is an inherent, inevitable disjunction between the lived and verbalized. This disjunction is the "gap." These are two different modes

---

[2]We thank Bruce Reis for calling this quote to our attention.

of expression not translatable one into the other. Also they are generated from different perspectives. The implicit is direct, subjective, and "lived through," while the verbal is a delayed view from outside the original implicit experience. This is the "gap" between word and experience that philosophers have pointed to as an inevitable product of translating lived experience into verbal expression.

Third, and here, our position differs markedly from the others. Disjunction, in itself, between the implicit and reflective-verbal should be viewed as an emergent property of the arising of the verbal from the implicit, and viewed in its own terms. It need not be conceptualized as a "gap" or distortion or fracture. There is not a problem or lack or loss in the process of emergence. In fact, it is because of the relatedness between word and experience that disjunctions, contradictions, and breaches in coherence, as well as complements and elaborations and harmonies, are created during the emergence of the reflective-verbal from the implicit. In this view, grasping the relations between the implicit and reflective-verbal, that is, the nature of the disjunction, is an additional and crucial property of the emergence. These three, the reflective, the implicit, and the disjunction between the two, make up one intuitively grasped package. That is where the music is.

In most cases, there is a high degree of coherence between implicit experience and its reflective-verbalization. Indeed we expect and rely on such coherence in conducting relationships within ourselves as well as with others. We are aware that some kind of a "coherence detector" will be needed to register the discrepancy between the implicit and verbal and to assign a value to the discrepancy, for example, conflicting, harmonizing, and so on.

Fourth, there are various forms of disjunction that must be separately conceptualized. In addition to the inherent disjunction that we have already described as discussed by the philosophers, there is second kind, which occurs when there is a more dramatic disruption and breach of harmony and coherence. It is these disjunctions that are of most interest to the clinician.

This position is not only consistent with a dynamic systems model. It is closer to a phenomenological description of what happens. During the emergence of the reflective-verbal (and its telling), we first receive-construct the intuition of a whole entity, a gestalt. It is this that is "experience-near." We do not immediately divide up the gestalt of implicit/verbal/disjunction into its "separate" parts and analyze each in relative isolation, academic style. It is this gestalt intuition that directs the second-by-second clinical inquiry.

We can now specify what we consider "meaning" to be. The gestalt of implicit experience, emergent reflective-verbalization, and the relation between these two that, all three taken together, make up meaning. Ultimately the meaning is captured in an intuitive grasp.

## A VIEW OF MEANING FROM THE
## TWO-PERSON INTERACTIVE PERSPECTIVE

So far, our discussion largely concerns the coherence of the implicit and reflective-verbal as it occurs in one person's mind and experience. We will now enlarge the discussion to bring in communication between two people. This is what the clinic is about.

The basic problem of the relation of the implicit and reflective-verbal is paralleled in the two-person situation in terms of what is spoken and what is reflectively heard. We consider the spoken to constitute an implicit experience for the listener for the following reasons. The listener hears the spoken message, infers the underlying implicit experience that gave rise to the words, and feels the difference between the two. He receives a "gestalt." He must then, in an act of reflection, make a whole meaning of this gestalt. Again in this act, a disjunction/coherence is introduced between the implicit experience of hearing/seeing/experiencing the speaker's performance and the listener's reflected meaning. When the listener then becomes the speaker, the process continues, only in the opposite direction.

The meanings (i.e., packages of implicit, reflective-verbal, and their disjunctions) build on each other and reorient the direction as the dialogue advances, resulting in more global or summarizing intuitive grasps. In other words, the meaning evolves in the course of the interaction. Clinically speaking, during the session, the patient reflects upon the interaction with the therapist, and intuits a meaning he or she has of the interaction (and vice versa). The meaning is never totally implicit, nor totally reflective-verbal, nor totally about their discrepancies.

The gestalt that gives rise to this meaning is a result of all three taken together captured in an intuitive grasp.

## CONCLUSION

We start with the assumption that mind and body evolved and developed together, deeply entwined within each individual. Spoken language is not possible without the experience of movement and gesture (Lakoff & Johnson, 1999; McNeill, 2005; Sheets-Johnstone, 1999). Equally, gesture requires language behind / within it.

We have explored how and why implicit and reflective-verbal are entwined and suffused with similar meaning. The distinction between linguistic and nonlinguistic is necessary for academic and philosophical reasons, but subjectively, the basic units of human communication are lived intentions. We assume and act as if the other is an embodied mind, like us, with intentions that can be multiply expressed and read. The exact form of expression is secondary to the intention.

We have mentioned several intertwinings between implicit experience and reflective-verbal that integrate the two. We note this integration is a precondition of potential and inevitable disjunctions between the two domains. Continuity of meaning across the implicit and explicit domains is discussed in this light. The reflective-verbal and implicit are not isomorphic but are necessarily deeply familiar to each other.

In the clinical situation, there will always be multiple intentions and meanings within any one act to communicate. We view such unscripted communications as emergent properties of a dynamic process comprised of three components which create a gestalt:

1.  The intention is implicitly experienced.
2.  A reflective-verbal version of this implicit experience is grounded in the nonverbal mental/body concepts contained in the implicit domain. The grounding is based on phylogeny, ontogeny, and culture.
3.  There is an inevitable disjunction between the implicit and the re-

flective-verbal. This is not a lack or a problem, it is just another property of the emerging gestalt.

All three come together during a process we have called the "intention unfolding process." During this process, a gestalt of all three, taken together, emerges and is captured in one intuitive grasp. It is this gestalt that gives out the multiple intentions and meanings that can shift and change over ongoing and repeated contemplation.

In the real world of dialogic communication one does not pay focal attention to the words that pass, or to the conventional gestures that are not mentally inhabited, nor to the disjunction between them. Instead, one is focused on the meaning of the total communication, and its intention. That is the phenomenological center.

# Forms of Relational Meaning:
# Response of the BCPSG
# to Commentaries

*A. Modell, S. Knoblauch, and D.B. Stern*

WE WANT TO EXPRESS OUR PLEASURE AT TAKING OUR TURN AS THE "AC-companists, audience, and even soloist as we read and experience our own embodied responses" to these papers. To continue Knoblauch's musical metaphor, these various commentaries constitute a "rich poly-rhythmic weave." We have not attempted to take up all the points mentioned in the commentaries; rather, we will address the key points that address central aspects of our thinking. The first point concerns our use of the term implicit memory; the second point involves the terms and notions, enactment, unformulated experience, and dissocia-tion; and the final response concerns the concept of objectivism in our use of ideas from other fields.

## THE STATUS OF THE CONCEPT
## OF IMPLICIT MEMORY

Modell expresses his concern about the limitations he attributes to the cognitive science view of procedural memory. However, from the be-ginning we have not been content to be confined by the existing definitions of procedural or implicit memory in cognitive science. In our earliest group publications, we pointed out the lack of consideration in cognitive psychology of the entire relational domain, namely what happens when someone is seen in ongoing interaction (Stern et al., 1998; Lyons-Ruth, 1999). Instead we offered the term "implicit relational knowing" to define the representation of the relational domain of interest to us and to psychoanalysis more broadly.

Modell mentions our reference to procedural memory; however, the entire quote regarding procedural memory goes beyond reference to the procedural memory of riding a bicycle to say:

> Most of the literature on procedural knowledge concerns knowing about interactions between our own body and the inanimate world (e.g. riding a bicycle). There is another kind that concerns knowing about interpersonal and intersubjective relations, i.e. how "to be with" someone (Stern, 1985, 1995). For instance, the infant comes to know early in life what forms of affectionate approaches the parent will welcome or turn away, as described in the attachment literature (Lyons-Ruth,1991). It is this second kind that we are calling *implicit relational knowing*. Such *knowings* integrate affect, cognition, and behavioral/interactive dimensions (p. 904).

This is a far cry from riding a bicycle.

The narrow frame surrounding procedural concepts is a lack in the cognitive sciences. Thus, much cognitive psychological literature on the topic of implicit memory is of limited relevance to our work. However, in contrast to experimental studies in cognitive psychology, studies of brain-damaged patients have clear relevance to our concepts in that they establish that implicit memory involves value-laden or emotion-laden action and can be recontextualized by experience in the absence of any capacity for explicit memory.

No human memory system lacks the potential for continual recontextualization in the light of further experience. As Modell notes, across human and animal species, traumatic threats to survival that produce extreme fear-based memories are more recalcitrant to change. However, this caveat applies across memory systems, and is not specific to

implicit memory. Freeman (1994) has demonstrated that recontextualization occurs even in the primitive case of the rabbit's olfactory memory, where he showed at the neuronal level that the existing synaptic
connections encoding a particular smell were reorganized when the
rabbit was exposed to a second smell.

All forms of memory—implicit, explicit, and autobiographical—are
subject to recontextualization in the light of further experience. In the
case of implicit memory, this is clearly demonstrated in the famous
case of the brain-damaged patient of Claparede (1911/1951), a woman
who had lost all explicit memory capacity. After many cordial meetings with Claparede, one day she refused to shake his hand. However,
she did not remember ever meeting with him before, nor did she know
why she refused to shake his hand. She was not able to recall that the
day before she had been pricked with a pin hidden in Claparède's extended hand (case cited in LeDoux, 1996). Additional examples of this
kind of dissociation of explicit/implicit are available in Damasio (1994),
and Ledoux (1996). These examples make clear that implicit non-conscious learning occurs in domains that are emotion-laden (value-lad-
en), relational rather than motor, available to recontextualization with
new experience, and potentially translatable to semantic memory.

We are in agreement with Modell that "an intent is the directing of
action," that "an intent represents *an unconscious selection of value*," and
that "meaning is achieved through action in the world." Modell's account leading up to this point, however, would imply that action is directed either by values that are unconscious and unintegrated (not
recontextualized in Modell's terms) or else by "salient autobiographical memories." We do not feel that these two alternatives are adequate
to capture the fluent and organized non-conscious knowings about
how to relate to others that characterize the relational domain, a domain that is arguably the largest area of human learning and experience. We continue to believe that we need the concept of relational
knowing in the implicit domain, as opposed to autobiographical memory or unintegrated unconscious memory, to account for this vast domain of knowing. We also believe, as we have stated (2007) that the
implicit is distinct from Freud's unconscious, which requires the idea
of repression.

It has been noted before that we don't refer to Freud very often, a point referred to again in these commentaries. We, as well as most readers, have been deeply involved with psychoanalytic thinking and with Freud's thinking in particular over many decades. However, we feel that citing his exact words is no longer necessary. Modern physicists don't continue to cite Newton. Elementary particle physicists don't continue to cite Einstein. Freud doesn't need to be continually cited. His ideas are common currency and taken for granted as a foundation for modern psychodynamic thinking.

## REGARDING ENACTMENT,
## UNFORMULATED EXPERIENCE,
## AND DISSOCIATION

The concept of implicit relational knowing would include enactments, but is broader than that of enactment, in that it encompasses the entire domain of implicitly represented relational knowing. Enactments may be one way that particularly dramatic or problematic ways of proceeding in relationships become clearer in the treatment. D. B. Stern feels that implicit relational knowing does not include the intensity of the personal relationship that analysis is, nor the specificity of the two persons involved. We feel that implicit relational knowing, which includes knowing about relations between patient and analyst, can certainly be intensely personal. However, the term *enactment*, which is generally used to refer to problematic clinical encounters, does not include the breadth and specificity of the term implicit relational knowing, and they should not be confused with one another.

In addition, while we agree with Donnel Stern's view that there are similarities between the concepts of "unformulated experience" and "implicit relational knowing," we want to point out that the concept of implicit relational knowing is much more specific regarding the primary form taken by the representation of relational experience. The notion of unformulated experience does not describe the form of the experience before it gets formulated. In contrast, implicit relational knowing advances a very clear model of how relational experience is initially represented.

Finally, the therapeutic utility of enactment is most commonly viewed as residing in the offering up of unconscious or dissociated content into the conscious domain for potential discussion and conversion into "formulated" or reflected-on experience. However, we do not see "reflection-upon" as a necessary ingredient of the change process in the implicit domain. Instead, we feel that change can occur in the process of the interaction itself, whether or not the form of the interaction becomes the subject of explicit discussion between patient and therapist.

Knoblauch raises the question of dissociation. The status of dissociation is an enormous topic beyond the purview of this response. Suffice it to say, we regard primary dissociation as part of the implicit domain.

## MAJOR MOMENTS IN THERAPY VERSUS MINOR, "BANAL" MOMENTS

There was a concern that BCPSG fails to include "intense personal entanglements" in its clinical considerations, so that its concepts are most appropriate for the less intense moments in a psychotherapy. In fact we began our inquiry as a group by taking up the particularly intense, unanticipated *now moments* in the therapeutic interaction. However, we recognized that much of therapeutic action takes place outside such heightened moments or enactments. Given this, we found it important to elaborate a model of change that could account for what is occurring in the less intense moments of the treatment. It has permitted us to see more clearly the uncertainty, unpredictability, and potential creativity that are features not only of heightened moments, but of all therapeutic interaction. It has also forced us to think about the inherent sloppiness of the spontaneous talk between therapist and patient as a co-creative emergence with much therapeutic potential. (See BCPSG, 2005).

## IS OUR POSITION OBJECTIVIST ?

We are perplexed by the critique that our position is "objectivist." This seems to stem from our using notions from dynamic systems theory, cognitive psychology, and developmental psychology in fashioning our account of meaning. We feel strongly that to further our understanding of the relational domain and to remain relevant as a field, we need to have continued dialogue with ideas from outside psychoanalysis per se.

The commentators ask, what have these imported notions "illuminated that would otherwise have remained invisible?" We would expand this question to include not only aspects of therapeutic action that might have remained invisible but also those aspects that might continue to be underspecified and poorly grasped.

In general, new developmentally and scientifically grounded vantage points allow us to see some of our traditional concepts in a fresh light, as well as to frame new concepts. In our own case, the new concepts that evolved from our exposure to other fields include psychodynamic theory's obvious need for a notion of relational representation beyond identification and incorporation, both during the preverbal period and throughout the life span; consideration of the various forms that such representations could take; the "sloppy" co-creative nature of spontaneous therapeutic interaction; a dynamical systems model that introduces emergent properties that offer therapeutic opportunities; the utilization of micro-analytic techniques of observation to bring into focus the "local level"; and, finally, a model of therapeutic change specific to the domain of implicit relational processes.

# Chapter 8

# An Implicit Relational Process Approach to Therapeutic Action

ONE OF THE MOST STRIKING INSIGHTS EMERGING FROM BOTH CLINICAL and research studies is that the qualitative nature of the whole therapeutic relationship appears to be the most important, specific element in the cure, more than any particular technical activity. In spite of that, we have shied away from elaborating the full implications of the awareness that the relationship in its entirety between the therapist and patient plays a major role in therapeutic cure. In this chapter we describe some of the paths that lead to this view and to some of its implications.

It becomes necessary to ask, how do we develop a useful current language for capturing the psychoanalytic process? Audio- and video-tapes impress upon us the utter complexity that has not been captured by previous conceptualizations of therapeutic action. Detailed process studies of psychoanalytic treatment (Waldron et al., 2004) make it clear that describing therapeutic action in terms of the commonly labelled analytic activities, interpretation, clarification, confrontation, fail to either describe or illuminate the complex multimodal process of exchange between the two interactants. Common terms such as "therapeutic alliance" attempt to speak to the overall state of the relationship but do little to advance our conceptual understanding of the relational field co-created in the therapy.

The concepts underlying psychodynamic thinking continue to change. The field is moving toward a new set of concepts in which the relationship between patient and therapist is at center stage in the cure. More emphasis is placed on the emerging dynamic process rather than on content or therapeutic technique. In addition, the nature of the unconscious and nonconscious is viewed differently and in a different relation to consciousness. Our aim here is to distil the basic elements of a relational process conception of therapeutic action.

## BASIC CONCEPTS OF AN IMPLICIT RELATIONAL PROCESS APPROACH

Throughout this volume, we have spoken of implicit relational knowing, how it is created, what it consists of, why it is the crux of what must be changed in therapy. We have even claimed that the task of therapy is to change implicit relational knowing. When one views therapy from this perspective, it changes one's notions about how therapy must work. The meanings that emerge from our interactions with others are communicated through multiple simultaneous channels with split-second timing, timing too rapid and too rapidly changing to be rendered in words. This dialogic process is at the heart of our view of any relational process. Engagement in this dialogue requires an active negotiation between the two partners, such that analyst and patient are working together back and forth to find a way to take the next steps forward. If they succeed, they will have established what we will call fittedness, which in turn gives rise to a jointly created direction and a more open, balanced, and inclusive relationship. This is not something the analyst brings, except perhaps as an orientation, but is a product of the interaction and communication between the two. While concepts such as directionality and fittedness are novel in the thinking of our field, we view them as the most basic orienting and structuring aspects of joint relational activity.

The process of creating a fitted joint direction serves to make more of the patient's world "relationable," that is, able to be brought into the relationship with another and thereby to create new relational possibilities. The more complex and inclusive the affective experiences that are included in the therapeutic exchange, the greater becomes the sense of valid agency within the patient and the more possibilities are enabled for the patient in relations with others as well as with the self. Concomitantly, more coherence will be created both within the patient's self experience and in regard to the patient's relational experiences with others. As we have previously stated, through certain kinds of exchange with others, you become more yourself.

## BASIC PREMISES

### 1. The Dyadic Nature of the Therapeutic Process

The relationship itself is the central force for change. It is not viewed as a "nonspecific" agent of change (see below), nor as a "context" for change, but as a highly specific set of transactions that directly produce change. Secondly, the relationship between therapist and patient is an ongoing process. All responses of both partners affect the state of the relationship. No activity has a privileged, a priori position in determining the nature of the relationship. The relationship creates a dyadic process and in turn is expanded by this process as it moves along.

### 2. Fittedness and Directionality in the Therapeutic Process

The relational process is directional. It has short-term and long-term goals. There must be a "fittedness" of direction between the partners. The goals need not be exactly or even well known at the beginning. They will be found en route. The initial chief complaint may provide one long-term goal that is relatively clear from the start, but could change. Instead, fitted directionality emerges out of encounters of the moment, from creative negotiation between the two partners as they begin to relate to each other.

This process of fitted directionality must be accomplished at the implicit level of lived interactions. The interactions may or may not be reflected upon explicitly, that is, verbally. This implicit experiencing creates "felt meanings" that can be lived and also further explored with words to give linguistic and narrative meanings, but need not be. Given the split-second signaling and multiple channels of affective and verbal meaning characteristic of any relational communication, most lived experience of the therapeutic relationship will, of necessity, never be explicitly verbalized or reflected upon.

### 3. Sloppiness and Creative Negotiation in the Therapeutic Process

Seeking, finding, and following a direction involves many tentative, exploratory initiatives, missed connections, repetitions, errors, misunderstandings, ruptures of shared directions, and repairs. Together we call these the "sloppiness" of the directional flow. These are intrinsic to the process and inevitable given indeterminacy in feeling one's way along in the dialogue, on both the patient's and the therapist's side.

### 4. Increasing Inclusiveness of the Therapeutic Process

The process of creative negotiation creates an increasing coherence in the relational field, and in the experiences of a relational self by the patient. This is experienced as a heightened sense of vitality and well-being when together and brings about a further expansion in the scope of the relationship and its shared intersubjective field.

### 5. Vitalization in the Therapeutic Process

Out of this process of feeling our way along to more fitted interactions comes increased feelings of vitality, trust, and caring in the therapeutic relationship. These are products of the success of the process of finding fitted directionality in the relationship, rather than characteristics that one or the other of the two participants brings to the relationship a priori.

THE CENTRALITY OF THE RELATIONSHIP
IN THE CURE: THE IMPLICIT RELATIONAL
PROCESS APPROACH AND THE
STATE OF THE FIELD

Both outcome-oriented and process-oriented research on psychodynamic psychotherapy are now underscoring the central role of relationship quality to positive changes in psychotherapy.

## Outcome Research in Psychodynamic Psychotherapy

In the last decades, there has been an increase in the number and conceptual importance of "relational" schools of psychoanalysis (see
(Aron, 1991; Beebe & Lachmann, 2002; Benjamin, 1988, 1995, 2004;
Ehrenberg, 1992; Knoblauch, 2000; Mitchell, 1998). These authors place
the relationship at the center of the therapeutic process, in a way different from the classical psychoanalytic emphasis on transference and
countertransference. Butler and Strupp (1986) state that psychotherapy
is the systematic use of a human relationship for therapeutic purposes.
Still earlier, since the 1950s, the Gestalt therapists have urged a shift in
therapeutic focus to the client–therapist relationship in the "here and
now" (Perls, Hefferline, & Goodman, 1951). Safran, Miran, and Proskurov (2008) point out that all techniques and interventions are relational acts. Moreover, research shows that what is termed the alliance
is a robust predictor of therapeutic outcome and that building and
maintaining the relationship is essential. Our work generally falls
within the designation of "relational," with some differences, but is
fully aligned with the notion of the centrality of the relationship.

The emphasis that relational schools place on the therapeutic relationship fits with a large body of evidence-based empirical literature
that has clearly situated the locus of therapeutic action in the relationship. Safran et al. (2008) credit Kohut with being first to point out that
ruptures and repairs in the relationship are important change events
in therapy. We would add that developmentalists have long known
and documented how the processes of rupture and repair within the
mother–infant relationship are essential experiences for developmental
progress (see chapters 1, 4, and 5).

Outcome studies (e.g., Safran et al., 2008) have found equivalent outcomes with a highly diverse range of therapies. This equivalence has been attributed to "common" or "nonspecific" factors, by which they mean that the relationship is the vital contributor to success. This body of work points to the centrality of the quality of the relationship as a whole in producing psychotherapeutic change.

## PROCESS STUDIES OF
## PSYCHOANALYTIC TREATMENT

In a very different tradition, and closer to the approach in this chapter, Waldron et al. (2004) have looked at the process between patient and analyst that leads to change in traditional analytic treatments. They began by noting that the way of measuring, and we would add, describing, psychoanalytic processes remains a problem more than 100 years after the invention of the procedure. Their ambitious study of the effect of the type and quality of the analyst's interventions on the patient's immediately subsequent analytic productivity, a focus on process, approaches the way we are thinking about therapeutic change.

Waldron et al. (2004) began with a definition of the psychoanalytic process as a special interactive dialogue between patient and analyst, aimed at lessening the patient's emotional conflicts. (We see this as one of the long-term goals, namely, that the patient and therapist must fit their overall directionality toward the chief complaint.) If the analysis is successful, the patient communicates increasingly unconstrained and affectively expressive associations and reflections.

Waldron et al. (2004) examined the effect of core analytic activities, including clarification, interpretation, and analysis of resistance, transference, and conflict, on the deepening of the therapeutic dialogue in tape-recorded sessions of psychoanalyses. Most importantly, the analyst's quality of intervention was rated on the basis of how well the analyst followed the patient's productions, as well as on the basis of the aptness of the type of intervention, the usefulness of its content, and the skill of presentation, including tact, timing, and language appeal.

Not surprising to current relational thinking, the therapeutic effect of different types of analytic activities was very dependent on the quality of those interventions, which varied across analysts and across sessions. Therefore, the quality rather than the type of intervention was overriding and was found to be the most important factor in the deepening of the patient's subsequent contribution. This relation between quality and productivity was found in each of the cases rated.

Furthermore, the deepening of the patient's productivity was, in turn, significantly related to the quality of the analyst's subsequent intervention, confirming the mutual influence occurring between patient and analyst in the quality of each other's contributions. They further found that the quality of an analytic intervention did not lie in aspects intrinsic to the contribution itself, but could only be reliably judged in relation to the prior context of the interaction.

This strong relationship between quality of intervention and patient productivity is the central finding of the study by Waldron et al. (2004). Regarding attunement to the patient's present state, the choice of an effectively fitted intervention and its timing and tactfulness was the most important element for the progress of the analysis. The quality of the analyst's contribution of any kind, so long as (s)he says "the right thing at the right time," is the essential element. In Waldron et al.'s words, "We do not dispute the major importance of interpretation, but with these three pairs we did conclude that the other core analytic activities seem equally important, and that none is very effective unless of high quality" (2004, p. 1106) They also note the convergence of their findings with the direction of our thinking. "Our investigation of the quality of treatment may turn out to represent another way of examining elements addressed by the Boston Change Process Study Group researchers (BCPSG, 2002; D. N. Stern et al., 1998) studying change from the vantage point of the moment-to-moment interaction—what they call 'the local level'" (p. 1111).

Waldron et al.'s work (2004), then, pushes us to move to a new and higher level of conceptualization of what leads to psychotherapeutic change. We are compelled to grapple with the qualities of the relationship itself, rather than with particular kinds of interventions.

## WHAT GOES INTO RELATIONSHIP QUALITY
## AS A SPECIFIC CURATIVE FACTOR
## IN PSYCHOANALYSIS?

As we saw above, the larger psychotherapy outcome literature points to the quality of the overall therapeutic relationship as critical to outcome, and Waldron's findings point to the quality of the analyst's moment-to-moment responses as most influential in whether the therapeutic dialogue deepens over time. So it becomes critical to model in more detail theoretically what "quality of intervention" might be capturing. Waldron et al. provide an initial list of attributes of an intervention rated high quality that included following the patient and offering an intervention characterized by aptness, usefulness, and skill, including tact, timing, and appealing language. These elements, attractive as they are, are based on the contributions of only one person and are not fully dyadic in conception.

When quality is considered from a two-person viewpoint, the criteria for judging quality shift dramatically. To move to a dyadic level of conception, we feel we need new terms, terms that move to an intrinsically dyadic rather than analyst-driven model of influence. We also need concepts that focus on the moment-to-moment relational exchanges and that encompass multilevel, simultaneous channels of communication that transmit primary aspects of meaning not based primarily on the semantic content of words.

### *Quality as Necessarily Dyadic*

In our model, quality is about "relational quality," not theoretical or technical proficiency on the part of the therapist. In our view, relational quality has to do with how well an act or statement on the part of the therapist or patient advances the directional fittedness and expands the shared relational field between them. While Waldron et al. (2004) first attempted to judge "quality" as a feature of a particular comment of the analyst, they quickly found that quality could not be judged apart from the context and current direction of the relational exchanges. This immediately recontextualizes quality as dyadic and fitted to the ongoing process between two people.

Second, while these authors focussed on the impact of the quality of the analyst's "interventions" on the patient's responses, they also found that when the quality of the patient's responses deepened, this was followed by higher-quality "interventions" by the analyst. This points to the mutuality of the process that is being engaged in, with each partner influencing the direction and the subsequent contribution of the other.

This dyadic relationship must also be conceptualized as an ongoing process. The therapeutic relationship and its appraisal and negotiation starts the first day the patient walks into the office. Either in the foreground or background of the patient's mind is, "Can I work with this person, can I get help here?" "Do I feel comfortable with him or her?" "Are the 'vibes' good enough?" The ongoing process of the relationship is there at every moment of therapy. Everything that is said and done pushes the relationship to evolve forward or backward or remain static.

While early psychoanalytic theorists viewed the therapist as apart, it is now generally accepted that there is no "stepping out of the relationship" to see elsewhere, or beyond the relationship, or deeper into the other's psyche. Appearing to "step out of it" for a moment, is yet another relational act. So is "evenly hovering attention." If for example the therapist and patient "step out of the immediately lived flow" in order to consider together what had just happened between them, or to look at the scope of an interpretation just made, where do they step to? They step into a different form of being together and relating, a different immediately lived flow, where they stand side by side to look at a "third" thing. This standing side by side is also part of the relationship.

In the therapeutic process, the partners experience things about each other that create a sense of how they do things together, as well as who the other is. We previously referred to this as the shared implicit relationship, highlighting how much of this may never be put into words, yet is part of the shared implicit relational knowing generated in the course of the therapeutic dyad moving along together. To illustrate, one need only look at the richness of a patient's picture of the analyst compared to the relative austerity of the analyst's utterances. How such a rich picture emerges cannot be explained by talking about things at the level of content because the process of interpersonal communication is multimodal, with many simultaneous levels of communication being registered in split-second intervals. Any semantic content is embedded in this simultaneous multimodal "affective commentary" in the form of facial, prosodic, and bodily cues that alter the meaning contained in the content itself. To give a simple example, the analyst can say "really" with so many different prosodic inflections that the meaning is fully dependent on the accompanying "nonverbal" features of the communication. "Really" can convey surprise, indifference, skepticism, contempt, or involved interest, depending on inflection and other relational cues accompanying the comment. The meaning inferred by the other will be folded into the other's implicit relational knowing.

This dependence of semantic meaning on the full interpersonal context of the utterance is characteristic of human communication. Getting at the full interpersonal meaning of a communication involves interpreting the verbal content as inflected by the accompanying prosodic, affective, and bodily cues. Interpreting the "real" meaning of another's communications becomes especially important to partners in relationships characterized by heightened affect and uncertainty, such as therapeutic or love relationships, where many hours can be taken up with scrutinizing the subtle inflections of word choice, timing, and affective cues that are part of any verbal statement.

With such an inclusive view of the relational process, we cannot separate particular highlighted analytic activities (e.g., clarification, interpretation, analysis of resistance, transference, and conflict, etc.) from the process of the relationship as a whole. These particular activities are part of what gives the relationship its specific form.

Other students of psychotherapy outcome have also focused on particular types of intervention as exemplifying crucial change agents in treatment, such as addressing core conflictual relationship themes (Luborsky, 1976), or a focus on interpretiveness (Gaston, 1990). Again, during these activities the relationship does not stop or get put on the back burner. These activities create a way of relating, the stuff of relating. This is also true of the smallest actions, of saying hello, good-bye, shifts in tone of voice, gestures, and so on.

Within psychoanalysis, there is a history (Freud, 1912/1958; Greenson, 1967; Sterba, 1934; Zetzel, 1966; for example) of dividing the relationship into what each theorist felt were its component parts. Two things stand out in these conceptualizations: First, the relationship is always divided into enabling and problematic facets, for example, un-objectionable positive transference versus transference neurosis. Sec-ondly, they mention only the patient's contribution to the relationship, whereas the therapist's part is more often described as "interventions." This subtly reflects the implicit assumption inherited from Freud that somehow the therapist is intervening into something from the outside, rather than engaging in an ongoing, multimodal contribution from in-side the dyad. Both evidence-based research and the relational schools have gone a long way toward correcting this implication that the thera-pist can work from a position in some sense "outside" the relationship. We would suggest that both parties are continually contributing to the therapeutic direction, whether it be through sound, gesture, or word. Even when the therapist is silent, he can be considered to be, among other things, listening, awaiting his/her turn, facilitating, withholding, withdrawing, putting pressure on, and so on.

Current theorists (e.g., Safran et al., 2008) approach the issue through discussion of the therapeutic alliance, a more familiar way of concep-tualizing the collaborative aspect of the therapeutic relationship. These authors conclude by proposing a reconceptualization of the alliance as an "ongoing process of intersubjective negotiation." This reconceptu-alization is quite close to our position in that we speak of the negotia-tion of joint direction as a central process in the treatment that is occurring at all times. Impressively, they cite evidence that a sense of the alliance that the patient has by the third to fifth session is predictive of outcome. In our terms, it would not be an "alliance" that would be fully in place by this time, but a sensing, based on the innate capacities for implicitly gauging fittedness or the possibility of it, of the likeli-hood of working collaboratively together.

These authors discuss the concept of rupture as relatively new, but having some overlap with ideas about impasses, strains, empathic fail-ures, resistance. They define a rupture as a strain or breakdown in the collaborative process, deterioration in the quality of relatedness or in communication. This focus on ruptures implicitly tags the importance we place on the negotiation of fittedness and shared direction.

Most often, the relationship between the patient and therapist is conceptualized as "nonspecific" because it exists in all approaches, or is at least the necessary "context" for therapy, or is held "in common" by all approaches. This view of "nonspecificity" permits people to forget that the relationship is the most mutative aspect of therapy. In so doing, the relationship escapes serious study and the focus falls on the specific techniques that differentiate different schools.

Our approach views the relationship as a specific modality of treatment that is both necessary and sufficient for change. Specific technical activities (e.g., desensitization or dream analysis) may add a great deal for certain patients or the same patient at different times, but the relationship is always there moving along. We posit a "real" relationship between two people who reveal in various ways their individualities, individualities that are not well captured by the concept of transference. We see the change process as occurring by way of the fitted directionality and shared experiencing of a real relationship, which includes the pasts of the two interactants, or in more familiar terms, transference material. The patient brings his habitual ways of responding into the "field of tension" that he and the therapist jointly create, and as the two members of the dyad gather information about each other and what is possible to do together, the relationship moves forward.

In a sense, the classical psychoanalytic position and ours are in agreement that the relationship is a necessary condition of change. However, we differ on whether it is a sufficient condition. Classical analysts have insisted that the relationship be interpreted and made conscious to be a sufficient element of change. That is not our view. We think that the relationship is also a sufficient condition for bringing about change.

In our view, the analyst's contributions to creating a joint direction are real, and reveal the "real" of himself or herself, through what is chosen to comment on and to ignore, through what is felt to be worth attending to, and through how the analyst goes about doing this.

### Quality as an Engaged Search for Directionality and Fittedness

The contributions of the therapist and patient must demonstrate the time, effort, and importance of finding directional fittedness—that it matters. These qualities must be felt by the other. They can be seen in the persistence and desire to "get it as right as possible." This is transmitted in the tension when ruptures of fittedness take place (some combination of anxiety, disappointment, frustration, etc.), and in the relaxation and reinvigoration when repairs are achieved. These efforts do require that the therapist is engaged emotionally in the relationship to an adequate extent (see below) and that this engagement is perceivable. Our view does not imply that this is explicitly understood by either patient or therapist. It is usually implicit.

This emphasis on the time, effort, and importance of searching is based on the notion that relational quality is neither theoretical nor technical proficiency, in the ordinary sense, on the part of the therapist. Instead, in the view elaborated here, relational quality has to do with how well an act or statement on the part of the therapist or patient advances the directional fittedness and expands the shared relational field. Waldron et al. (2004) also found that when the quality of the patient's responses deepened, higher-quality "interventions" by the analyst followed. In our reading of Waldron et al.'s (2004) work, we see the clinician raters as perceiving higher-quality contributions when they see the analyst as grasping and furthering the multileveled mutual directionality taking shape over the last few sessions between patient and analyst. This quality cannot be judged by the contribution itself, but only by how it relates to what came before, as well as what comes next.

The complex process of fitting together requires an active negotiation between the two partners, such that analyst and patient are working together back and forth in finding direction and fit. This is a hit-or-miss endeavor. It is useful to keep in mind that finding fittedness can appear as a mundane process, although one that is also time-consuming and effortful. Attempts to achieve fittedness involve the full complex of explicit and implicit features that make up our communications with one another.

As illustration of the ongoing ordinariness of what we are referring to as searching for a fit and fittedness, two vignettes from an audiotaped analysis by Merton Gill (1972), reprinted courtesy of the Psychoanalytic Research Consortium, are presented. The first is from the initial hour. Clearly there is rich dynamic material here that we are not explicating, as it is not part of the focus of the current chapter.

P:   I . . . I'm nervous.

T:   Yeah, I see you are, but just take it easy and tell me a little about yourself.

P:   Mmmm—well, I don't know what Kenny told you.

T:   Very little.

P:   Very little. Okay. I'm married. I've two children. I don't work. I'm a housewife—but that's work.

T:   Yes, I know it is.

P:   Mmm—want to get right down to what the basic problem is? . . .

An immediate direction is created, dealing with the patient's nervousness. The analyst's responses are succinct but homey, accepting, trying to put the patient at ease, conveying that he appreciates that being a mother/housewife is work, not to be devalued. You can talk to me, he seems to be implying, you're safe, I'm not about to look down on you.

By the fourth session, in what follows, one can see the two groping, trying things out, with the patient seeking clarification and the analyst implicitly giving her a sense of what it's like to be with him, what the procedure is like.

T:   I think—yeah—I think maybe you're also sort of wanting me to know that this is a strange and unusual and very new situation for you and you are sort of wanting me to know that I should have some degree of patience and give you time to get—to get used to do it. To know how to do it. You're perhaps afraid that I'll expect you to jump in and do everything exactly right the first minute and so on.

P:   Yeah, I guess it goes back to what we discussed too. Uh—geez, my mind (laughs) I forgot. I think of something when you're saying and then—then I forget it (sighs). Must start taking up my vitamin pills again. Uh, it's like, uh, I don't want you to give up on me, you know, that's what it is.

T:   Oh, yes, that's a better way to put it than I did.

The analyst, in conveying he doesn't need to be right, to be the boss, that he welcomes the patient as a full participant and co-leader, enhances the patient's agency and freedom to proceed. In this remark, he is showing her that she has an ability to express herself that he recognizes.

A little later, after the two have worked on a dream together, the patient begins to remember two incidents where her father was uncharacteristically complimentary toward her.

T:   And these events are so few that they stand out in your memory so sharply.

P:   Yeah. And most of the other ones are always ones I don't even want to say or bring up because, uh, I don't want to talk about my father that way, you know, it's—I guess, I respect him so much. That was one big thing, they used to always harp on the word, "respect your parents" "respect, respect," that uh, to talk about them, uh, in a way that I thought they hurt me or did something wrong would be disrespect them to them and maybe that's why I sort of don't want to come here—don't want to talk about my mom or my dad in a bad way. (pause) It, uh—it hurts.

T:   Yes. I think that might even have something to do with the dream—that uh, you have a feeling if you start to talk freely, you might say just terrible things, it would be awful.

P:   Mmmm—there's a lot—like I told Nick, I haven't even told you. Uh, this is terrible—yet it's good to me. Uh-oh (sighs). Nick and I were not married until Ericka was like a year and a half old—I had—I got pregnant and Nick and I were gonna get married and then he just decided he couldn't do it and copped out and I was all by myself and I was living at home with my parents. . . .

Here we see that the establishment of fittedness leads to a freeing up of constraints and a heightening of spontaneity within the patient. Feeling that the analyst is in tune with her, she summons up the resolve to broach the shameful issue of her out-of-wedlock pregnancy.

Confrontation or flagging a misalignment or difference is also included under searching for a fit. Hobson describes an intake interview with a young man, who, "seemed to be conveying to me how I might succeed in helping him, where everyone else had failed. Yet it did not feel to me that this man had any confidence in what I might achieve on his behalf. For example, he had been speaking for ten minutes, and at no time did he seem interested in my view of his story. . . . In the end I decided to interrupt . . . to say, 'I wonder if I might stop you for a moment there. You are speaking to me as if I had been very helpful to you at the beginning, and as if you have confidence in me and what I might offer. . . . Yet I wonder what is really going on'" (2002, p. 23).

Hobson registers the disjunction between what is being said versus enacted (I have confidence in you but no interest in what you have to say) and how he feels in response. His own input is a way of adjusting the exchange, based on his parsing of intention. Although he is confronting his patient, we see this as in the service of finding a more adapted fittedness. He continues, "at this point, the patient looked dumbfounded, then exclaimed, 'You want me to be honest?' I said yes, I wanted him to be honest" (2002, p. 23).

Hobson, in saying "we are not fitted at the moment," has implied that he would like to establish a more adapted fit, and in so doing, initiated a change in the intersubjective field.

What is most pertinent here is how much time and effort both of the analysts cited above spend working toward directional fittedness. In order to reach it both partners must constantly try to grasp the other's intentional direction, again something not necessarily in awareness. Directional fittedness must be attended to at many levels simultaneously and over time. We are not close to having any complete account of the multiple levels at which fittedness is constantly being monitored between two interacting partners, including patient and therapist. Some of these levels of fit come readily to mind, such as: From the therapist's side, there are many levels of fit that can be delineated. These would include fit with the immediately preceding contribution of the patient; with the patient's contradictory simultaneous affective states; with the direction the patient wants to go ultimately in the treatment; with the speed or pace of change felt to be tolerable to both partners; with the patient's sensitivities and self-esteem; and with the personalities and temperaments of the patient and therapist. With little modification these many levels of fit can also be seen to be pursued by the patient in regard to the therapist.

We have referred to the subjective aspect of shared directionality as recognition process (Chapters Three and Five), that is, an apprehension by the two partners of the achievement of a shared subjective fit.

### Quality as Creative Negotiation of Sloppiness and Indeterminacy

Given the multiple levels of the experience of both parties in any given moment, and the multiple levels at which communication between two people is continually occurring, it is a given that fitting together of any two subjectivities will require much negotiation, disambiguation, feedback in many modalities, and missed possibilities. Indeterminacy is an unavoidable concomitant of the process. This gives rise to an inevitable sloppiness. The therapist's ability to apprehend and participate in such ambiguous, fluid, and emotionally charged situations must be felt by the patient and vice versa, and will be critical to the outcome of the treatment.

The question of how the dyad gets to the point of engaging in "high-quality" exchanges that deepen the material is important. It appears that the analyst and the patient are bringing diverse elements of their mutual experiences together in more complex forms of fittedness. We see such an exchange of high-quality fittedness, the most intense of which we have termed "moments of meeting," as most often building on a prior process of creative negotiation, rupture, and repair that is inherently sloppy and indeterminate.

While much of the therapeutic literature focusses on the high-intensity moments of rupture or meeting, most of therapeutic work is not of this kind, yet it is equally or more vital to the progress and success of the work. What is quality during the less dramatic moments of the treatment? We see quality residing in the trying out and trying on of the search for where the two should go next. This requires a higher-level awareness of why this process is critical to the treatment.

Winnicott (1958) refers to "a degree of inexactness" in the parent's response to the infant as an essential precondition to developmental progression of the infant in order to allow the entry of reality and frustration, so that the baby needs to work to be known to the parent. An awareness of the importance of inexactness is also important to the therapist, so that the therapist is not foreclosing the uncertainty of what it takes to know another mind. Frameworks that become implements of explanation of the other's mind lead to a shutting down of the openness of the therapist in approaching the patient.

It is this openness and awareness of the indeterminancy of the process that is therapeutic, because it is communicated to the patient as a way of proceeding that respects the subjectivity of the other. It is a way of implicitly communicating to the patient an awareness of the complexity of mind. The openness that has to be a part of two independent subjectivities finding ways to communicate and share with each other is a necessary precondition to emotional growth in therapy.

### *Quality as Increasing Inclusiveness in the Relational Field*

Psychoanalysis has always been oriented toward bringing as much of mental process as possible into a free associative mode where unconscious material becomes conscious and verbal. We would now reframe this concept from a two-person perspective. The more one's experiences are shared with a responsive other, the more one's thoughts and feelings will be experienced as human and "relationable," that is, able to be included in one's relationships with others and thereby with oneself. Sharing of meanings and experiences converts experiences of shame, guilt, or deviance into expressions of a joint humanity. And that converts one's subjective mental life into something acceptable and bearable, and something that can be included in one's exchanges with important others.

We see this increased scope of the dialogue as emerging from the small steps in fitting together that are negotiated moment by moment in the treatment process. To the extent that a successful exchange has occurred around less charged affective material, the two participants take small steps toward engaging issues of greater dynamic import for the patient's self-image and sense of cohesion. Negotiating increasingly broad-ranging dialogues in the treatment, a process that brings more aspects of the patient's difficult feelings and life experiences into interchange with the therapist, is the hallmark of a treatment with direction and fittedness. Instead of viewing this process from the viewpoint of the patient's increasing self-awareness of dynamic conflict, we view it from the viewpoint of the patient's becoming able to participate in vital relationships in a different way than before.

Increased inclusiveness thus refers to how much of the patient's experience can be included in the therapeutic relationship. Sharing with another is a way of making experience as human as possible. Sharing is less about expression of content than about how a dialogue is conducted with another, about learning to exchange affectively charged material in a relationship. This would include, on the part of the therapist, a willingness to use a wide, but appropriate, spectrum of the therapist's subjectivity, life experience, and individuality.

### *A Word on Products of Quality*

Sander (personal communication, July 28,1999) has noted that an upshot of fitting together is vitalization, experienced by both partners, which in turn leads to a greater feeling of liking each other. This vitalization serves as a directional element, in that it encourages the two to repeat ways of being together that generate such inner experiences, thus being a hallmark of dyadic quality.

Similarly, increased levels of trust can be seen to follow upon a heightened sense that the relational quality exists and will continue to exist. When present, the patient will progressively make difficult feelings and experiences relationable. Not simply verbalized to a listener for the patient's and analyst's reflection for interpretive reading, but palpably folded into the nature of the evolving relationship—furthering the quest for who each person is for the other.

### SUMMARY

In summary, we offer a shift in conceptual framework from the notion that therapeutic change depends on the quality of the interventions of the analyst. Working from a dyadic perspective, we would frame conceptions of quality within a relational model that stresses features of the process between two persons. From this vantage point, we located psychotherapeutic quality in an engaged search for directionality and fittedness, in the creative negotiation of sloppiness and indeterminacy, and in efforts to increase the breadth of affectively charged experiences that can be brought into the therapeutic relationship. To the extent that these dyadic processes are realized, we would expect to see an emerging feeling in the treatment relationship of trust and mutual vitalization. These dynamic processes, once in motion, move toward increasing integration, coherence, and fluency in the patient's ability to make their experiences "relationable," that is, to be guided by their own feelings and directions in a balanced way in significant exchanges with others.

# References

Ainsworth, M., Blehar, M., Waters, E., & Wall, S. (1978). *Patterns of attachment*. Hillsdale, NJ: Erlbaum.

Aron, L. (1991). The patient's experience of the analyst's subjectivity. *Psychoanalytic Dialogues, 1*, 29–51.

Atwood, G., & Stolorow, R. (1984). *Structures of subjectivity*. Hillsdale, NJ: Analytic Press.

Bahktin, M. (1981). *The Dialogic Imagination*. Austin: University of Texas Press.

Baricco, A. (2002). *Lands of glass* (A. Goldstein, Trans.). London: Penguin.

Basch, M. (1975). Toward a theory that encompasses depression. In E. J. Anthony & T. Benedek (Eds.), *Depression and human existence* (pp. 485–534). Boston: Little, Brown.

Bateman, A., & Fonagy, P. (2004). *Psychotherapy for borderline personality disorder: Mentalization-based treatment*. Oxford, UK: Oxford University Press.

Beebe, B., Jaffe, J., Lachmann, F., Feldstein, S., Crown, C., & Jasnow, M. (2000). Systems models in development and psychoanalysis: The case of vocal rhythm coordination and attachment. *Infant Mental Health Journal, 21*(1), 99–122.

Beebe, B., & Lachmann, F. (1988). The contribution of mother–infant mutual influence to the origins of self and object representations. *Psychoanalytic Psychology, 5*, 305–337.

Beebe, B., & Lachmann, F. (1994). Representation and internalization in infancy: Three principles of salience. *Psychoanalytic Psychology, 11*, 127–165.

Beebe, B., & Lachmann, F. (2002). *Infant research and adult treatment: Co-constructing interactions*. Hillsdale, NJ: Analytic Press.

Beebe, B., & Stern, D. (1977). Engagement-disengagement and early object experiences. In M. Freedman & S. Grand (Eds.), *Communicative structures and psychic structures* (pp. 35–55). New York: Plenum Press.

Benjamin, J. (1988). *The bonds of love: Psychoanalysis, feminism, and the problem of domination*. New York: Random House.

Benjamin, J. (1995a). *Like subjects, love objects.* New Haven, CT: Yale University Press.

Benjamin, J. (1990). Recognition and destruction: An outline of intersubjectivity. In: *Relational Psychoanalysis: The Emergence of a Tradition,* S.A. Mitchell & L. Aron, eds. The Analytic Press: Hillsdale, NJ, pps 193–200.

Benjamin, J. (2004). Beyond doer and done-to: An intersubjective view of thirdness. *Psychoanalytic Quarterly, 73,* 5–46.

Bollas, C. (1987). *The shadow of the object: Psychoanalysis of the unthought known.* New York: Columbia University Press.

Boston Change Process Study Group. (1998a). Report 1. Non-interpretive mechanisms in psychoanalytic therapy: The "something more" than interpretation. *International Journal of Psychoanalysis, 79,* 908–21. (see Stern et al., 1998, below).

Boston Change Process Study Group. (1998b). Report 2. Interventions that effect change in psychotherapy: A model based on infant research. *Infant Mental Health Journal, 19,* 277–353. (see Tronick et al., 1998a below).

Boston Change Process Study Group. (2002). Report 3. Explicating the implicit: The local level and the microprocess of change in the analytic situation. *International Journal of Psychoanalysis, 83,* 1051–1062.

Boston Change Process Study Group. (2005a). The something more than interpretation revisited: Sloppiness and co-creativity in the psychoanalytic encounter. *Journal of the American Psychoanalytic Association, 53*(3), 693–729.

Boston Change Process Study Group. (2005b). Response to commentaries. *Journal of the American Psychoanalytic Association, 53*(3), 761–769.

Boston Change Process Study Group. (2007). The foundational level of psychodynamic meaning: Implicit process in relation to conflict, defense, and the dynamic unconscious. *International Journal of Psychoanalysis, 88,* 843–860.

Boston Change Process Study Group. (2008). Forms of relational meaning: Issues in the relations between the implicit and reflective/verbal domains. *Psychoanalytic Dialogues, 18,* 125–148.

Bowlby, J. (1973). *Attachment and loss: Vol. 4. Separation.* New York: Basic Books.

Braten, S. (1998). Infant learning by altero-centric participation: The reverse of egocentric observation in autism. In S. Braten (Ed.), *Intersubjective communication and emotion in early ontogeny* (pp. 105–124). Cambridge, UK: Cambridge University Press.

Bruschweiler-Stern, N., Harrison, A., Lyons-Ruth, K., Morgan, A., Nahum, J., Sander, L., Stern, D.N., & Tronick, E.Z. (1998) Reflections on the process of psychotherapeutic change as applied to medical situations. *Infant Mental Health Journal, 19,* 320–323.

Brentano, F. (1973). Psychology from an empirical standpoint. London: Routledge & Kegan Paul. (Original work published 1874)

Bretherton, I. (1988). Open communication and internal working models:

Their role in the development of attachment relationships. In R. Thompson (Ed.), *Nebraska symposium on motivation: Socio-emotional development* (pp. 57–113). Lincoln: University of Nebraska Press.

Bruner, J. (1986). *Actual minds, possible worlds.* Cambridge, MA: Harvard University Press.

Bruner, J. (1990). *Acts of meaning.* New York: Basic Books.

Bruner, J. (2002). *Making stories: Law, literature, life.* New York: Farrar, Strauss, and Giroux.

Butler, S., & Strupp, H. (1986). Specific and non-specific factors in psychotherapy: A problematic paradigm for psychotherapy research. *Psychotherapy 23,* 30–39.

Carpenter, M., Akhtar, N., & Tomasello, M. (1998). Fourteen- through 18-month-old infants differentially imitate intentional and accidental actions. *Infant Behavior and Development, 21,* 315–30.

Claparede, E. (1951). Recognition and "me-ness." In D. Rapaport (Ed.), *Organization and pathology of thought* (pp. 58–75). New York: Columbia University Press. (Original work published 1911).

Clark, A. (1997). *Being there: Putting brain, body, and world together again.* Cambridge, MA: MIT Press.

Clyman, R. (1991). The procedural organization of emotions: A contribution from cognitive science to the psychoanalytic theory of therapeutic action. *Journal of the American Psychoanalytic Association, 39,* 349–381.

Damasio, A. (1994). *Descartes' error: Emotion, reason, and the human brain.* New York: Grosset/Putnam.

Damasio, A. (1999). *The feeling of what happens: Body and emotion in the making of consciousness.* New York: Harcourt Brace.

Decety, J., & Chaminade, T. (2003). When the self represents the other: A new cognitive neuroscience view on psychological identification. *Consciousness and Cognition, 12,* 577–596.

Derrida, J. (1967). *L'écriture et la différence.* Paris: Editions du Seuil.

Dilthey, W. (1976). *Selected writings* (H. P. Rickmen, Ed.). Cambridge: Cambridge University Press.

Edelman, G. (1987). *Neural Darwinism.* New York: Basic Books.

Edelman, G. (1992). *Bright air, brilliant fire.* New York: Basic Books.

Ehrenberg, D. (1992). *The intimate edge.* New York: Norton.

Erikson, E. (1950). *Childhood and society.* New York: Norton.

Feldman, C., & Kalmar, D. (1996). Autobiography and fiction as modes of thought. In D. Olson & N. Torrence (Eds.), *Modes of thought: Explorations in culture and cognition* (pp. 106–122). Cambridge, UK: Cambridge University Press.

Fenichel, O. (1941). *Problems of psychoanalytic technique.* New York: Psychoanalytic Quarterly.

Ferenczi, S., & Rank, O. (1924). *The development of psychoanalysis.* Madison, CT: International Universities Press, 1986.

Fivaz-Depeursinge, E., & Corboz-Warnery, A. (1995). Triangulation in relationships. *The Signal, 3*(2), 1–6.

Fivaz, E., Fivaz, R., & Kaufmann, L. (1979). Therapy of psychotic transaction families: An evolutionary paradigm. In C. Muller (Ed.), *Psychotherapy of schizophrenia*. Amsterdam: Excerpta Medica.

Fivaz-Depeursinge, E., Fivaz, R. & Kaufmann, L. (1982). Encadrement du développment, le point de vue systemique. Fonctions pédagogique, parentale, thérapeutique. Cahiers critique de thérapie familiale et de practiques de réseaux, 4-5, 63–74.

Fivaz, R. (1996). Ergodic theory of communication. *Systems Research 13*, 127–144.

Fonagy, P. (1991). Thinking about thinking. Some clinical and theoretical considerations in the treatment of the borderline patient. *International Journal of Psychoanalysis, 72*, 639–656.

Fosshage, J. (2005). The explicit and implicit domains in psychoanalytic change. *Psychoanalytic Inquiry, 25*(4), 516–539.

Freeman, W. (1995). *Societies of brains: A study in the neuroscience of love and hate*. Hillsdale, NJ: Erlbaum.

Freeman, W. (1999). *How brains make up their minds*. London: Weidenfeld and Johnson.

Freud, S. (1958). The dynamics of transference. In J. Strachey (Ed. & Trans.), *The standard edition of the complete psychological works of Sigmund Freud* (Vol. XII, pp. 97–108) London: Hogarth Press. (Original work published 1912)

Freud, S. (1958. Project for a scientific psychology. In J. Strachey (Ed. & Trans.), *The standard edition of the complete psychological works of Sigmund Freud* (Vol. 3, p. 108). London: Hogarth Press. (Original work published 1895)

Gallese, V. (2001). The "shared manifold" hypothesis: From mirror neurons to empathy. *Journal of Consciousness Studies, 8*(5–7), 33–50.

Gaston, L. (1990). The concept of the alliance and its role in psychotherapy: Theoretical and empirical considerations. *Psychotherapy, 27*, 143–153.

Gergely, G., & Csibra, G. (1997). Teleological reasoning in infancy: The infant's naive theory of rational action. A reply to Premack and Premack. *Cognition, 63*, 227–233.

Gergely, G., Nadsasdy, Z., Csibra, G., & Biro, S. (1995). Taking the intentional stance at 12 months of age. *Cognition, 56*, 165–193.

Gergely, G., & Watson, J. (1999). Early social-emotional development: Contingency, perception, and the social biofeedback model. In P. Rochat (Ed.), *Early social cognition* (pp. 101–136). Hillsdale, NJ: Erlbaum.

Gianino, A., & Tronick, E. (1988). The mutual regulation model: The infant's self and interactive regulation. Coping and defense capacities. In T. M. Field, P. M. McCabe, & N. Schneiderman (Eds.), *Stress and coping across development* (pp. 47–68). Hillsdale, NJ: Erlbaum.

Gill, M. (1994). *Psychoanalysis in transition*. Hillsdale, NJ: Analytic Press.

Goldin-Meadow, S. (2003). *Hearing gesture: How our hands help us think*. Cambridge, MA: Harvard University Press.

Gopnik, A., & Meltzoff, A. (1998). *Words, thoughts and theories*. Cambridge, MA: MIT Press.

Greenberg, J. (1996). Psychoanalytic words and psychoanalytic acts. *Contemporary Psychoanalysis, 32*, 195–213.

Greenson, R. (1967). *The technique and practice of psychoanalysis: Vol. 1*. New York: International Universities Press.

Guntrip, H. (1975). My experience of analysis with Fairbairn and Winnicott. *International Journal of Psychoanalysis 2*, 145–156.

Harrison, A., Bruschweiler-Stern, N., Lyons-Ruth, K., Morgan, A., Nahum, J., Sander, L., Stern, D.N., & Tronick, E.Z. (1998). The case of sophie. *Infant Mental Health Journal, 19*, 309–314.

Harrison, A. (2001, May 1). *Setting up the doll's house*. Beata Rank lecture presented at the Boston Psychoanalytic Society, Boston, MA.

Hartmann, H. (1958). (Original work published 1939) *Ego psychology and the problem of adaptation*. International Universities Press: New York

Heidegger, M. (1982). *On the way to language*. New York: Harper & Row.

Hertsgaard, L., Gunnar, M., Erickson, M., & Nachmias, M. (1995). Adrenocortical response to the strange situation in infants with disorganized/disoriented attachment relationships. *Child Development, 66*, 1100–1106.

Hobson, P. (2002). *The cradle of thought*. Oxford, UK: Oxford University Press.

Hoffman, I. (1998). *Ritual and spontaneity in the psychoanalytic process: A dialectical constructivist view*. Hillsdale, NJ: Analytic Press.

House, J. & Portuges, S. (2005). Relational Knowing, Memory, Symbolization, and Language: Commentary on the Boston Change Process Study Group. *Journal of the American Psychoanalytic Association, 53*(3), 731–744.

Husserl, E. (1962). *Ideas pertaining to a pure phenomenology and to a phenomenological philosophy: First book. General introduction to pure phenomenology* (B. Gibson, Trans.). New York: Collier.

Husserl, E. (1989). *Ideas pertaining to a pure phenomenology and to a phenomenological philosophy. Second book: Studies in the phenomenology of constitution* (R. Rojcewicz & A. Schuwer, Trans.). Dordrecht, Netherlands: Kluwer Academic Publishers. (Original work published 1930)

Jacoby, L., & Dallas, M. (1981). On the relationship between autobiographical memory and perceptual learning. *Journal of Experimental Psychology: General, 110*, 300–324.

Jaffe, J., Beebe, B., Feldstein, S., Crown, C., & Jasnow, M. (2001). Rhythms of dialogue in infancy. *Monographs of the Society for Research in Child Development, 265*(66, Serial No. 2).

James, T., & Gautier, I. (2003). Auditory and action semantic features activate sensory-specific perceptual brain regions. *Current Biology, 13*, 1792–1796.

Kandel, E. (1999). Biology and the future of psychoanalysis: A new intellectual framework for psychiatry revisited. *American Journal of Psychiatry, 156*(4), 505–523.

Kihlstrom, J., & Cantor, N. (1983). Mental representations of the self. In L. Berkowitz (Ed.), *Advances in experimental social psychology* (Vol. 17, pp. 1–47). San Diego, CA: Academic Press.

Knoblauch, S. (2000). *The musical edge of therapeutic dialogue*. Hillsdale, NJ: Analytic Press.

Knoblauch, S. (2005). Body rhythms and the unconscious. *Psychoanalytic Dialogues, 15*(6), 807–827.

Knowlton, B., Ramus, S., & Squire, L. (1992). Dissociation of classification learning and explicit memory for specific instances. *Psychological Science, 3,* 172–179.

Kohut, H. (1984). *How does analysis cure?* Chicago: University of Chicago Press.

Lacan, J. (1977). *Ecrits, a selection*. New York: Norton.

Lachmann, F., & Beebe, B. (1996). Three principles of salience in the patient-analyst interaction. *Psychoanalytic Psychology, 13,* 1–22.

Lakoff, G., & Johnson, M. (1980). *Philosophy in the flesh*. New York: Basic Books.

LaPlanche, J., & Pontalis, J. (1988). *The language of psychoanalysis* (D. Nicholson-Smith, Trans.). London: The Institute of Psychoanalysis and Karnac Books. (Original work published 1967)

Le Doux, J. (1996). *The emotional brain*. New York: Touchstone.

Lewicki, P., Hill, T., & Czyzewska, M. (1992). Non-conscious acquisition of information. *American Psychologist, 47,* 796–801.

Lichtenberg, J. (1983). *Psychoanalysis and infant research*. Hillsdale, NJ: Analytic Press.

Litowitz, B. (2005). When something more is less: Comments on the Boston Change Process Study Group. *Journal of the American Psychoanalytic Association, 53*(3), 751–759.

Loewald, H. (1971). The transference neurosis: Comments on the concept and the phenomenon. *Journal of the American Psychoanalytic Association, 19,* 54–66.

Luborsky, L. (1976). Helping alliances in psychotherapy. In J. L. Clanghorn (Ed.), *Successful psychotherapy* (pp. 92–116). New York: Brunner/Mazel.

Lyons-Ruth, K. (1991). Rapprochement or approchement: Mahler's theory reconsidered from the vantage point of recent research on early attachment relationships. *Psychoanalytic Psychology, 8,* 1–23.

Lyons-Ruth, K. (1998). Implicit relational knowing: Its role in development and psychoanalytic treatment. *Infant Mental Health Journal, 19*(3), 282–289.

Lyons-Ruth, K. (1999). The two-person unconscious: Intersubjective dialogue, enactive relational representation, and the emergence of new forms of relational organization. *Psychoanalytic Inquiry, 19*(4), 576–617.

Lyons-Ruth, K. (2000). "I sense that you sense that I sense . . .": Sander's recognition process and the specificity of relational moves in the psychotherapeutic setting. *Infant Mental Health Journal, 21*(1), 85–98.

Lyons-Ruth, K. (2003). Dissociation and the parent–infant dialogue. *Journal of the American Psychoanalytic Association, 51*(3), 883–911.

Lyons-Ruth, K., Bruschweiler-Stern, N., Harrison, A., Nahum, J., Sander, L., Stern, D., et al. (1998a). Implicit relational knowing: Its role in development and psychoanalytic treatment. *Infant Mental Health Journal, 19*, 282–289.

Lyons-Ruth, K., Connell, D., Zoll, D., & Stahl, J. (1987) Infants at social risk: Relationships among infant maltreatment, maternal behavior, and infant attachment behavior. *Developmental Psychology, 23*, 223–232.

Lyons-Ruth, K., & Jacobvitz, D. (1999). Attachment disorganization: Unresolved loss, relational violence, and lapses in behavioral and attentional strategies. In J. Cassidy & P. Shaver (Eds.), *Handbook of attachment theory and research* (pp. 520–554). New York: Guilford Press.

Lyons-Ruth, K., & Zeanah, C. (1993). The family context of infant mental health. Part I: Affective development in the primary caregiving relationship. In C. Zeanah (Ed.), *Handbook of infant mental health* (pp. 14–37). New York: Guilford Press.

Main, M., Kaplan, N., & Cassidy, J. (1985). Security in infancy, childhood and adulthood: A move to the level of representation. In I. Bretherton & E. Waters (Eds.), *Growing points of attachment theory and research. Monograph of the Society for Research in Child Development, 50*(1–2, Serial No. 209), 66–104.

Main, M., Tomasini, L., & Tolan, W. (1979). Differences among mothers of infants judged to differ in security of attachment. *Developmental Psychology, 15*, 472–473.

Malatesta, C., Culver, C., Tesman, J., & Shepard, B. (1989). The development of emotion expression during the first two years of life. *Monograph of the Society for Research in Child Development, 54*(1–2, Serial No. 219).

Martin, L., Spicer, D., Lewis, M., Gluck, J., & Cork, L. (1991). Social deprivation of infant Rhesus monkeys alters the chemoarchitecture of the brain: I. Subcortical Regions. *Journal of Neuroscience, 11*, 3344–3358.

Maturana, H., & Varela, F. (1980). *The tree of knowledge.* Boston: Shambhala.

Maturana, H., & Varela, F. (1987). *The tree of knowledge: The biological roots of human understanding.* Boston: New Science Library.

Mayes, L. (2005). Something is different but what or why is unclear: Commentary on the Boston Change Process Study Group. *Journal of the American Psychoanalytic Association, 53*(3), 746–750.

McNeill, D. (2005). *Gesture and thought.* Chicago: University of Chicago Press.

Meltzoff, A. (1995). Understanding the intentions of others: Re-enactment of intended acts by 18-month-old children. *Developmental Psychology, 31*, 838–850.

Meltzoff, A., & Gopnik, A. (1993). The role of imitation in understanding persons and developing a theory of mind. In S. Baron-Cohen, H. Tager-Flusberg, & D. J. Cohen (Eds.), *Understanding other minds: Perspectives from autism* (pp. 335–366). New York: Oxford University Press.

Merleau-Ponty, M. (1962). *Phenomenology of perception* (C. Smith, Trans.). New York: Humanities Press. (Original work published 1945)

Merleau-Ponty, M. (1968). *The visible and the invisible* (C. Lefort, Ed., A. Lingis, Trans.). Evanston, IL: Northwestern University Press (Original work published 1964)

Mitchell, S. (1993). *Hope and dread in psychoanalysis.* New York: Basic Books.

Mitchell, S. (1997). *Influence and autonomy in psychoanalysis.* Hillsdale, NJ: Analytic Press.

Mitchell, S. (1998). The analyst's knowledge and authority. *Psychoanalytic Quarterly, 67,* 1–31.

Modell, A. (2003). *Imagination and the meaningful brain.* Cambridge, MA: MIT Press.

Morgan, A., Bruschweiler-Stern, N., Harrison, A., Lyons-Ruth, K., Nahum, J., Sander, L., Stern, D.N., & Tronick, E.Z. (1998). Moving along to things left undone. *Infant Mental Health Journal, 19,*

Nahum, J. (1994). New theoretical vistas in psychoanalysis: Louis Sander's theory of early development. *Psychoanalytic Psychology, 11*(1), 1–19.

Nahum, J., Harrison, A., Lyons-Ruth, K., Morgan, A., Sander, L., Stern, D. N., & Tronick, E. (1998). Case illustration: Moving along . . . and, is change gradual or sudden? *Infant Mental Health Journal, 19*(3), 315–319.

Nahum, J. (2000). An overview of Louis Sander's contribution to the field of mental health. *Infant Mental Health Journal, 21*(1–2), 29–41.

Natorp, P. (1912). *Allgemeine psychologie.* Tubingen, Germany: J. C. B. Mohr.

Ogawa, J., Sroufe, L., Weinfield, N., Carlson, E., & Egeland, B. (1997). Development and the fragmented self: Longitudinal study of dissociative symptomatology in a nonclinical sample. *Development and Psychopathology, 9,* 855–879.

Ogden, T. (1997). *Reverie and interpretation.* Northvale, NJ: Jason Aronson.

*Oxford English Dictionary.* (1971). 2nd ed. New York: Oxford University Press.

Pally, R., & Olds, D. (1998). Consciousness: A neuroscience perspective. *International Journal of Psychoanalysis, 79,* 971–988.

Perls, F., Hefferline, R., & Goodman, P. (1951). Gestalt therapy: Excitement and growth in the human personality. New York: Dell.

Piaget, J. (1952). *The origins of intelligence in children.* New York: International Universities Press.

Piaget, J. (1971). *Biology and knowledge.* Chicago: University of Chicago Press.

Pipp, S., & Harmon, R. (1987). Attachment as regulation: A commentary. *Child Development, 58,* 648–652.

Prigogine, I. (1997). *The end of certainty: Time, chaos, and the new laws of nature.* New York: Free Press.

Prigogine, I., & Stengers, I. (1984). *Order out of chaos: Man's new dialogue with nature.* New York: Basic Books.

Quine, W.V. (1960). *Word and Object.* Cambridge: MIT Press.

Renik, O. (1999). Playing one's cards face up in analysis. *Psychoanalytic Quarterly, 68,* 521–540.

Rizzolatti, G., Fogassi, L., & Gallese, V. (2001). Neurophysiological mechanisms underlying the understanding and imitation of action. *Neuroscience, 2*(9), 661–670.

Rochat, P. (Ed.). (1999). *Early social cognition.* Hillsdale, NJ: Erlbaum.

Rommetveit, R. (1974). *On Message Structure: A Framework for Language*and Communication. New York: Wiley Press.

Ruby, P., & Decety, J. (2001). Effect of subjective perspective taking during simulation of action: A PET investigation of agency. *Nature Neuroscience, 4*(5), 546–550.

Sabbagh, M. (2004, June). Understanding orbitofrontal contributions to theory of mind reasoning: Implications for autism. *Brain and Cognition, 55*(1), 209–219.

Safran, J., Muran, J., & Proskurov, B. (2008). Alliance, negotiation, and rupture resolution. In R. Lvey & J. Ablon (Eds.), *Handbook of evidence-based psychodynamic psychotherapy* (pp. 201–225). New York: Humana Press/Springer.

Sander, L. (1962). Issues in early mother-child interaction. *Journal of the American Academy of Child and Adolescent Psychiatry, 1,* 141–166.

Sander, L. (1965). Interactions of recognition and the developmental processes of the second 18 months of life. Talk presented at Tufts-New England Medical Center, Boston, MA.

Sander, L. 1975. Infant and caretaking environment: Investigation and conceptualization of adaptive behavior in a system of increasing complexity. In E. James Anthony (Ed.), *Explorations in child psychiatry* (pp. 129–166). New York: Plenum Press.

Sander, L. (1980). Investigation of the infant and its caregiving environment as a biological system. In S. Greenspan & G. Pollock (Eds.), *The course of life: Vol. 1. Infancy and early childhood* (pp. 177–201). Adelphi, MD: National Institute of Mental Health.

Sander, L. (1983). Polarity, paradox, and the organizational process in development. In J. Call, E. Galenson, & R. Tyson (Eds.), *Frontiers of infant psychiatry* (pp. 333–346). New York: Basic Books.

Sander, L. (1984). The Boston University Longitudinal Study—prospect and retrospect after twenty five years. In J. Call, E. Galenson, & R. Tyson (Eds.), *Frontiers of infant psychiatry* (Vol. 2, pp. 137–145). New York: Basic Books.

Sander, L. (1985). Toward a logic of organization in psychobiological development. In H. Klar & L. Siever (Eds.), *Biologic response styles: Clinical implications* (American Psychological Association Monograph). Washington, DC: American Psychological Association.

Sander, L. (1987). Awareness of inner experience: A systems perspective on self-regulatory process in early development. *Child Abuse and Neglect, 11,* 339–346.

Sander, L. (1988). The event-structure of regulation in the neonate-caregiver system as a biological background for early organization of psychic structure. In A. Goldberg (Ed.), *Frontiers in self psychology* (pp. 64–77). Hillsdale, NJ: Analytic Press.

Sander, L. (1991, June). *Recognition process: Specificity and organization in early human development.* Paper presented at the conference on The Psychic Life of the Infant, at the University of Massachusetts, Amherst, MA.

Sander, L. (1995a). Identity and the experience of specificity in a process of recognition. *Psychoanalytic Dialogues, 5,* 579–593.

Sander, L. (1995b, April). *Thinking about developmental process: Wholeness, specificity, and the organization of conscious experiencing.* Invited address presented at the annual meeting of the Division of Psychoanalysis, American Psychological Association, Santa Monica, CA.

Sander, L. (1997). Paradox and resolution: From the beginning. In S. Greenspan, S. Wieder, & J. Osofsky (Eds.), *Handbook of child and adolescent Psychiatry: Volume 1. Infants and preschoolers: Development and syndromes* (pp. 153–159). New York: Wiley.

Sandler, J. (1987). *Projection, identification, projective identification.* New York: International Universities Press.

Sandler, J., & Fonagy, P. (Eds.). (1997). *Recovered memories of abuse: True or false.* London: Karnac Books and International Universities Press.

Sartre, J-P. (1976). *L'être et le néant.* Paris: Tel Gallimard. (Original work published 1943)

Schacter, D., & Moscovitch, M. (1984). Infants, amnesia and dissociable memory systems. In M. Moscovitch (Ed.), *Infant memory* (pp. 173–216). New York: Plenum.

Schafer, R. (1992). *Retelling a life.* New York: Basic Books.

Schiller, C. (Ed.). (1957). *Instinctive behavior: The development of a modern concept.* New York: International Universities Press.

Schore, A. (1994). *Affect regulation and the origins of the self: The neurobiology of emotional development.* Hillsdale, NJ: Erlbaum.

Schwaber, E. (1998). The non-verbal dimension in psychoanalysis: 'State' and its clinical vicissitudes. *International Journal of Psychoanalysis, 79,* 667–680. It's fine this way.

Searle, J. (1969). *Speech acts: An essay in the philosophy of language.* New York: Cambridge University Press.

Sheets-Johnstone, M. (1999). *The primacy of movement.* Amsterdam: John Benjamins.

Spangler, G., & Grossmann, K. (1993). Biobehavioral organization in securely and insecurely attached infants. *Child Development, 64,* 1439–1450.

Spitz, R.A. (1957). *No and yes—On the genesis of human communication*. New York: International Universities Press.

Sroufe, A. (1999). Implications of attachment theory for developmental psychopathology. *Development and Psychopathology, 11*, 1–13.

Stechler, G. (1993). *CasePresentation*. Paper presented at the symposium on the Enigma of Change in Psychodynamic Therapy II, Boston, MA., May 1993

Stechler, G. (2003). Affect: The heart of the matter. *Psychoanalytic Dialogues*. 13, 711–726.

Sterba, R. (1934). The fate of the ego in analytic therapy. *International Journal of Psychoanalysis, 15*, 117–126.

Sterba, R. (1940). The dynamics of the dissolution of the transference resistance. *Psychoanalytic Quarterly, 9*, 363–379.

Stern, D. B. (1997). *Unformulated experience: From Dissociation to Imagination in Psychoanalysis* Hillsdale, NJ: Analytic Press.

Stern, D. N. (1971). A micro-analysis of mother–infant interaction: Behaviors regulating social contact between a mother and her three-and-a-half-month-old twins. *Journal of the American Academy of Child Psychiatry, 10*, 501–517.

Stern, D. N. (1977). *The first relationship: Infant and mother*. Cambridge, MA: Harvard University Press.

Stern, D. N. (1983). The early development of schemas of self, other, and "self with other." In J. Lichtenberg & S. Kaplan (Eds.), *Reflections on self psychology* (pp. 49–84). Hillsdale, NJ: Analytic Press.

Stern, D. N. (1985). *The interpersonal world of the infant: A view from psychoanalysis and developmental psychology*. New York: Basic Books.

Stern, D. N. (1994). One way to build a clinically relevant baby. *Infant Mental Health Journal, 15*(1), 9–25.

Stern, D. N. (1995). *The motherhood constellation: A unified view of parent–infant psychotherapy*. New York: Basic Books.

Stern, D. N. (2004). *The present moment in psychotherapy and everyday life*. New York: Norton.

Stern, D.N., Hofer, L., Haft, W., & Dore, J. (1984) Affect attunement: The sharing of feeling states between mother and infant by means of intermodal fluency. In T. Field & N. Fox (Eds.), *Social Perception in Infants*. Norwood, NJ: Ablex, 1984, 249–268.

Stern, D. N., Sander, L., Nahum, J., Harrison, A., Lyons-Ruth, K., Morgan, A., et al. (1998). Non-interpretive mechanisms in psychoanalytic therapy: The "something more" than interpretation. *International Journal of Psychoanalysis, 79*, 903–921. (see above, Boston CPSG Report I).

Stern-Bruschweiler, N., & Stern, D. N. (1989). A model for conceptualizing the role of the mother's representational world in various mother–infant therapies. *Infant Mental Health Journal, 10*, 142–156.

Stolorow, R. (1997). Dynamic, dyadic, intersubjective systems: An evolving paradigm for psychoanalysis. *Psychoanalytic Psychology, 14*(3), 337–346.

Stolorow, R. (2007). Trauma and the "ontological unconscious." Ch 5, pp 23-31. In: Stolorow, R., *Trauma and human existence: Autobiographical, psychoanalytic, and philosophical reflections.* New York: Routledge.

Stolorow, R., & Atwood, G. (1992). *Contexts of being.* Hillsdale, NJ: Analytic Press.

Stolorow, R., Atwood, G., & Brandchaft, B. (Eds.). (1994). *The intersubjective perspective.* Northvale, NJ: Jason Aronson.

Strachey, J. (1934). The nature of the therapeutic action of psychoanalysis. In M. Bergmann & F. Hartman (Eds.), *The evolution of psychoanalytic technique* (pp. 331–360). New York: Basic Books.

Thelen, E. (1989). Self-organization in developmental processes: Can systems approaches work? In M. Gunnar & E. Thelen (Eds.), *Minnesota symposia in child psychology* (pp. 22, 77–117). Hillsdale, NJ: Erlbaum.

Thelen, E., & Smith, L. (1994). *A dynamic systems approach to the development of cognition and action.* Cambridge, MA: MIT Press.

Thomä, H., & Kachele, H. (1987). *Psychoanalytic practice: Vol. 1. Principles.* Berlin: Springer-Verlag.

Toíbín, C. (2004). *The master.* New York: Scribner.

Tomasello, M. (1999). *The cultural origins of human cognition.* Cambridge, MA: Harvard University Press.

Tomasello, M., Carpenter, M., Call, J., Behne, T., & Moll, H. (2005). Understanding and sharing intentions: The origins of cultural cognition. *Behavioral and Brain Sciences, 28,* 675–691.

Tranel, D., & Damasio, A. (1993). Covert learning of affective valence does not require structures in hippocampal system or amygdala. *Journal of Cognitive Neuroscience, 5,* 79–88.

Trevarthen, C. (1979). Communication and cooperation in early infancy: A description of primary intersubjectivity. In M. Bullowa (Ed.), *Before speech* (pp. 321–347). London: Cambridge University Press.

Trevarthen C. (1980). The foundations of intersubjectivity: Development of interpersonal and cooperative understanding in infants. In D. Olson (Ed.), *The social foundations of language and thought* (pp. 382–403). New York: Norton.

Trevarthen, C. (1993). Brain, science and the human spirit. In J. B. Ashbrook with P. D. MacLean (Eds.), *Brain, culture and the human spirit* (pp. 129–181). Lanham, MD: University Press of America.

Tronick, E. (1989). Emotions and emotional communication in infants. *American Psychologist, 44*(2), 112–119.

Tronick, E. (Ed.). (1998). Interactions that effect change in psychotherapy: A model based on infant research [Special issue]. *Infant Mental Health Journal, 19*(3), 277–353.

Tronick, E., Als, H., & Adamson, L. (1979). Mother–infant face-to-face communicative interaction. In M. Bullowa (Ed.), *Before speech: The beginnings of human communication* (pp. 349–373). Cambridge, UK: Cambridge University Press.

Tronick, E., Als, H., Adamson, L., Wise, S., & Brazelton, T. B. (1978). The infant's response to entrapment between contradictory messages in face-to-face interaction. *Journal of the American Academy of Child and Adolescent Psychiatry, 17,* 1–13.

Tronick, E., Bruschweiler-Stern, N., Harrison, A. M., Lyons-Ruth, K., Morgan, A. C., Nahum, J. P., Sander, L. W., & Stern, D. N. (1998). Dyadically expanded states of consciousness and the process of therapeutic change. *Infant Mental Health Journal, 19(3),* 290–299.

Tronick, E., & Cohn, J. (1989). Infant–mother face-to-face interaction: Age and gender differences in coordination and the occurrence of miscoordination. *Child Development, 60,* 85–92.

Tronick, E., & Weinberg, K. (1997). Depressed mothers and infants: The failure to form dyadic states of consciousness. In L. Murray & P. Cooper (Eds.), *Postpartum depression and child development* (pp. 54–85). New York: Guilford Press.

van IJzendoorn, M. (1995). Adult attachment representations, parental responsiveness, and infant attachment: A meta-analysis on the predictive validity of the Adult Attachment Interview. *Psychological Bulletin, 117,* 387–403.

Varela, F., Lachaux, J. P., Rodrigues, E., & Martinerie, J. (2001). The brainweb: Phases synchronization and large-scale integration. *Nature Reviews Neuroscience, 2*(4), 229–239.

Varela, F. J., Thompson, E., & Rosch, E. (1993). *The embodied mind: Cognitive science and human experience.* Cambridge, MA: MIT Press.

Von Bertalanffy, L. (1952). *Problems of life.* New York: Harper.

Vygotsky, L. S. (1962). *Thought and language* (E. Hanfmann & G. Vakar, Trans.). Cambridge, MA: MIT Press. (Original work published 1934)

Vygotsky, L. S. (1986). *Thought and language* (A. Kosulin, Trans. and Ed., Rev. ed.). Cambridge, MA: MIT Press. (Original work published 1934)

Waldron, S., Scharf, R. D., Crouse, J., Firestein, S. K., Burton, A., & Hurst, D. (2004). Saying the right thing at the right time: A view through the lens of the Analytic Process Scales (APS). *Psychoanalytic Quarterly, 73,* 1079–1125.

Weiss, P. (1947). The problem of specificity in growth and development. *Yale Journal of Biology and Medicine, 19,* 234–278.

Weiss, P. (1949). The biological basis of adaptation. In J. Romano (Ed.), *Adaptation* (pp. 1–22). Ithaca, NY: Cornell University Press.

Weiss, P. (1970). Whither life science? *American Scientist, 58,* 156–163.

Westen, D., & Gabbard, G. (2002a). Developments in cognitive neuroscience: I. Conflict, compromise, and connectionism. *Journal of the American Psychoanalytic Association, 50*(1), 53–98.

Westen, D., & Gabbard, G. (2002b). Developments in cognitive neuroscience:

II. Implications for theories of transference. *Journal of the American Psychoanalytic Association, 50*(1), 99–134.

Winnicott, D. (1953). Transitional objects and transitional phenomena. In D. Winnicott, *Collected papers: Through pediatrics to psychoanalysis*. New York: Basic Books.

Winnicott, D. (1957). *The child and the family*. London: Tavistock.

Winnicott, D. (1965). The capacity to be alone. In D. Winnicott, *The maturational processes and the facilitating environment: Studies in the theory of emotional development*. London: The Hogarth Press and The Institute of Psychoanalysis.

Winnicott, D. (1971). Mirror role of mother and family in child development. In D. Winnicott, *Playing and reality* (pp. 111–118). London: Tavistock.

Zahavi, D. (1999). *Self-awareness and alterity: A phenomenological investigation*. Evanston, IL: Northwestern University Press.

Zahavi, D. (2003). How to investigate subjectivity: Natorp and Heidegger on reflection. *Continental Philosophy Review, 36*, 155–176.

Zetzel, E. R. (1956). Current concepts of transference. *International Journal of Psychoanalysis, 37*, 369–376.

Zetzel, E. (1966). The analytic situation. In R. E. Litman (Ed.), *Psychoanalysis in America* (pp. 86–106). New York: International Universities Press.

# Index